KING OF THE MOONSHINERS

KING
of the
MOONSHINERS

Lewis R. Redmond
in Fact and Fiction

Edited by Bruce E. Stewart
With a Foreword by Durwood Dunn

The University of Tennessee Press
Knoxville

The Appalachian Echoes series is dedicated to reviving and contextualizing classic books about Appalachia for a new generation of readers. By making available a wide spectrum of works—from fiction to nonfiction, from folk life and letters to history, sociology, politics, religion, and biography—the series seeks to reveal the diversity that has always characterized Appalachian writing, a diversity that promises to confront and challenge long-held stereotypes about the region.

Copyright © 2008 by The University of Tennessee Press / Knoxville.
All Rights Reserved. Manufactured in the United States of America.
First Edition.

This book is printed on acid-free paper. The paper in this book meets the requirements of American National Standards Institute / National Information Standards Organization specification Z39.48-1992 (Permanence of Paper). It contains 30 percent post-consumer waste and is certified by the Forest Stewardship Council.

Library of Congress Cataloging-in-Publication Data

King of the moonshiners: Lewis R. Redmond in fact and fiction / edited by
Bruce E. Stewart; with a foreword by Durwood Dunn.—1st ed.
    p. cm. — (Appalachian echoes series)
    Includes bibliographical references and index.
ISBN-13: 978-1-57233-640-7 (pbk.: alk. paper)
ISBN-10: 1-57233-640-4 (pbk.: alk. paper)
    1. Distilling, Illicit‹North Carolina—History—19th century. 2. Liquor industry‹Taxation—North Carolina. 3. Redmond, Lewis Richard, 1854–1906. 4. Outlaws‹North Carolina—Biography. I. Stewart, Bruce E.

HJ5021.K56 2008
364.1¹33—dc22
[B]   2008005804

For My Parents
"And now these three remain:
faith, hope, and love.
But the greatest of these
is love."

CONTENTS

Foreword
Durwood Dunn
ix

Acknowledgments
xi

Introduction: The Life and Legacy of Lewis R. Redmond
xiii

C. McKinley's Interview of Redmond, 1878
C. McKinley
1

The Entwined Lives of Miss Gabrielle Austin,
Daughter of the Late Rev. Ellis C. Austin, and of Redmond,
the Outlaw, Leader of the North Carolina "Moonshiners"
Edward B. Crittenden
31

The True Life of Maj. Lewis Richard Redmond, the Notorious
Outlaw and Famous Moonshiner, of Western North Carolina,
Who Was Born in Swain County, N.C., in the Year 1855,
and Arrested April 7th, 1881
R. A. Cobb
99

Index
125

ILLUSTRATIONS

1. Lewis R. Redmond, c. 1880s   xiv
2. Redmond Family   xvii
3. Lewis Redmond's Grave   xiv
4. Cover of *Entwined Lives,* by Bishop Crittenden   30
5. The Innocent Girl Arrested for Theft   44
6. The Horrors of the Whipping Post   50
7. Valley of the Shadow of Death   54
8. Redmond's Placard   56
9. Bray Shot Dead by His Chieftain   67
10. Charlie Hashagen Made Captive   72
11. Front Cover of *The True Life of Redmond,* by R. A. Cobb   98
12. The Killing of Duckworth   107
13. Home of Redmond   113
14. The Capture of Redmond   118

FOREWORD

Durwood Dunn

On March 1, 1876, at almost the very moment when Lewis Richard Redmond, a young moonshiner from Transylvania County in the Blue Ridge Mountains of southwestern North Carolina, shot and killed Alfred Duckworth, a U.S. deputy marshal pursuing him for illicit distilling, Redmond stepped into the realm of defining myth from which he would never escape. His instant popularity and celebrity with Southerners fused the unpopularity of a federal liquor tax and Reconstruction in the myth of this heroic ex-Confederate who seemed to defy, in an effortless manner, the full force and weight of the federal government's effort to capture him and bring him to justice. In a later interview with a sympathetic reporter, C. McKinley, of the *Charleston News and Courier*, Redmond himself played an active role in the myth-making process, portraying himself as a victim of unjust federal taxes on corn whiskey that impoverished southerners were ill-equipped to pay.

The catapulting of Redmond as a defiant, heroic outlaw onto the national stage was not just the work of unreconstructed southerners, however. Historian Daniel Boorstin demonstrated how the love of an antihero was an *American* characteristic, stemming from the early nineteenth century. It was this broader appeal that made Redmond's tale irresistible for expropriation by an unscrupulous writer of dime novels, Edward B. Crittenden, whose *The Entwined Lives of Miss Gabrielle Austin, Daughter of the Late Rev. Ellis C. Austin, and of Redmond, the Outlaw, Leader of the North Carolina "Moonshiners"* was almost completely fictional, woven out of Victorian values then popular in the American North. In Crittenden's treatment of Edmond, the moonshiner outlaw nevertheless perfectly exhibits what Boorstin considered quintessential elements of the American antihero: Good Bad Men who fell afoul of the law because of some injustice, but who otherwise, despite their criminal deeds, exhibited unimpeachable character, foremost of which was chivalry toward helpless women and children.

FOREWORD

Redmond thus filled a need in both North and South for a hero, and the popularity of Crittenden's *Entwined Lives* in the North well illustrates the fact that, as historians Fitzhugh Brundage and Nina Silber have argued, the northern audience was clearly an important participant in this reconstruction of southern identity through novels and short stories. Most fascinating, however, is that the Redmond myth was evolving, shaping but also being shaped by changing currents in the postwar South. By the 1880s, proponents of the doctrines of the New South saw illicit moonshining as destructive of modernization and industrialization, the very antithesis of progressive change they now sought for their section. In this context, New South booster, temperance reformer, and newspaper editor Robert A. Cobb wrote *The True Life of Maj. Lewis Richard Redmond* in 1881, condemning illicit distillers who had become a symbol of backwardness which threatened this progress.

Historian Bruce E. Stewart contextualizes both Crittenden's dime novel on Redmond and Cobb's critical rebuttal, as well as the 1878 interview of the outlaw by C. McKinley of the *Charleston News and Courier,* which was widely reprinted throughout the United States. These texts illuminate both the myth in its making and its subsequent deconstruction in painstaking but fascinating detail. As Stewart so ably demonstrates, at the very instance when the New South was ridding itself of the Redmond mythology in the wake of changing southern public opinion, local colorists and other northern journalists transformed the illicit distiller to become the cornerstone of a new mythic region—Appalachia. Moonshining and its attendant violence would early become a key element in this new regional mythology. If, as Charles Beard maintained, history is just a cat being dragged by its tail to places it scarcely wants to go, nothing seems stranger than the Redmond mythical character being dragged out of a postwar Confederacy he was never really part of into this new "strange land and peculiar people" of Appalachia. Unlike Billy the Kid and other mythic American outlaws, Redmond is hardly remembered today. But his new imaginary matrix, Appalachia, seems as indestructible as Beard's historiographical cat.

ACKNOWLEDGMENTS

It is a great pleasure to thank those who helped me as I worked to complete this book. John Inscoe, who served as my major professor and mentor at the University of Georgia, read several versions of the manuscript and encouraged me to submit it to the University of Tennessee Press. I hope to one day live up to the high standards John sets for all of his graduate students. It was also a joy to work with Durwood Dunn and Scot Danforth, both of whom showed great enthusiasm for this project and supported me from the very beginning. I also gratefully acknowledge the assistance of Dan Pierce and Gordon McKinney. Both carefully read the manuscript and offered invaluable suggestions.

I am grateful to other individuals who have contributed to this project in various ways. I would like to thank Neal Hutcheson at Sucker Punch Pictures for providing me with several photographs of Lewis R. Redmond. Neal went far beyond the call of duty to help me. The staff at the North Carolina Collection at UNC–Chapel Hill also assisted me in scanning illustrations from the dime novels included in this book. I appreciate the sharp editing skills of Karin Kaufman and Stan Ivester; both have worked hard to improve my prose. Moreover, the research for this project would not have been possible without the financial aid of the Dean's Award in Humanities at the University of Georgia.

I would also like to acknowledge those who have supported me throughout the years. Pete Carmichael and Richard Starnes took me under their wings at Western Carolina University and introduced me to the rigors of academia. At the University of Georgia, I had the opportunity to work with Paul Sutter, Kathleen Clark, and Stephen Mihm, all three of whom, along with John Inscoe, served on my dissertation committee. While at UGA, I also had the great fortune to work with a talented group of graduate students. You know who you are, and I thank you for six wonderful years. I would also like to thank my new colleagues at Appalachian State University, all of whom have made

ACKNOWLEDGMENTS

my transition from a graduate student to an assistant professor an enjoyable experience.

I also owe a debt of gratitude to my family. My grandmother, aunts, uncles, cousins, sisters-in-law, and nieces have supported me. My brothers, William and Jason, have always believed in me, and I cannot thank them enough. I also express admiring appreciation to Karen Strait, whose faith in me never wavers. She is my best friend.

Lastly, I would like to thank my parents, William and Miriam, who served as my first role models. This book is dedicated to them.

INTRODUCTION

The Life and Legacy of Lewis R. Redmond

During the early 1870s, Lewis Richard Redmond was a little-known moonshiner from Transylvania County in the Blue Ridge Mountains of southwestern North Carolina. That would change on March 1, 1876. In February, the federal government had issued a warrant for Redmond's arrest, believing (correctly) that he was guilty of illicit distilling. U.S. Deputy Marshal Alfred Duckworth, with this warrant in hand, set out to capture Redmond.[1] Upon finding the twenty-one-year-old Lewis and his future brother-in-law, Amos Ladd, on a road near the community of East Fork on March 1, Duckworth ordered the men to stop their wagon.[2] He then drew a pistol from his jacket, announced that Redmond was under arrest, and read the warrant out loud. Redmond supposedly responded: "All right, put up your pistol, Alf, I will go along with you."[3] The deputy marshal lowered his gun. Redmond quickly grabbed a small derringer from Ladd and fired point-blank at Duckworth, shooting him in the throat. The two outlaws then jumped off the wagon and fled into the woods on foot. Duckworth attempted to pursue them but collapsed due to loss of blood and died shortly thereafter. Now wanted for murder, Redmond fled to Pickens County in northwestern South Carolina, where, within three years, he gained national notoriety, earning the nickname "King of the Moonshiners."[4]

More than any other individual moonshiner in southern Appalachia, Redmond captured the imagination of middle-class Americans during the late nineteenth century. Like Billy the Kid and Jesse James, he became a legendary figure, reflecting people's hopes, needs, and fears.[5] Most mountain residents (and other Southerners) viewed him as a folk hero, an outlaw who valiantly fought against the Bureau of Internal Revenue and its "infernal" liquor tax. He supposedly killed in self-defense and for a noble cause: to protect his community from an "oppressive" federal government. Many people from outside the South, however, insisted that Redmond was a violent criminal, the product of an uncivilized region that required reforming. Nearly a decade before the

INTRODUCTION

Earliest known photograph of Lewis R. Redmond, probably taken in the 1880s. Courtesy of Neal Hutcheson.

Hatfield-McCoy and other feuds made national headlines in the late 1880s, newspaper stories and dime novels about Redmond perpetuated images of a violent and lawless Appalachia that persist today.[6]

This book includes three publications that helped to transform Redmond into a national celebrity during the late 1870s and early 1880s. The first is C. McKinley's interview of Redmond in June 1878. A reporter for the *Charleston News and Courier* and opponent of the Bureau of Internal Revenue, McKinley's sympathetic portrayal of the moonshiner made Redmond a household name. The second publication is Edward B. Crittenden's *The Entwined Lives of Miss Gabrielle Austin, Daughter of the Late Rev. Ellis C. Austin, and of Redmond, the Outlaw, Leader of the North Carolina "Moonshiners."* Published in 1879, this dime novel solidified Redmond's reputation as the most dangerous man in southern Appalachia. Largely due to *Entwined Lives*, which went through at least three printings in English and one in German, Redmond's capture and conviction in 1881 made front-page news throughout the country. That year, perhaps wanting to capitalize on the outlaw's fame (or infamy), Robert A. Cobb, a native western North Carolinian from Burke County, wrote *The True Life of Maj. Lewis Richard Redmond, the Notorious Outlaw and Famous Moonshiner, of Western North Carolina, Who Was Born in Swain County, N.C., in the Year 1855, and Arrested April 7, 1881,* which is the final piece included in this book. Taken together, these publications are unique because they provide us with different viewpoints about Redmond and moonshining in general during the late-nineteenth century.

But these publications also provide us with incomplete, sometimes biased, and often inaccurate accounts of Redmond's life. Moreover, generations of mountain residents have passed down legends about Redmond, retelling them as truth. Redmond's life remains shrouded in myth and mystery. To better understand his exceptional story, we must re-create the world in which Redmond lived during the turbulent years of Reconstruction in the Carolina highlands and other communities across the South. Government documents, manuscripts, and newspapers, along with the three publications included in this book, reveal that moonshiners' resistance to liquor law enforcement was neither the product of ethnic origins nor the result of geographical isolation, as many historians have argued.[7] This lawlessness reflected a number of grievances that certain elements in mountain (and southern) society had against the federal government following the Civil War.[8] Former Confederates, for instance, resented the presence of United States troops to enforce liquor taxation, while others protested the expansion of federal authority via the Bureau of Internal Revenue. In this political context, many white Southerners embraced Redmond as a hero, an unreconstructed Confederate who refused to surrender to the national government.

If we are to believe his gravestone, Lewis Richard Redmond was born on April 15, 1854.[9] More likely than not, he was born in Rabun County, located in northern Georgia, where his parents lived in 1850.[10] We do know that he was the son of Richard Harris Redmond. Richard was born in North Carolina (probably in Transylvania County) around 1810. In the 1830s, the elder Redmond moved to nearby Pickens County in northwestern South Carolina,

INTRODUCTION

where he married a local farmer's daughter, Malinda Reece. In 1836, Malinda gave birth to Morgan, the first of her ten children. Sometime before 1850, Richard relocated his family to Militia District 536 in Rabun County. In 1856, when Lewis Redmond was two years old, his father moved the clan to western North Carolina. By 1860, the Redmond family had settled in Davidson's River Township in what was then part of Henderson County (now Transylvania County).[11]

Little is known about Lewis Redmond's childhood. He probably labored on his father's small farm, where he cultivated corn, vegetables, and other crops to feed the family and sometimes satisfy market demands.[12] It was there that Redmond's father also taught the boy how to distill corn into alcohol. One of the region's first industries, liquor manufacturing allowed many antebellum farmers living in more rugged and isolated areas to obtain cash and participate in the larger market economy.[13] Maybe one night Richard also sat beside Lewis in the family's cabin and recalled the famous Whiskey Rebellion of 1794 in which seven thousand southwestern Pennsylvanians rebelled against the federal government's first attempt to levy taxes on imported and domestically manufactured spirits.[14] Perhaps the boy was shocked (and proud) to discover that opposition to these duties inflamed farmers all along the backcountry, including western North Carolina.[15] Soaking in these tales, maybe Lewis came to believe at an early age that he had an inherent right to distill alcohol.

Too young to enlist in the Confederate army, Lewis, whose older brothers would serve in the famous Thomas Legion, continued to live on the Redmond farm during the Civil War.[16] According to legend, the boy spent most of his time at a nearby Confederate camp, where soldiers eventually gave him the complimentary nickname "Major."[17] More likely than not, Redmond was exposed to violence during the war. By 1863, guerrilla warfare in western North Carolina had blurred the lines between combatants and noncombatants, resulting in such atrocities as the Shelton Laurel massacre in Madison County, where local Confederates executed thirteen civilians, including a twelve-year-old suspected of treason.[18] Vigilantism increased in Transylvania County and other parts of the region as residents scrambled to protect themselves from marauding bushwhackers and home guardsmen alike. This extralegal violence continued to be a feature of mountain (and southern) life during Reconstruction.[19] It may also have influenced how Redmond and other moonshiners would respond to the Bureau of Internal Revenue and its "infernal" federal liquor tax.

Following the Civil War, many southern highlanders struggling to rebuild their shattered communities resumed the antebellum practice of distilling their crops into alcohol. However, a new problem emerged. In 1862, the

Redmond family. Courtesy of Neal Hutcheson.

U.S. Congress had levied duties on liquor, tobacco, and other luxuries to raise revenue for the Union war effort. It had also established the Office of the Commissioner of Internal Revenue (commonly known as the Bureau of Internal Revenue) to collect these taxes.[20] Mountain residents who wanted to manufacture alcohol at war's end quickly discovered that they had to pay a federal liquor tax.[21] Many of these distillers, largely small farmers, challenged the legitimacy of the Bureau of Internal Revenue and resisted federal agents in their collection efforts. As historian Wilbur R. Miller points out, they became moonshiners because "a distant federal government 'criminalized' part of their way of life by imposing a tax on home-distilled whiskey they had produced for generations."[22]

Moonshiners would not fight the Bureau of Internal Revenue alone. As long as distillation did not deprive their communities of foodstuffs, southern highlanders who did not produce alcohol regarded liquor manufacturing as an inalienable right. During Reconstruction, moonshiners gained sympathy among these residents by claiming that they had the right, just as their fathers did, to make a living unmolested by the federal government. George Atkinson from West Virginia, for instance, pointed out that highlanders there "claimed that inasmuch as this is a free government—a Republic—every citizen should be allowed to make a living for himself and family as best he can; and if he does not steal, or trample upon the rights of his neighbors, the Government should not interfere with him."[23] Like most illicit distillers, mountain residents also believed that the liquor tax placed a heavy burden on small producers. One Caldwell County farmer in western North Carolina, who had never "made a drop of liquor" and drunk only a "wee bit," protested in 1869 the "unjust and oppressive operation of the internal revenue laws of the national government." Since distillers in the mountain counties had little means and lived in one of the "most inaccessible regions," this man believed that their crops would ruin before getting to market if not distilled. With the burden of paying a liquor tax, the "plain countrymen" would be unable to support their families.[24]

Moreover, supporters of the moonshiners viewed liquor law enforcement as a tool used by the federal government to prevent them from restoring "home rule."[25] For former mountain Confederates, liquor taxation reaffirmed their fears of "Yankee centralization" following the Civil War. In 1870, for instance, South Carolina moonshiners attacked a group of revenue agents, shouting that "they had been Confederate Soldiers for four years, had often fought and whipped Yankees."[26] Denizens in northern Georgia had "a lurking sentiment that the United States is yet a foreign government, and that its officers and agents are intruders upon their reserved rights."[27] These mountain residents also associated revenuers with former Unionists during the Civil War, and for good reason. Wartime Unionism was often a prerequisite for men hired by the Bureau of Internal Revenue. South Carolina Collector of Internal Revenue L. Cass Carpenter, for instance, was a Unionist "carpetbagger" who had moved to the state in 1867 and helped organize the Republican Party. Another Palmetto State revenuer, Charles Dennis O'Keefe, was a member of the Union League, serving as its president and secretary.[28] Unquestionably, former Confederates developed a hatred for revenue agents who were Unionists and viewed them as the purveyors of radical change in the post–Civil War South.

By 1870, federal liquor taxation and Reconstruction had become inseparable issues, thereby producing a climate in which southerners' resistance to revenuers took a violent turn. Mountain moonshiners increasingly intimidated, assaulted, and (sometimes) killed bureau agents.[29] President Ulysses S. Grant responded by sending the Seventh U.S. Cavalry and companies of the Second and Eighteenth infantries to protect revenuers conducting raids in southern Appalachia. Bureau agents' authority to summon federal soldiers increased with the passage of the Force Act of 1871. Aimed at combating the

Ku Klux Klan (KKK) by giving federal officials power to use troops for protection when making arrests, this act also granted revenuers the same authority. The use of troops, however, reminded many white southerners of their failure to overthrow Reconstruction and evoked cries of "bayonet rule."[30]

Meanwhile, Democratic politicians did little to discourage moonshiner violence and often encouraged it. Resentful that the Bureau of Internal Revenue provided Republicans with "hundreds of patronage jobs," they condemned federal liquor taxation by linking it with Radical Republicanism and the question of "home rule."[31] Democrat and former North Carolina Governor Zebulon B. Vance, for instance, chastised the entire revenue system as corrupt and called bureau agents "red-legged grasshoppers." Holding up to his mountain audience a grasshopper preserved in alcohol, he proclaimed in 1876: "This fellow . . . eats up every green thing that God ever gave to man, and he only serves the universal dissolution. The time has come when an honest man can't take an honest drink without having a gang of revenue officers after him."[32] That same year, Democrat Wade Hampton from South Carolina also used liquor law enforcement as a rallying point to unify mountain whites against Reconstruction, blaming Republicans for the "oppressive" tax.[33] It was in this politically charged setting that many Southerners, including Hampton, would regard Lewis Redmond as a hero who refused to surrender to an "oppressive" federal government.

Following the Civil War, Lewis continued to labor on the family farm in Transylvania County, where he also helped his father operate a moonshine distillery. "I worked on the farm all day and at the still at night to make a living for us," he told a newspaper reporter in 1878. "I would be so tired the next day that I have gone to sleep in the corn row between the plough handles, and would wake up only when my horse stopped at the end of the furrow."[34] An ambitious teenager, Lewis also began to transport his neighbors' moonshine to market during the mid-1870s. Rumors of his illegal activities soon reached federal authorities, who promptly issued a warrant for the young man's arrest.[35] According to legend, revenue agents then visited Redmond's home and arrested his father. Lewis supposedly recalled what happened next: "They took [my father] down to the church near by. They captured several other men in the church, and the preacher stopped in the midst of his sermon and sat down. My father and several gave bail—the rest they took away with them. My mother was badly frightened by it all and died in a few days afterwards. My father had to go to Asheville. The journey and exposures made him ill, and he, too, died a few weeks later."[36] More likely than not, this tale about the death of Redmond's parents was nothing more than propaganda. Lewis (or the newspaper reporter who interviewed him) probably created it as a means

INTRODUCTION

of building local and national sympathy for the young moonshiner. What we do know, however, is that on March 1, 1876, Lewis mortally wounded deputy marshal Alfred Duckworth and quickly fled to nearby Pickens County in northwestern South Carolina.[37]

That Redmond viewed Pickens County as a safe haven should come as no surprise. In the 1830s, his father had lived in that county and probably maintained ties with many kinfolk and friends there after he moved to Georgia and (later) North Carolina.[38] Lewis was also already acquainted with several Pickens County inhabitants such as the Ladd family, most of whom resided in Eastatoe Township. In fact, he married one of the Ladd daughters, Adeline, in 1878.[39] Redmond knew that these people would protect him from revenue agents. Moreover, other Pickens County denizens sympathized with the moonshiners. By 1876, the Democratic *Pickens Sentinel* had become an outspoken opponent of the Bureau of Internal Revenue. In July, for instance, the newspaper's editor, D. F. Bradley, launched an attack on Deputy Marshals E. H. Barton and William F. Gary, accusing them of accosting an innocent widow during a raid.[40] Two months later, Bradley argued that federal liquor law enforcement was a tool of Radical Republicanism. "We ask the men of the mountains," the *Sentinel* read, "if they have not seen their people hounded down like wolves by Radical Revenue officials, and in many instances shot down like dogs.... Yes, you have seen all this and more too."[41] In this atmosphere, Redmond was assured to gain the support of local communities.

Redmond's arrival in Pickens County did not escape the notice of federal authorities. By the fall of 1876, South Carolina Collector of Internal Revenue L. Cass Carpenter had ordered Deputy Marshal E. H. Barton from Easley, a town located in southeastern Pickens County, to apprehend the young outlaw. On January 11, 1877, Barton, who had thus far been unsuccessful in discovering the moonshiner's whereabouts, received information from a "trusty scout" that Redmond was selling alcohol near the town of Liberty. Barton immediately organized a raiding party of four deputies, including Van B. Hendricks and William F. Gary. Around 1:00 A.M. on the twelfth, the party had surrounded the residence where Redmond was operating his illegal business. Posing as a potential customer, Hendricks then approached the house, knocked on the door, and, upon seeing Redmond, lit a match as a signal for Barton and the other deputies to storm the dwelling. In a report to Commissioner of Internal Revenue Green B. Raum, Carpenter explained what happened next:

> Everything was carried out successfully. Barton entered, secured two prisoners, Redmond and one other, and at once tied Redmond's arms. Not having quite rope enough to tie his legs, he went out the door to where his wagon

was standing to get a portion of the harness to complete the bindings. Scarcely had Barton reached the open air before Redmond sprang from among those around him, left the same door where Barton had just gone out, and made for the timber, about 50 yards away. The snow was at least four inches deep at the time, and the night quite dark. Barton immediately brought his double-barreled shot-gun to bear upon the flying fugitive, but it missed fire the first time, and before he could get the other barrel ready, Redmond had got so far into the timber as to be invisible.

Following Redmond's escape, Barton and his men confiscated a wagon, several horses, and other personal items belonging to the outlaw and started toward Easley. The party was only able to travel about half a mile before riding into an ambush. Barton heard a loud bang and felt an intense pain as buckshot from Redmond's gun ripped through his right forearm and thigh. Hendricks received more serious wounds. "Several buck shot passed through his scrotum and testicles, one through his penis, and one though the fleshy part of his thigh," Barton informed Carpenter. After returning fire, the party retreated to a nearby house, where the owner, Mr. Pepper, reluctantly allowed the deputies to dress Hendricks's wounds and rest for the night.[42] At daybreak, Barton's party separated. Two of the deputies rode with Barton to his house in Easley, while Gary accompanied Hendricks to Liberty. Before reaching Liberty, Hendricks and Gary once again confronted Lewis and two other men, who "asked for Barton; and upon being told he had gone the other way, and was probably several miles on his way home, gave up further pursuit and left."[43]

Redmond, however, was not yet ready to end his dispute with Barton. Three days after the outlaw's escape, a Pickens County official reported that a group of twenty-five mounted men, "armed with guns, pistols, axes, &c.," had informed a local African American that "they intended to have the horses, &c., that Barton and his guard captured." "I am uneasy for Barton every moment, and would not be surprised to hear of his being murdered at any time," Carpenter wrote to Raum on January 18.[44] Redmond soon enacted his revenge. On the morning of January 20, Lewis, "with nine of his heavily armed mountain roughs," surrounded Barton's house. Barton's wife stopped them at the gate, allowing her husband, who had been sleeping, to put on his clothes. The deputy marshal then informed Redmond that he was coming out and that the outlaw "could dispose of [him] as he liked." Standing outside the house, Lewis demanded that Barton return the horses, wagon, and other personal belongings that the raiding party had captured. Barton informed Redmond that the horses were miles away in the town of Greenville in Greenville County. Redmond responded by forcing Barton's wife to take two of the deputy's horses and accompany him to Easley, where she cashed a check for $105 to pay for the confiscated horses. The outlaw then, according to Barton, "made her dismount in the public streets, took the best horse I had, worth at least $100, and returned to her the other one."[45]

Redmond's escape from federal authorities and subsequent raid on Barton's house in January 1877 alarmed Carpenter, who believed (correctly) that the outlaw had organized a large illicit distilling operation around "Rocky Bottom," located in northern Pickens County on the North Carolina–South Carolina border. He immediately requested that Commissioner of Internal Revenue Raum deploy more federal troops to assist revenue agents in the capture of the young moonshiner.[46] "This man Redmond is a desperate fellow, ready to take human life whenever one interferes with his plans in any way," Carpenter explained to his superior that January. "His capture and conviction would do much towards breaking up the traffic."[47] Raum agreed: "[T]hese high-hand outrages . . . ought to be stopped, and the majesty of the law vindicated."[48] In late January, Raum ordered Revenue Agent Jacob Wagoner, who had conducted several successful raids in western North Carolina, "to inaugurate a vigorous movement to suppress frauds and arrest violators of the law in [Carpenter's] district."[49] Three months later, Raum instructed Lieut. W. A. Miller of the U.S. Eighteenth Infantry, stationed in Greenville, to use a detachment under his command to help federal officials arrest Lewis and other moonshiners operating in Pickens County.[50]

With the help of federal troops, revenue agents captured several members of "Redmond's band," which, Lieut. Miller exaggerated, numbered "at least one hundred and fifty men." On April 23, 1877, for instance, federal authorities conducted a raid in "Rocky Bottom," where they confronted two known associates of Redmond, both of whom "resisted arrests and attempted to cut the collector and marshal with a cavalry saber and shoot them with a revolver."[51] That following day, another raiding party operating in northern Pickens County destroyed two large distilleries and captured a Mr. Porter. Carpenter reported what happened next: "Redmond, who lives in the vicinity of Porter's place, was sent for, and an effort [was] made to capture the three deputies who had gone two miles or more ahead of the soldiers." "These people are more bold and defiant than ever," an angry Carpenter confessed.[52]

By the summer of 1877, Redmond's continued resistance against federal liquor law officials had begun to garner him national attention. On June 6, the *New York Times* published what would be the first of several exposés on the outlaw and his band. "In Pickens and the adjoining counties an organization is known to exist which embraces a large proportion of the male population, who have thus far evaded all efforts of the authorities to detect and capture them," the *Times* read. "This organization is under the direction of a man named Redmond, and is reported to be well armed and disciplined for offensive and defensive operations."[53]

Editors of the *Times* and revenue agents alike argued that South Carolina Democrats encouraged Redmond and other moonshiners to evade the law. In June 1877, Carpenter believed that Wade Hampton, who in his 1876 campaign had "told the people that if he were elected governor they could have their little stills on every branch if they desired," was responsible for these "outrages." "They [illicit distillers] seem to have got the impression from somewhere that Wade Hampton can save them from any further payment of tax to the United States Government," he wrote to Raum, "and they flatly refuse to have anything more to do with revenue matters."[54] U.S. Marshal R. M. Wallace agreed. That September, he revealed that "one of the most serious difficulties with which we have to contend [in South Carolina] is the universal hostility of the democratic State officials" whose refusal to cooperate with revenue agents inspired mountain distillers to break the liquor law.[55]

While federal authorities intensified their efforts to apprehend Redmond, the moonshiner's popularity increased in Pickens County and other parts of South Carolina. For many native whites, Redmond was becoming a hero, an unreconstructed Confederate waging war against an "unjust" federal government. As such, local residents defended Redmond's misdeeds and protected him from revenue agents. In January 1877, for instance, the *Pickens Sentinel* blamed Barton, who allegedly "struck and kicked Redmond after he was tied," for making the outlaw "angry" and forcing him to commit violence.[56] The *Charleston News and Courier* agreed that Barton's behavior in the raid was "outrageous" and labeled revenue enforcement "as part of the Yankee oppression resulting from the late war."[57] Nor did citizens of Easley condemn Redmond's raid on Barton's house later that same month. According to Carpenter, they cheered, "*Hurrah for Redmond;* he has done right," as Barton's wife gave the outlaw $105 and a horse.[58] By the fall of 1877, federal authorities found it impossible to capture Redmond, largely because local residents would give him (and other moonshiners) ample warning of a raiding party's approach.[59] "The entire population sympathize with him, and shield him whenever necessary," Lieut. John Anderson of the U.S. Eighteenth Infantry complained in June 1877. "In fact, it has become the pride of many to boast of their connection with Redmond."[60]

Commissioner of Internal Revenue Green B. Raum, headquartered in Washington, D.C., was not intimidated, however. "I am fully determined that the illicit manufacture and sale of spirits . . . shall be suppressed," he informed a Palmetto State revenue agent in January 1878.[61] To accomplish this

INTRODUCTION

goal, Raum launched a counteroffensive against the moonshiners of southern Appalachia. Effective enforcement, he believed, required "a force of deputies, armed when necessary, as will demonstrate the ability and determination of the government to collect its revenues and enforce its laws."[62] More so than any other commissioner before him, Raum would rely heavily on civilian posses, arguing (correctly) that the use of federal troops "was a constant irritation to the people" and "should not be long continued."[63] With these posses, newly appointed South Carolina Collector of Internal Revenue E. M. Brayton coordinated the first of many seasonal sweeps throughout the region in February 1878, focusing on moonshine strongholds located in Greenville, Oconee, Pickens, and Spartanburg counties.[64]

Meanwhile, Redmond, who had thus far maintained a low profile, would regain the attention of Raum in March 1878, when he "rescued" three fellow moonshiners from the Pickens County jail. According to Collector Brayton, Redmond, with "a body of men numbering about fifteen," arrived in Easley on the night of March 9, where they proceeded to the local jail and called for Sheriff Joab Mauldin, who was guarding several prisoners inside. The unmasked desperados opened the door and ordered Mauldin to hand over three men who had been incarcerated earlier that day for illicit distilling.[65] The startled sheriff (whom Brayton believed had behaved "grossly negligent" during the jailbreak) recalled what happened next: "I was perfectly helpless to resist them, they having guns presented at me. They demanded and took the keys of the jail from me, and I, in order to save as many of the prisoners from being released or escaping as possible, went with them to the prisoners' room, when they released the three men and took them off on horseback."[66] As soon as the jail breakers had left, Mauldin ran across town to U.S. Commissioner John E. Thornley's house. Thornley then sent for Deputy Collector E. G. Hoffman, who arrived minutes later. But he was too late. The outlaws had escaped.[67]

Three days later, on the morning of March 12, Redmond and fourteen companions returned to Easley. They first stopped at a store and purchased some goods before paying H. B. Hendrix an unwelcome visit. According to Brayton, the outlaws threatened to kill Hendrix if he continued to board Hoffman and other revenue agents. "Searching the house," Brayton explained, "[Redmond] took everything, including some overcoats which he thought belonged to the officers." (The overcoats belonged to deputy marshals William Springs and Charles Cummings.) The band then rode to the nearby town of Liberty, where they ransacked the house of William Gary, who continued to work with the Bureau of Internal Revenue as a guide and informer. Federal authorities once again arrived too late to capture Redmond and his band.[68] "This is high-handed business," Hoffman wrote to Brayton on March 13. "It confirms the information I had received that there was a regularly organized force in the mountains, banded to violate the revenue laws and to fight revenue officers."[69]

Commissioner of Internal Revenue Green Raum was livid over the news. The credibility of the Bureau of Internal Revenue (and the federal government) was at stake. Lewis Redmond had become Public Enemy Number One. On March 12, 1878, Raum authorized Brayton to employ 100 men to apprehend Redmond and the other jail breakers. "Do not fail to use all necessary means to overcome resistance," he telegraphed the collector that following day. "Arrest Redmond . . . at any cost." Three days later, Raum sent another message to Brayton, instructing him to offer a reward of $300 for Redmond's capture. "I regard it as extremely important that this outlaw be captured," he concluded.[70] Brayton was not optimistic, however. "I fear he will either flee temporarily from the State, or hide in the mountains out of the reach of the officers," he warned Raum. "The difficulties which have to be overcome to capture him are almost insuperable."[71] Nonetheless, Brayton followed orders and assembled a team of "courageous and reliable men" to apprehend the moonshiner.

By the end of March, these revenue agents had begun to make headway, capturing several rumored associates of Redmond.[72] Then, on April 27, E. G. Hoffman, with "a force of deputies," encountered the infamous outlaw. That morning, Hoffman and his men crossed the Keowee River into "Rocky Bottom," where they learned that Lewis had been spotted nearby the night before. The agents then "struck [Redmond's] trail which led directly to the house of his mistress, Miss [Adeline] Ladd." They proceeded to surround the house. To the dismay of Hoffman, however, "Redmond discovered two of our men on the hill to the left of the house who had carelessly exposed themselves to view." Lewis immediately ran into the woods. After searching for three hours, Hoffman decided to "move back a few miles and to hide our horses, then return to the vicinity of the Ladd house on foot and lay in the wood for Redmond." The planned failed. As the revenue officers rode off, they heard a loud bang. Hoffman remembered: "Three shots were fired before we could dismount. . . . On our arrival at the spot from whence the shots came we only heard retreating footsteps . . . and our pursuit proved of no avail." One of Hoffman's guides also lay wounded. "It is generally believed that unless immediate steps are taken to prevent it," Hoffman concluded in his report to Brayton, "Redmond or some of his friends will murder both of the guides who led us into Rocky Bottom."[73]

Meanwhile, Redmond continued to enjoy a broad base of support in Pickens County and other parts of South Carolina. Deputy Collector Hoffman believed that local officials refused to cooperate with him because they had "sympathies for the blockade business." "True they made a fine parade and eloquent speeches... but the sheriff's force did nothing [to capture Redmond]," Hoffman complained about Oconee County authorities in March 1878.[74] Nor were Pickens County residents willing to take stern legal action against the outlaw. Circuit Judge T. J. Mackey, for instance, tried to secure an indictment against Redmond and several other men for their role in the jailbreak. The judge, however, soon discovered that "public sympathy was strongly in favor" of the accused. Mackey then attempted to convince the Pickens County Grand Jury to indict Redmond for stealing the overcoats of Deputy Marshals Springs and Cummings. After the jury twice returned a verdict of "No Bill," Mackey removed one of the jurors, who was reportedly "a close ally and intimate associate of Redmond." Only then did it indict Lewis "on the plainest and most reliable evidence."[75]

Supporters of the moonshiners quickly came to Redmond's defense. According to the *Keowee Courier* in April 1878, the young outlaw was "a peaceable, quiet citizen" who had been "badly treated" by revenue agents. "In the past the people [Redmond and other alcohol distillers] have been made to feel that their only redress lay in their own hands, and hence they have been often driven to resistance, when otherwise they would have readily submitted," the newspaper read. "The people have rights as well as these officers."[76] Members of the Pickens County grand jury agreed. Shortly after indicting Redmond for larceny, they convinced Mackey to launch an investigation on the alleged abuses of several revenue agents in northwestern South Carolina. "[S]ufficient facts appear," Foreman R. E. Steele explained to Mackey in late May, "that these officers have, for several years, committed the grossest outrages upon the persons and property of many of our law-abiding citizens, on the mere pretext or suspicion, without any legal proof whatever." Foreman then denounced revenue officials as "'Carpet-Baggers' of infamous character" and listed a number of charges that residents had brought against them: "[Citizens] have been seized under their own roofs or while ploughing in their fields and, without any warrant issued for their arrest, have been manacled and thrown into jail, where, after remaining several days, they have been released, on the ground that there was no evidence against them. These officers have searched private dwellings, both by day and at night, without any search warrant; and have, in several instances, beaten, kicked and otherwise maltreated the victims of their lawless conduct, who protest against the wrong thus done them."[77]

The grand jury investigation and subsequent publication of revenue "outrages" in the *Keowee Courier, Pickens Sentinel,* and other state Democratic newspapers increased South Carolinians' hatred for the Bureau of Internal Revenue.[78] That April, for instance, Hoffman reported that when he asked a

Pickens County boy who was deemed worse, "a revenue officer or a horse-thief," the five-year-old responded: "A revenue officer."[79] Such discontent further legitimized the moonshiners' fight against the federal government and escalated the potential for violence. U.S. Marshal R. M. Wallace noted in April that violations of the liquor law in Pickens, Oconee, Spartanburg, and Greenville counties had become "more frequent and more daring" than "for years previous."[80] Bloodshed soon followed. In Greenville County, on the night of April 19, moonshiners ambushed and mortally wounded Deputy Marshal Rufus H. Springs. Wallace, who considered Springs a "very intelligent, energetic, and efficient officer," was troubled over the news and never able to apprehend the murderers. "The officers have not dared to go out without combining together for mutual protection and they have been shot at repeatedly, but without serious results previous to this time," he wrote to U.S. Attorney General Charles Devens.[81]

In June 1878, tensions between South Carolinians and Bureau of Internal Revenue agents erupted when deputy collectors, searching for Redmond, killed his friend and future wife's brother, Amos Ladd. This homicide ultimately brought national attention to the so-called moonshine wars of southern Appalachia and made Redmond "the most notorious character in America."[82] According to South Carolina District Attorney L. C. Northrop, the four revenuers—Hugh Kane, William H. Durham, G. W. Moose, and R. P. Scruggs—shot the twenty-one-year-old Amos in self-defense. Northrop explained that, on the night of June 8, the raiding party arrived in "Rocky Bottom" with a warrant to arrest Redmond, Ladd, and twenty other moonshiners. They then walked to the house of Redmond's girlfriend Adeline Ladd, where the noted outlaw and "his trusty henchman," Amos, were rumored to have been residing. The deputy collectors hid in the woods for a day and, when they determined that the suspects were inside the domicile, advanced. Kane walked toward the front of the dwelling and was the first agent to confront Amos. The moonshiner reportedly raised his pistol at the deputy collector and pulled the trigger. Fortunately for Kane, the gun misfired. Amos then ran to the rear of the house where Durham, "seeing him [Amos] armed and not knowing whether he had shot Kane or not, fired upon him." Three bullets entered Amos's body, killing him instantly. Meanwhile, Moose and Scruggs captured another unnamed man who had fled the abode. The four revenuers then decided that it was best for them to leave the vicinity.[83] "We immediately started for Pickens C. H. to surrender to the sheriff of that county," Kane wrote to Collector Brayton on June 10. "This latter idea we abandoned after considering the imminent danger our lives would be in if we were confined in Pickens jail. We hired a horse and I rode to Easley Station and took the train for Greenville. When I reached the latter place I procured a team and went to bring in the other men, which I did, and then surrendered to Sheriff Gilreath to-day."[84]

Outraged, the South Carolina press reported a different version of Ladd's death. The *Pickens Sentinel* called it "cold blooded" murder. "It appears that that the young man [Amos] was standing, or rather leaning, against the door facing, when the Revenue officers . . . walked up . . . and deliberately shot him dead on the spot without a moment's warning or an intimation of their designs," editor D. F. Bradley of the *Sentinel* wrote on June 13. "We pronounce this one of the most fiendish, cold blooded murders ever committed in this County."[85] Other newspapers soon joined the chorus of opposition. The *Charleston News and Courier* denounced Ladd's "killers" as "a gang of bullies." It then warned that the "atrocious murder" would provoke more violence "unless the people can see that there is protection and safety to be had by lawful means."[86] The *Greenville Enterprise and Mountaineer* agreed: "The killing was unjustifiable upon any ground whatever—a cowardly, brutal and atrocious murder. . . . For years they [revenuers] have held a reign of terror in the mountains, and it is getting high time they were being taught that there is still a God in Israel and law in the land. We are tired, in common with the honest public, of the fearful murders in which these ruffians are the principle actors. The revenue service of South Carolina must be reformed or an outraged and indignant people will take the law into their own hands."[87]

State officials promptly charged Kane, Scruggs, Durham, and Moose with first-degree murder. The deputy collectors were worried, and for good reason. Writing to Attorney Charles Devens on June 15, one of their attorneys, William E. Earle, explained: "The press of this State is united in the cry for the blood of these men. And its popular effect has been immediate. A trial means conviction."[88] Collector Brayton bewailed that "in any other country the people would praise and honor" the accused "instead of hating and persecuting them."[89] Although unable to initially have the case removed to federal court, where the deputy collectors believed they would be acquitted, Earle and District Attorney L. C. Northrop succeeded in transferring the trial from Pickens County to Anderson.[90] That August, after Northrop had earlier issued a writ of habeas corpus, the deputy collectors were then peacefully transferred to federal custody.[91] The trial, largely due to jurisdictional quarrels and prosecuting attorneys' inability to locate several witnesses, dragged on until 1882, when the four deputy collectors were finally acquitted of the state murder charges in federal court.[92] By then, as we shall see, support for the moonshiners had declined in South Carolina and other former Confederate states.

When the news of Ladd's death reached Charleston, the *News and Courier* instructed C. McKinley "to go and find Redmond." Little is known about McKinley. The journalist had been working for the *News and Courier* since at least January 1878, when he covered a story about a Union County militia group that accosted several revenue agents who had confiscated some illicit tobacco. Shortly thereafter, McKinley became the paper's regular correspondent for news in northwestern South Carolina.[93] Arriving in Pickens County on June 20, the reporter made inquiries about Redmond's whereabouts. Despite local residents' distrust of "strangers," he eventually made contact with two of Redmond's band and asked them if he could interview the outlaw. On June 24, McKinley received a note from Redmond granting him permission to do so. McKinley quickly packed his belongings and walked out of town alone "into the adjacent woods and by a circuitous route reached the rendezvous appointed for the night." There, he met W. T. Field, a local probate judge who had agreed to take the reporter to Redmond's hideout.[94] That next day, after an exhausting journey, McKinley and his guide at last met Redmond. The subsequent interview (which Redmond affirmed took place) turned the young outlaw into a national celebrity.[95]

An opponent of the Bureau of Internal Revenue, McKinley clearly sympathized with Lewis. He described the outlaw as "little more than a boy in years" and "one of the handsomest men I ever saw." Nor did McKinley believe that Redmond possessed the qualities of a "bad man." "His frank open manner, innocent young eyes, and more than all his honest sun-browed face and pleasant smile, which no man could wear and yet be a villain," the reporter explained, "inspired me at once with perfect confidence, and placed me so much at ease." In McKinley's view, Redmond was a devoted brother, a loyal Democrat, and a philanthropist. He wrote:

> The simple-hearted women of the mountains all admire if they do not love him, and neither his name nor his presence have any terrors for them. Why it was only last year, say they, that he paid off the taxes which were hanging over the heads of I am afraid to state how many poor families. ... And besides all this, did he not ride five consecutive days "working for Hampton" during the last campaign, and on election day did he not hitch up his own wagon and team and send eight or ten old men who couldn't walk and who hadn't voted for years, all the way from their homes to the poll at Eastatoe, where he dared not go himself? And, outlaw as he is, is he not now supporting his three sisters, who have no other dependence, and one of whom has been a cripple for eleven years?

INTRODUCTION

McKinley insisted that Lewis was the quintessential Southerner, an honorable man who protected his family and community from corrupt federal revenue agents. "What can I do for him [Redmond]," he concluded. "Nothing but to feebly write down his far off impassioned appeal to the executors of that stern law which had outlawed him, and to await the answer I must send [for Redmond to live peace]. What shall it be? Will they give him a chance or not? I do not know."[96]

As McKinley wrote down the outlaw's words "almost verbatim" in a notebook, Redmond said little to refute the journalist's flattering portrayal of him. Lewis first recalled the tragic death of his elderly parents, which he blamed on revenue agents. Redmond then insisted that he had killed Duckworth in self-defense. "Duckworth," the moonshiner explained, "swore he 'would take me, warrant or no warrant, or would kill me in the attempt.'" Moreover, Redmond argued that his raid on Barton's house was warranted because the deputy marshal had treated him dishonorably. Lewis then insisted that he was in North Carolina during the Pickens County jailbreak. As for his role in the Gary and Hendrix raids, Lewis maintained that they were not his "doing." "I did not lead the party, and at first refused to go with them," he told McKinley. "They said they had gone with me when I needed them, and now I refused to help them when they needed me. So I went." According to McKinley, Redmond concluded the interview with a tearful plea for mercy: "It looks hard for me to have to go through all this. If I had done anything worthy of it I would not mind, but I have not done more than other people, and why should I have to bear it all? . . . I have settled my troubles with Barton and Hendri[x], and this very week Gary sent me word that if I would let him alone he would quit the revenue service and go to work on his farm. . . . I only want peace, so I can go back to my farm and work for myself and my sisters, without being shot at every day like a dog. They have shot at me twenty-six times already, and I think that ought to be enough."[97] Like Jesse James and other southern outlaws, Redmond played an active role in the myth-making process, promoting himself as the victim of an "unjust" federal government.

Published in the *Charleston News and Courier* from July 2 to 4, 1878, Redmond's interview quickly captured the interest of several northern newspapers. By July 20, both the *New York Times* and the *National Police Gazette* had printed portions of the interview. Both newspapers were hesitant to champion Redmond and his fight against the Bureau of Internal Revenue. Reflecting the views of many northern Republicans, the *New York Times* argued that the Democratic Party encouraged Redmond and other moonshiners to commit violence for political gain. "To throw a romantic air over the fight for federal patronage, and indeed, to give it the appearance of a missionary enterprise, the editors of the *News and Courier* sent McK. to Pickens to interview the outlaw Lewis R. Redmond and his lawless companions," the *Times* reported on July 15. "He [McKinley] retailed, with an air of truth, the many virtues and trials of the 'moonshiners,' and placed United States revenue officers in a most questionable light." The *Times* believed that nothing could have been further from the truth. It dismissed the interview as propaganda (which was true) and provided readers with its own description of Redmond. The newspaper charged that Redmond lived with several "concubines" and seldom cared for his sisters. Editors also noted that Redmond had murdered Alfred McCreary, an informer who "was shot in his field while surrounded by his little children." "[It] is fear of the outlaw that seals the lips of his neighbors," the *Times* concluded in explaining why Lewis had thus far avoided capture.[98]

For northern Democrats, however, Redmond's interview confirmed what many of them had long believed: that Republicans used the Bureau of Internal Revenue as a tool to expand federal authority and punish white Southerners. The Democratic *New York World,* for instance, condemned revenuers' alleged maltreatment of Redmond. It also protested District Attorney L. C. Northrop's attempt to transfer the murder case against Durham, Moose, Kane, and Scruggs to federal court. "There is a revenue law, and it is to be obeyed unfalteringly, no matter how unjust or oppressive individuals may think it," the *World* read in July 1878. "But there are also laws which govern the officials appointed to enforce that revenue law, and when they are violated the offender must be punished by the same process as any other criminal."[99] The *Springfield Republican* in Massachusetts agreed, adding that Commissioner of Internal Revenue Green B. Raum could avoid further bloodshed in the mountain South by appointing more honest men. It explained: "The true way to deal with it [moonshiner resistance to federal liquor law enforcement] is to place the execution of the law in the hands of men whom the people trust, and then tone up the public sentiment to support them."[100]

Meanwhile, the *Charleston News and Courier* emerged as the mouthpiece for the pro-moonshiner movement in South Carolina. Following its publication of Redmond's interview, the newspaper, fearful that the federal government used the Bureau of Internal Revenue to expand its authority, printed a series of articles defending the outlaw and other illicit distillers.[101] These men reportedly opposed federal liquor taxation for two reasons. First, the moonshiner believed that he had an inherent right to distill alcohol and was simply "doing precisely that same thing that his father and father's father did with impunity and a clear conscience for years before he was born." More important, moonshiners supposedly broke the law out of economic necessity. Because of the mountain region's rugged terrain and poor roads, mountain

INTRODUCTION

farmers had to distill their corn into alcohol to make a living. But the *News and Courier* believed that the federal liquor tax had significantly reduced farmers' profit margin and forced them to become moonshiners. The newspaper explained: "It cost a farmer ten dollars to haul to market twenty bushels of corn that sold for eight dollars. The whole value of the corn [is] absorbed, with two dollars additional, by payment for a wagon and for the subsistence of the farmer and his team. When distilled the same corn would have produced fifty gallons of whiskey, worth seventy-five dollars, at the rate of $1.50 per gallon. What wonder is it that the illicit manufacture of whiskey continues, despite the risk and danger. . . . [I]t is distill or starve with the large majority of the small farmers on the Ridge."[102]

These articles solidified many white South Carolinians' belief that the federal government had overstepped its legal authority. An opponent of the Bureau of Internal Revenue, Governor Wade Hampton quickly sought to profit from this groundswell of support for Redmond and other illicit distillers. In mid-July, he demanded that the federal government offer amnesty to Palmetto State moonshiners, much to the delight of state Democrats.[103] "It will carry joy to many a mountaineer who has borne the indignities of the revenue officials for doing that which to his mind was perfectly correct," the *Ninety-Six Guardian* in Hampton County rejoiced. "This action of Governor Hampton will doubly endear him to the people of the State."[104] Hampton then publicly announced that he opposed defense attorney W. E. Earle's attempt to transfer the Ladd murder case to federal court.[105] Finally, in late July, the governor withdrew a $200 reward that he had authorized following the Pickens County jailbreak for the capture of Redmond.[106] "Hampton found he had been a little too premature in offering a reward for the arrest of Redmond for breaking open the Pickens County jail," Earle remembered. "It was proven to him that Redmond neither led the party nor aided in the rescue of the illicit distillers."[107]

Faced with such growing discontent in South Carolina (and other former Confederate states), Commissioner of Internal Revenue Green B. Raum took immediate action. On July 29, he instructed newly appointed Revenue Agent W. H. Chapman to visit the counties of Pickens, Greenville, Oconee, and Spartanburg and discuss with "leading citizens" there "a peaceful and orderly" solution to local residents' resistance to federal liquor taxation. "I earnestly desire that the internal revenue laws shall be enforced peaceably and quietly and without the necessity of using an armed force," he then explained to Chapman and other subordinates. "This can only be done where the officers are supported by a public sentiment favorable to the observance and enforcement of the laws."[108] That following month, Raum allowed District Attorney

L. C. Northrop to grant amnesty to Palmetto State moonshiners if they pled guilty in federal court and pledged not to distill alcohol illegally again.[109]

South Carolinians responded favorably to Raum's lenient course of action. That August, the Greenville County Grand Jury expressed its "hearty approval and commendation of the wise and beneficent policy adopted by the government towards this class of the violators of its laws."[110] State and mountain newspapers agreed. "This is glad tidings," the *Charleston News and Courier* wrote on August 10 in praising Raum's decision to enact clemency. "By a word the Government has worked a revolution in the condition of the moonshiners. They need live no longer like hunted animals."[111] Meanwhile, the *Speight's Spartanburg Daily* applauded the "magnanimity and clemency of the government."[112] The *Keowee Courier* in Oconee County also extolled the amnesty order. "This is a right step of the government, both as a corrective and preventative," the newspaper read. "It will accomplish more, and promptly, in securing obedience to the law than all the marshals and commissioners in the State could effect in a year of turmoil . . . and confusion."[113] Even D. F. Bradley of the *Pickens Sentinel* admitted that the federal government had acted wisely and urged distillers to obey the law.[114]

To Raum's delight, hundreds of moonshiners in northwestern South Carolina quickly turned themselves into federal and state officials. "The announcement [of amnesty] was hailed with joy by many men who had been engaged in various violations of the law," U.S. Marshal R. M. Wallace wrote to Attorney General Charles Devens on August 7. "[N]early all defendants even the most guilty soon asked to be allowed to enter the plea of guilty."[115] Three days later, the *Charleston News and Courier* reported that 167 moonshiners had traveled to Greenville, where they surrendered to revenue agents and offered to plead guilty in federal court.[116] Overall, the number of convictions for evading federal liquor taxation in South Carolina rose from 85 in 1877 to 632 in 1879, an increase of 644 percent.[117] Moreover, federal records suggest that Raum's lenient policy encouraged many Palmetto State moonshiners to become legitimate, as the number of registered stills multiplied from 7 in 1876 to 109 in 1879.[118]

Raum, however, made sure that South Carolinians did not interpret his benevolence as a sign of weakness. He quickly ordered revenue agents to continue their operations against the illicit distillers. Raum also announced that Redmond would not receive amnesty, much to the dismay of the *Charleston News and Courier*. "The Government cannot afford to treat him as if he were a notorious criminal, instead of what he is, one as much sinned against as sinning," the newspaper read on August 21.[119] Raum disagreed. He argued that Redmond's case was an exception to the rule. "I will say that the apologist of

INTRODUCTION

Redmond shows him to have been a violator of the law of the most desperate character, pursuing the business of defrauding the Government for a livelihood, and shooting officers without mercy who undertook his arrest," Raum explained to attorney W. E. Earle. "His gross misconduct led directly to the death of Ladd [and] I cannot consent to grant any leniency to Redmond while Deputies Kane and others are incarcerated or in jeopardy."[120]

The news of Raum's refusal to extend Redmond amnesty further propelled the outlaw into the national spotlight. Along with the *Charleston News and Courier,* the *New York Times* and the *Washington Post* closely watched the events unfolding in northwestern South Carolina and asked their readership "Will Redmond Come In?"[121] That August, C. McKinley and several Pickens County residents visited Lewis and tried to convince him to surrender. According to the *New York Times,* however, the moonshiner "saw through this a scheme to claim the reward offered for his capture, and left them abruptly." "It will be dangerous for these benevolent persons to visit that locality again," the *Times* concluded.[122] Meanwhile, District Attorney L. C. Northrop, having just secured an indictment against the outlaw for his role in the Pickens County jailbreak, believed that the noose was tightening around Redmond's neck. "I am advised that the people are doing their best to get Redmond out of the country, before his inevitable capture or death," he wrote to Attorney General Charles Devens on August 30. "[H]is own gang have betrayed him and I understand, that he himself . . . is advising the people to quit distilling and to obey the law."[123]

Nonetheless, Redmond's unwillingness to surrender solidified his status as a folk hero. For many South Carolinians, he remained a symbol of defiance to federal authority. On August 30, for instance, revenue agents visited Pumpkintown in Pickens County, where hundreds of denizens had congregated to vote in the Democratic primary election. An "old man" quickly greeted the federal officials and bragged that Redmond would never surrender. "After leaving the voting place," one of the revenuers remembered, "we could distinctly hear the crowd cheering the name of Redmond. . . . I really did not think the sentiment of the masses would be favorable to Redmond, but I fear it is so."[124] That same day, E. G. Hoffman and his special force arrived at Pickens Court House and "found an excited crowd cheering for Redmond." The crowd also advised the raiding party not to enter Redmond's base of operations in Eastatoe Township. "It was predicted," Hoffman explained to Commissioner of Internal Revenue Green Raum, "that a visit from us would bring about bloodshed, and I have no doubt that under the circumstances somebody would have been hurt."[125] Raum was furious over the news. On September 7, he wrote to Collector E. M. Brayton: "I want you and them [Redmond's supporters] to understand that if there is a manifestation of an organization on the part of illicit distillers for the purpose of resisting the law, that instead of attacking them with a handful of men I will authorize you to employ such a force as will be overwhelming, so as to avoid bloodshed on either side."[126]

By 1879, Redmond and other South Carolina moonshiners found themselves in retreat. Raum's leniency had begun to reduce illicit distillers' resistance to federal liquor taxation and encouraged many local residents to tolerate the Bureau of Internal Revenue.[127] Raum also ordered Palmetto State revenuers to intensify their search for Redmond, who had reportedly resumed his illegal activities.[128] In February, federal officials captured two members of "Redmond's band," Joseph Chapman and Joseph Dodgers. Both men (in exchange for clemency) testified that Redmond had led the Pickens County jailbreak and subsequent raids on Hendrix's and Gary's abodes.[129] These arrests, along with revenuers' success in locating and destroying stills, prompted District Attorney Northrop to declare in March: "[Redmond's] gang is broken up."[130]

Lewis agreed and quickly fled to western North Carolina, where he eventually settled near Charleston (now Bryson City) in Swain County.[131] By the spring of 1879, North Carolina's Sixth District collector John J. Mott learned that Redmond, still wanted for the 1876 murder of Duckworth, had moved to the mountain region and ordered revenue agents to apprehend him. According to Deputy Collector Robert A. Cobb, U.S. Marshal A. C. Bryan almost captured the outlaw shortly thereafter.[132] In October, U.S. Marshal Robert M. Douglas also reportedly "ran across" Redmond, but, concluding that his force was "inferior" to the outlaw's "band of 25 or 30 desperate characters," withdrew "from the vicinity without much ceremony." "The only reason why Redmond has not been apprehended is believed to be on the account of the insufficiency of the reward offered by the government [for Duckworth's murder]—$250," the *Asheville Citizen* reported after Douglas's near confrontation with the moonshiner. "Marshal Douglas says if the government will make the reward $1,000 he will wager that Redmond will be forthcoming."[133] To the dismay of Douglas, however, Redmond evaded federal authorities (and bounty hunters) for two more years.

The year 1879 also marked the publication of Edward B. Crittenden's *The Entwined Lives of Miss Gabrielle Austin, Daughter of the Late Rev. Ellis C. Austin, and of Redmond, the Outlaw, Leader of the North Carolina "Moonshiners."* Published in Philadelphia, this dime novel, which went through at least three printings in English and one in German, must have thrilled its Victorian audience. The narrative begins in 1878 in Virginia, where the angelic Gabrielle Austin is falsely accused of larceny, convicted, and sentenced to be whipped

INTRODUCTION

by an African American constable. Stripped to the waist, she is rescued from the public flogging by a "mysterious knight of modern times," who leaves without telling Gabrielle his name. Gabrielle then travels to Asheville, North Carolina, to live with her cousin, whose husband, Dick Allison, is a revenue agent. One day, while traveling with Dick, Gabrielle's wagon is attacked by a band of moonshiners. After killing Dick, the men seize Gabrielle and take her to their hideout, a large cave located on Mount Mitchell. There, she learns that their leader is the same man who had saved her from the whipping post, Lewis Redmond. The young captive also discovers that Redmond is a tormented man. Although educated and refined, he lives only to avenge his father's death at the hands of federal authorities. "One night a body of Federal troops surrounded our house, and demanded my father's surrender," he explains to Gabrielle. "Like a brave man he refused, and gave up his life rather than sacrifice his liberty. The shock of that terrible night's occurrence killed my mother, and I, a boy in years and in experience with the rugged side of life's journey, was an orphan." Unable to shed innocent blood, Lewis ultimately allows Gabrielle and her fiancé, who attempted to rescue her, to leave unscathed. Nonetheless, Redmond refuses to reform himself. "Redmond the outlaw," Crittenden writes, "still defies the authority of the law, daily commits crimes unparalleled in history, has startling adventures and hairbreadth escapes."[134]

Crittenden concludes *Entwined Lives* by giving Redmond's own account of his life. In it, Redmond claims that he had attended Princeton University, where his fellow students were "all Northern born and especially intolerant toward the South," and that he had lived in Europe during the Civil War. In 1867, after learning that "anarchy [now] ruled supreme" in the South, he returns to live with his family in North Carolina. Months later, his father, who was a devoted Confederate and member of the Ku Klux Klan, is murdered by federal troops. Only then does Redmond become an illicit distiller, hoping to enact revenge on an "unjust" federal government. "We have a right to protest against laws which injure us," Lewis writes in justifying why he had killed fifty-four revenue officials. "If our protest is not heeded, the document which declared us a free and independent nation instructs us to exercise our right and duty, and 'throw off such government' . . . which forbids us to manufacture the products of our own land without first paying . . . a tax."[135]

Despite Crittenden's claim that "I emphatically endorse this narrative as true in every particular . . . the honest stamp of truth in every line," *Entwined Lives* was a hoax. Bishop Crittenden, Gabrielle Austin, and most of its other characters never existed. In fact, Redmond (in 1886) and revenue agents alike denounced the dime novel as a fraud.[136] "Some two or three years since, a pamphlet, purporting to give a correct narrative of Redmond's life and adventures, was given to the public, and had a wide sale," revenuer George Atkinson wrote in 1881. "From personal knowledge of my own, and from facts derived from United States officers in the two Carolinas, I pronounce the whole story a fabrication and a myth."[137] Robert A. Cobb from Burke County, North Carolina, agreed: "I have not the time to speak . . . of this print, which grossly libels the people of my native mountains. It is the life of an outlaw, but not the kind of outlaw Major Redmond is."[138] Even Redmond's wife, Adeline, complained about *Entwined Lives*. "Why they even printed a whole book about him and it was full of lies," she told a newspaper reporter in 1927. "I put a stop to the sale of that book around here. They had in it that Mr. Redmond killed lots of people and lived in a cave up in the mountains. My man never lived in a cave in his life and he never killed but one man [Alfred Duckworth]."[139]

Although factually incorrect, *Entwined Lives* exemplified the struggle white southern men believed themselves to have been engaged in following the Civil War and solidified Redmond's status as a hero. In it, Redmond attempts to defend white males' mastery over their households and communities against the impositions of federal authority. When saving Gabrielle from the whipping post, for instance, Lewis valiantly fights with and defeats the African American constable. Charged with the protection of white women and restoration of the racial status quo in the post–Civil War South, Redmond is acting like any other honorable gentleman. Nor does Crittenden depict Redmond as a ruthless murderer. The revenue agents he kills deserved their fate. They were often "desperate" and "irascible" individuals who had provoked Redmond to commit violence. More important, these men worked for the Bureau of Internal Revenue, an agency that promoted the expansion of federal authority. Many white southern males, hoping to reassert their own hegemony, could relate to the themes in *Entwined Lives* and champion Lewis as a former Confederate who refused to surrender.

Meanwhile, Redmond's life as an outlaw was about to come to an end. In 1881, bureau agents intensified their search for Lewis, who, despite apologists' claims that he had become a law-abiding citizen, continued to manufacture and distribute moonshine near Charleston in Swain County, North Carolina.[140] That February, Deputy Collector Robert A. Cobb's raiding party (which probably consisted of six men) almost captured the young outlaw. Having left Charleston four hours earlier, Cobb and his force arrived near Redmond's home around 3:00 A.M. on the twenty-ninth. They quickly dismounted from their horses and proceeded to crawl on their knees toward the domicile. Before reaching the house, however, several of Redmond's dogs began to bark, awakening the outlaw and his wife. Cobb immediately "called for [Redmond's] wife to make a light, which she did very reluctantly." The raiding party then entered

INTRODUCTION

the house, but Lewis was not inside. He had supposedly escaped through a small hole in the rear of the dwelling (or through "a low, wide chimney"). According to Cobb, Redmond, who was then hiding in the woods, screamed: "I will let you off this time without hurting you, but the next time you come back I will be better prepared for you." As Cobb's men ran in the direction from where Lewis had yelled, the moonshiner fired two rounds over their heads and ran deeper into the forest. "[T]he night being very dark, and Redmond having all advantage of the location, further attempt to pursue him that night was deemed unwise," Cobb ended his account of the incident.[141]

The outlaw's luck would soon run out, however. On the morning of April 7, another raiding party reached the vicinity of Redmond's house and hid themselves in the woods. Redmond's dogs again began to bark, but this time the revenue force remained quiet. The moonshiner supposedly told a *National Police Gazette* correspondent what happened next: "It was 10 o'clock one morning 'long 'bout the first week in this month, when my wife asked me to stop out into the edge of the clearin' 'round the house and kill her a squirrel or two. She said that she heard the dogs a barkin' up on the edge of the woods, and she 'lowed they'd treed one up thar. I got down the shot-gun and started up the ridge on t'other side 'o the house. When I got in 'bout fifty yards o' the dogs, 'bout half a dozen men stepped out from behind a cliff, and hollered, 'Halt.'"[142] According to Cobb, Redmond then raised his shotgun at the revenue agents, who immediately fired their weapons. Shot (perhaps) six times, Lewis attempted to flee from the scene. He was able to run a half a mile before exhaustion and blood loss forced him to surrender.[143] Federal authorities had at last apprehended the "King of the Moonshiners," a feat that quickly made national headlines and would become immortalized in the 1881 publication of Robert A. Cobb's *The True Life of Maj. Lewis Richard Redmond, the Notorious Outlaw and Famous Moonshiner, of Western North Carolina, Who Was Born in Swain County, N.C., in the Year 1855, and Arrested April 7, 1881*.[144]

Six days after Redmond's capture, deputy marshals transported the prisoner to Asheville, where a doctor tended to his wounds.[145] Although Lewis eventually recovered, he talked "in a very hoarse tone, as if he was in pain with the drawing of each breath," due to several bullet wounds near his lungs and throat.[146] In August, federal authorities, perhaps having heard rumors of an impending rescue, transferred Redmond to Greenville, much to the delight of South Carolinians.[147] When Redmond's train stopped at Spartanburg, for instance, hundreds of spectators assembled around the station to catch a glimpse of the outlaw. Greenville residents gave Redmond a hero's welcome. The *Atlanta Daily Constitution* reported that women there were "universally struck" by the moonshiner and had presented him a bouquet of flowers.[148]

According to the *Keowee Courier* on August 18, over five hundred people had visited Redmond in jail, giving him cigars, food, and whiskey.[149] Meanwhile, the *Greenville Daily News* encouraged denizens to "forget [Redmond's] faults in admiration of his undaunted courage and unmistakable dash." Lewis remained a hero, one of the last Confederates who continued to defy the federal government. "Disgusting as it must appear to sensible people," the *New York Times* complained, "it is a fact that Redmond is at this time the most popular man in South Carolina."[150]

Amid this outpouring of sympathy, Redmond's trial began at 10:00 A.M. on August 25, 1881. The federal government, however, would not prosecute Redmond for the murder of Duckworth. Instead, it charged the moonshiner with eight violations of the internal revenue laws and two counts of conspiracy (for his role in the Barton and Gary raids). Redmond "admitted that he had done wrong," but insisted that "some big men" had encouraged him to break the law.[151] After his client pled guilty to all charges, defense attorney A. C. Garlington then asked Judge George S. Bryan for leniency, arguing that Redmond had reformed himself and had suffered enough: "[Redmond] has expressed himself to the mandates of the law, when the authority was shown him. But in April last, while at home in peace, he was fired upon, and severely wounded. Thirteen balls penetrated his body and clothing. Four balls are now in his body; and he is injured perhaps for life. In all the fusillades fired upon him, he numbers one hundred and sixty-two shots. He is now suffering from his grievous wounds. Is this not enough?"[152] Judge Bryan remained unconvinced. On August 29, he sentenced Redmond to serve ten years at the federal penitentiary in Auburn, New York.[153]

News of Redmond's conviction and subsequent prison term garnered national attention.[154] The *New York Times* believed that the outlaw's conviction was "a victory for the cause of law and order." "This man has been, for years, a terror to the officers of the Government instructed with the enforcement of the revenue laws," it read on August 26. "After a hard fight ... [t]he Redmond gang has been broken up."[155] The *Washington Post* also believed that justice had been served and printed a letter from Collector Brayton in which he wrote to Green Raum: "This is a great triumph for the Government."[156] Many South Carolinians, however, disagreed. "These sentences appear to be reasonable and just compared to the offences with which the parties were charged," D. F. Bradley of the *Pickens Sentinel* explained in September, "but we are not prepared to say how they would appear compared to justice, yet we can say who justice would send to Albany [federal penitentiary] with them if it had its way."[157]

Although Redmond remained a celebrated figure, the same could not be said for other illicit distillers. In fact, support for the moonshiners had begun to decline in South Carolina and other former Confederate states before Redmond's capture in 1881. As already discussed, Raum's amnesty order in 1878 had increased Palmetto State residents' tolerance for the Bureau of Internal Revenue. This change in sentiment was also due to the Democratic Party's acceptance of federal liquor taxation beginning in the late 1870s. In 1878, Democrats gained control of both houses of Congress and, despite previously denouncing it as tyrannical, left the Bureau of Internal Revenue intact. Committed to reducing the national tariff, southern Democrats championed this course of action. If the U.S. Congress eliminated the bureau and its liquor tax, which had become the country's leading source of internal revenue, they feared that most Republicans would reject tariff reform. Consequently, by the early 1880s, federal liquor taxation had become a bipartisan issue and moonshiners increasingly lost the support of southern Democrats.[158]

More important, the reputation of moonshiners declined in northwestern South Carolina (and other parts of southern Appalachia) as the region experienced an unprecedented era of economic modernization. Largely due to the completion of the Atlanta & Charlotte Air Line in 1871, capital invested in manufacturing rose 146 percent in Spartanburg, Greenville, Pickens, and Oconee counties between 1870 and 1880.[159] During that decade, Palmetto State highlanders also witnessed dramatic increases in urbanization. In 1870, for instance, census enumerators recorded four communities (Walhalla in Oconee County, Pickens in Pickens County, Greenville in Greenville County, and Spartanburg in Spartanburg County) in the mountain region with a population of over one hundred residents.[160] Ten years later, that number had multiplied to seventeen.[161]

By 1880, industrial development had facilitated the rise of an urban, professional middle class in northwestern South Carolina. These townspeople wanted to create a New South, one in which industry, commercial farming, and cheap labor would become the backbone of the region's economy.[162] They also increasingly argued that alcohol impeded commercial and moral prosperity. "[Alcohol] is . . . an incubus that weighs down our moral, religious, educational, and material progress," the *Keowee Courier* explained in June 1880. "It pollutes society, degrades humanity, and breeds domestic wretchedness and woe."[163] With the support of the *Keowee Courier, Pickens Sentinel,* and other Palmetto State newspapers, urban highlanders embraced the temperance movement during the early 1880s. They chastised the "traditional" drinking mores of their rural neighbors, whom they had begun to view as backward and unrefined, and passed local-option laws to curtail alcohol consumption in their communities.[164] Through such efforts, the town middle class sought to legitimize its control over local affairs and force residents to conform to the demands of the new industrial social order.

The rise of anti-alcohol sentiment ultimately encouraged a growing number of South Carolinians to become more hostile toward the moonshiners. These men and women no longer viewed illicit distillers as valiant Southerners who protected them from "outsiders." Instead, reformers labeled them as the purveyors of violence, crime, and intemperance.[165] In July 1881, for instance, the murder of deputy marshal Thomas Brayton in Pickens County outraged many South Carolinians.[166] The *Charleston News and Courier,* which had been a strong opponent of the Bureau of Internal Revenue, believed that it was "one of the most brutal and heartless murders ever committed in South Carolina." The newspaper then lashed out at the moonshiners:

> Those who are engaged in the illicit whisky trade do not represent any of the conservative elements of society, and are entitled to very little consideration on account of their intelligence, property interests, or general refinement of character. They are as a class men with little property and no education, who openly and defiantly violate the laws for their own personal gain. They are not innocent law-breakers.... The sympathy of those who are moved by the pitiful story of the wrongs of the "moonshiners" is absolutely wasted. It would take a very wide stretch of imagination and the genius of a writer of yellow-back novels to make either a hero or martyr out of the average manufacturer of moonshine whisky.[167]

Mountain residents, most of whom had earlier chastised revenue agents, agreed. According to the *Greenville News,* the "entire population" in Pickens County condemned Brayton's murder. "Nobody that knew him [Brayton] would believe that he could have done anything to provoke the deadly assault," the *News* read on July 24. "He was always kind, courteous, and obliging to the extreme, and was an efficient and popular officer and citizen."[168] The *Keowee Courier* revealed that Brayton's killing was "obnoxious to the law abiding citizens" in Oconee County. "This paper and the large bulk of our people," it continued, "desire to see the illicit liquor traffic utterly suppressed and have used every moral force to this end."[169]

By the 1880s, the broad base of support that illicit distillers had enjoyed in northwestern South Carolina (and other parts of southern Appalachia) was diminishing. "Unlike white supremacy," historian Wilbur Miller has argued, "moonshining itself was becoming increasingly disreputable, and many people did not accept the violence employed to defend it."[170] Even Wade Hampton, fearing that moonshiner violence had become a political liability, declared in August 1881 that he would no longer tolerate "infractions of revenue laws."[171]

INTRODUCTION

Celebrated as heroes during Reconstruction, illicit distillers found themselves under attack from Hampton and other former allies, much to the delight of Commissioner of Internal Revenue Green B. Raum. In 1882, Raum reported that illicit distilling in South Carolina and other former Confederate states had "become the exception rather than the rule" largely due to southerners' increased tolerance for federal liquor taxation. "There is no longer organized resistance to the authority of the government, the people render obedience to the laws, and the taxes are collected without unnecessary friction," he proclaimed.[172] The tide had begun to turn against the moonshiners.

Nonetheless, Lewis Redmond's popularity remained unabated in South Carolina. In 1884, Palmetto State temperance reformers Sally Taylor and Grace Elmore launched a movement to release the moonshiner from jail.[173] Taylor's and Elmore's reasons for organizing this campaign are unknown. Both were advocates of the Lost Cause and would later join the Daughters of the Confederacy, suggesting that they may have supported Redmond (and overlooked his transgressions) as a means of challenging the federal government one final time. Whatever their motives, Taylor and Elmore quickly found a receptive audience. That March, 158 Greenville denizens signed a petition demanding that U.S. Attorney General Benjamin Brewster transfer Redmond from Auburn, New York, to the state penitentiary in Columbia, South Carolina. Believing that the moonshiner was dying of tuberculosis and had "proven his penitence for his misdeeds," the petitioners then asked Brewster to pardon Redmond. They concluded: "We are sure that the fact that his further confinement at Auburn will be equivalent to a sentence of death and that he has a wife and a large family of children who will be left entirely destitute will be sufficient to obtain the measure of clemency asked for."[174]

In April, Brewster agreed to move Redmond to Columbia.[175] Taylor and Elmore could not have been more pleased. With the help of other "ladies" in the community, they began to collect money, cloths, and toys for the outlaw and his family.[176] "The girls dashed gallantly to achievement," Taylor remembered years later. "They took the Main Street and allowed no one to give over twenty-five cents in contribution to their Redmond fund. One gentleman began to harangue about law breakers and immoral charity, etc. Sally Seibels [who was taking donations] pulled her companion, and rushingly said: 'Come along, we are getting more than twenty-five cents worth of *spread eagle*' and would not receive anything from this lawyer orator, even words."[177] Meanwhile, on May 16, 1884, President Chester Arthur, at the requests of Senator Wade Hampton and Attorney General Brewster, granted Lewis a full and unconditional pardon.[178]

Shortly after Redmond's arrival to Columbia in mid-May, Taylor, Elmore, and several other women visited the prisoner, who, although "wheezing from the shot in his windpipe" and standing on crutches, was "handsome and pleasing looking, with a grave and settled expression in deep blue eyes." According to Taylor, Lewis was unaware that President Arthur had pardoned him or that local citizens had collected donations for his family. When Taylor and her friends entered Redmond's jail cell carrying cloths, "a little trunk of toys," and $55, the outlaw stood "in a daze on his wooden supports, not apprehending their words as they itemized his future possessions." Elmore then announced: "And here, Mr. Redmond, is the best of all—your pardon." Redmond immediately sat down in disbelief. "The man," Taylor recalled, "did not know of the surprise except that Senator Hampton had mentioned to him: 'I expect to have good news for you.'"[179]

On May 28, Hampton and South Carolina Governor Hugh S. Thompson accompanied Redmond to the train station in Columbia, where "a number of ladies and gentlemen" greeted them and provided the outlaw with refreshments "for his homeward trip." Lewis waved farewell to the crowd, entered the train, and sat down. "Along the route," the *New York Times* reported, "a number of persons boarded the train and shook hands with the physically wrecked hero of many hairbreadth escapes."[180] That night, the train arrived at Easley in Pickens County. There, Redmond met his family and rode to his new home in nearby Sunny Dale. Six months later, he wrote a letter to the *Charleston News and Courier,* thanking the paper for sending McKinley "to interview me when I was a 'wild man' in the mountains and styled an 'outlaw.'" Lewis then declared: "Thank God I am a free man to-day; out of prison, out of the clutches of the law, and out of the revenue or blockade business; at home with my wife and babies and surrounded by a host of true and tried friends! Breathing the pure mountain air, in the enjoyment of improving health, I desire to engage in some honorable, legitimate business for a support for myself and family."[181] The moonshiner would never again write or speak to the press.

Redmond remained a law-abiding citizen until his death in 1906.[182] After writing to the *Charleston News and Courier* in 1884, he moved his family to Slabtown in Anderson County, South Carolina, where he rented some land from Holbert Pickens and farmed. In 1886, Lewis relocated near the town of Walhalla in Oconee County.[183] There, Dietrich Biemann hired the former moonshiner to run a government distillery. Redmond's legal whiskey quickly became a hit with customers. "F. W. Wagener & Co. at Charleston bought all he could make," Redmond's wife, Adeline, remembered in 1927. "This was the finest corn whiskey that could be made and they called it 'Redmond's Hand

Mash.'"[184] To further boost sales, F. W. Wagener & Company reproduced Redmond's picture on the bottle labels and barrel heads.[185]

In the late 1890s, Redmond moved his family to the Lidell farm, located five miles east of Seneca in Oconee County. He continued to operate a legal distillery until his health began to decline around 1905. Redmond also remained a local celebrity. By then, however, he refused to talk about his past. Ironically, in March 1906, deputy marshal H. E. Barton's grandson, Edwin Parker McCravy, was one of the last people to visit Redmond. The famous outlaw, who had raided Barton's house in January 1877, had always fascinated McCravy. "When I was a child, he was the most talked about man second to Wade Hampton," McCravy remembered. "Naturally I had the curiosity to meet and know the man personally."[186] Years earlier, McCravy had met Lewis in Walhalla, where the outlaw treated him "with the utmost courtesy." Upon learning of Redmond's ailing condition, McCravy decided to see his grandfather's nemesis one final time. As he approached the house, Lewis was sitting in a rocking chair on the front porch. McCravy remembered: "He invited me in and said that the boys were plowing, his wife was cooking dinner, and he insisted that I stay and take dinner with him. I had to deny myself that pleasure. His feet and legs were horribly swollen and he looked anything but well." After speaking to Redmond about the location of a nearby abandoned still, McCravy "shook his hard old hand 'goodbye' and that was the last time that I saw the famous 'moonshiner' and killer."[187]

On April 5, 1906, Lewis Redmond died a "quiet, almost obscure death" from pneumonia. Shortly afterward, the *Seneca News* fondly recalled that Lewis was a noble man and devoted father:

> We remember an incident connected with the man and his home life, which was one of the most pathetic we ever witnessed, convincing us that there was a big, warm, tender heart beneath the rough exterior of Redmond's character. Some years ago we were at the Southern depot here and Redmond was also there with his family, among them the little unfortunate deaf mute, a daughter. She was there to be taken by the mother to Cedar Springs, our institute for deaf, dumb, and blind. Although closely embraced in his arms and during the long wait for the train, the tears never ceased in their flow down his rugged cheeks, gently fondling her, constantly smoothing her hair or patting her cheek or arranging her hat, totally oblivious to the crowd of curious faces around him. . . . We knew thenceforth that Lewis Redmond was not as "black as he had been painted."[188]

Redmond's wife (who would pass away in 1933), his nine children, and his thirty-eight grandchildren wanted the world to remember him the same. They

Lewis Redmond's grave in Oakway's Return Baptist Church Cemetery in Oconee County. Photograph by the author.

buried Lewis in Oakway's Return Baptist Church cemetery in Oconee County and had inscribed on his gravestone: "He was the sunshine of our home."

When compared to Billy the Kid and Jesse James, Redmond's career as an outlaw is unspectacular. Contrary to myth, he killed only one man, Alfred Duckworth. Nor was "Redmond's band" as large as revenue agents, journalists, and Southerners claimed. Although Lewis was its leader, the band probably consisted of no more than fifteen moonshiners. But Redmond's life as an illicit distiller occurred at a time when many white Southerners were searching for heroes. Defeat on the battlefield, emancipation, and Reconstruction had forced white Southerners to explain why they, as supposedly God's chosen people, had met such a dismal fate. Many soon embraced the so-called Lost Cause movement, an omnibus term that explicates how Southerners celebrated the vanquished Confederacy in the late nineteenth century.[189] Redmond gave these people hope. In their eyes, he continued to fight for the Confederacy. Lewis became a symbol of the Lost Cause, an unreconstructed Rebel who against all odds evaded capture and refused to surrender to an "unjust" federal government.

INTRODUCTION

Perhaps Redmond's most enduring legacy, however, relates to the creation of the myth of violent Appalachia during the late nineteenth century. Since the 1970s, historians have demonstrated conclusively that stereotypes about the mountain region often reflected Victorian middle-class America's desire to stress the benefits of industrialization and "progress." "In an age of faith in American, and more generally Western, intellectual, cultural, and social superiority over the other 'races' of the world," historian Anthony Harkins writes, "these [stereotypes] were designed to show not cultural difference so much as cultural hierarchy—to celebrate modernity and 'mainstream' progress."[190] Perceived by northerners (and a growing number of southerners) as a remnant of the colonial era, Appalachia became a "strange" and backward place. In short, outside observers believed that the region and its people were economically, geographically, and culturally at odds with modern America.[191]

Hoping to reaffirm their cultural superiority, among other reasons, Victorian whites also depicted Appalachia as a place where lawlessness and brutality prevailed. Most historians have emphasized the role that feuding played in the construction of this violent Appalachia. During the late 1880s, they agree, the national media's coverage of the Hatfield-McCoy and other feuds convinced middle-class citizens that mountain whites were inherently more violent than other Americans.[192] Although correct, these scholars have underestimated the impact that moonshiner violence had on the formation of such misconceptions.[193] Coinciding with the emergence of "local color" writing, a literary genre that grew out of new literary magazines and stressed the "peculiarities" of mountain life, newspaper accounts and dime novels about Redmond brought national attention to the moonshine wars.[194] Consequently, illicit distilling became synonymous with Appalachia and its people.

Following the publication of Redmond's interview in 1878, *Harper's Weekly, Appleton's Journal,* and other northern urban-based magazines began to focus considerable attention on moonshining in Appalachia.[195] That August, for instance, *Appleton's Journal* printed Constance Fenimore Woolson's "Up in the Blue Ridge." In it, Woolson feared that mountain residents would never adapt to modern society, largely because geographical isolation had forced them to rely on moonshining to make a living. The story chronicles the adventures of Stephen Wainwright, a Northerner who visits the mountains of North Carolina and falls in love with a "mountain girl." Wainwright, however, soon discovers that his life is in danger, as many local residents, including a Baptist preacher, believe he is a revenue agent attempting to capture the notorious moonshiner Richard Eliot. Eliot, Woolson explains, was a typical highlander, who, unable to adapt to modern society and find a civilized profession, became an illicit distiller. Although Wainwright convinces locals that he is not a revenuer, his cousin and fellow New Yorker John Royce pledges to capture Eliot, who had murdered a bureau agent named Allison. The story ultimately pits civilized America against savage Appalachia, as Royce and Eliot square off in a gunfight. After wounding Royce, Eliot escapes and vows to continue his illegal profession. "The moonlight-whiskey is made up in the mountain, and still the revenue-detectives are shot," Woolson concludes. "The wild, beautiful region is not yet conquered."[196]

In August 1879, perhaps hoping to capitalize on the popularity of Crittenden's *Entwined Lives*, *Harper's Weekly* printed "Law and Moonshine," an exposé on moonshiners in western North Carolina. Like "Up in the Blue Ridge," this work argued that illicit distillers were the products of geographical isolation. However, it added a new theme, suggesting that moonshiner violence was the result of genetics. According to the anonymous author, most mountain whites were not only illicit distillers but also naturally "wild" and "grotesque." Predisposed to reject authority, they were stubborn individualists who remained loyal to kinfolk and neighbors. "It is impossible," the author explains, "to convince these big-boned, semi-barbarian people that the revenue official who comes with an armed posse into their haunts, searching for and destroying their stills, is not an emissary of a tyrannical and unjust government, for whom the sly bullet is but too good a welcome."[197] Unlike "Up in the Blue Ridge," which tended to sympathize with the illicit distillers, "Law and Moonshine" places blame squarely on the shoulders of highlanders, whose culture and genetic makeup encourages them to act irrationally and commit violence.

By the 1880s, many Americans agreed that moonshining was largely the result of both geographical isolation and genetics. In short, it was one of the peculiarities of southern Appalachia. Like other mountain residents, illicit distillers, living "far from all railroads or civilization of any kind," remained ignorant and refused to embrace "change."[198] The *Atlantic Monthly* reported in 1882 that moonshining was "partly a feature of the old warfare of the mountaineers against the civilization and the people of the towns." These "tall, finely-built, powerful, loose-jointed" men were also a breed apart, a distinct, racialized "other" genetically and culturally predisposed to break the law.[199] According to Donald Baines in "Among the Moonshiners" in 1885, illicit distillers in Macon County, North Carolina, remained "semi-barbarians" and as such knew "no law of right and justice."[200] Inevitably, Baines and other writers pointed out, these traits, along with a fondness for alcohol, made moonshiners and other "backward" highlanders prone to commit violence.[201] To make matters worse, they believed that illicit distilling, among other reasons, had encouraged white Appalachians to embrace feuding, a practice that became synonymous with the region and its people during the late 1880s. Kentucky journalist James Lane Allen explained in 1886: "The special origins of [feuding] are various: blood heated and temper lost under the influence of 'moonshine'; reporting on the places and manufacturers of this; local politics; the survival of resentment engendered during the civil war—these, together with all causes that lie in the passions of the human heart and spring from the constitution of all human society, often make the remote and insulated life of these people turbulent, reckless, and distressing."[202]

These writers and other Victorian Americans, however, argued that mountain residents could find salvation. They insisted that industrialization was the antidote to the region's economic and social ills. Once again, the moonshiner served as a symbol of what was wrong with southern Appalachia. Like other highlanders, he was the product of an isolated environment, one that promoted ignorance, idleness, and violence. But the moonshiner also became a prime example of how "outsiders" could improve mountain society. Education, religion, and, above all, economic modernization promised to bring an end to illicit distilling and other traditional practices that plagued the mountain region. Railroads, factories, and other industrial projects ushered in a new era of progress by discouraging highlanders from engaging in illicit distilling, binge drinking, and violence.[203] As Donald Baines concludes in "Among the Moonshiners": "In a few more years, when the march of progress shall have sounded through these woods and dales the 'moonshiners' occupation will be gone, and in his stead we shall find industrious, hard-working farmers, cultivating the rich soil that is now running to waste; the hum of the spindle shall succeed the bubbling of the still, and where now is nought but desolation, squalor and ignorance, there shall be cultivation and plenty, happiness and wealth, education and intelligence."[204]

The final publication in this book, Robert A. Cobb's *The True Life of Maj. Lewis Richard Redmond,* is important, among other reasons, because it exemplifies Baines' and other Victorian Americans' belief that moonshiners were a threat to civilization, a symbol of rural "backwardness." In it, Cobb, who became a prominent temperance reformer, New South booster, and newspaper editor in Burke County during the 1880s, chastised illicit distillers for harming the mountain region's reputation and economic potential.[205] In his eyes, the days of moonshining were over and Redmond was not a hero. "Compare the life of Redmond with that of the most humble citizen who honors and obeys the laws of his country and of his God," Cobb explained. "See the man who abides by and supports the laws of his country, whether rich or poor, old or young, he moves on in the even tenor of his way. . . . But see the man that is at enmity with his fellowman, his country, and his God. He 'fleeth when no man pursueth,' and his slumbers are as the raging water casting up mud and clay. So it has been with Maj. Redmond."[206] Having helped make moonshining synonymous with Appalachia, Lewis Redmond's life ultimately served as a warning to other mountain residents engaged in illicit distilling. They would have no place in the new industrial social order.

Notes

1. Several persons reported that another deputy, Mr. Lankford, accompanied Duckworth in his search for Redmond. See John Preston Arthur, *Western North Carolina: A History from 1730 to 1913* (Raleigh, NC: Edwards & Broughton Printing Co., 1914), 304; and *Keowee Courier,* Nov. 25, 1925.

2. One source claims that it was Redmond's uncle, Mr. Belcher, rather than Amos Ladd who was with Redmond on Mar. 1. See *Keowee Courier,* Nov. 25, 1925. In an 1878 interview, Redmond failed to give the name of the person who was with him on that fateful day. See *Charleston News and Courier,* July 2, 1878.

3. C. C. Duckworth to J. P. A., May 1, 1912, quoted in Arthur, *Western North Carolina,* 304.

4. For accounts of Duckworth's murder, see *Charleston News and Courier,* July 2, 1878; R. A. Cobb, *The True Life of Maj. Lewis Richard Redmond, the Notorious Outlaw and Famous Moonshiner, of Western North Carolina, Who Was Born in Swain County, N.C., in the Year 1855, and Arrested April 7, 1881* (Raleigh, NC: Edwards, Broughton, & Co., 1881), 9–11; Arthur, *Western North Carolina,* 304; *Keowee Courier,* Nov. 25, 1925; Jim Bob Tinsley, *The Land of Waterfalls: Transylvania County, North Carolina, including Stories about Locally-Made Gillespie Rifle-Guns, Long Hunters of the Taxaway and Upper French Broad Rivers, and Major Lewis R. Redmond, Famous Carolina Mountain Outlaw and Moonshiner* (Brevard, NC: J. B. and Dottie Tinsley, 1988), 157; and George Ellison, "'Major' Lewis R. Redmond," *Appalachian Quarterly* 11 (Mar. 2006): 45.

5. For more recent discussions on Jesse James, Billy the Kid, and other American outlaws, see T. J. Stiles, *Jesse James: Last Hero of the Civil War* (New York: Alfred A. Knopf, 2002); Michael Wallis, *Billy the Kid: The Endless Ride* (New York: W. W. Norton & Co., 2007); and Frank Richard Prassel, *The Great American Outlaw: A Legacy of Fact and Fiction* (Norman: Univ. of Oklahoma Press, 1993).

6. For studies on the Hatfield-McCoy feud and the role that feuding played in the creation of so-called violent Appalachia, see Altina L. Waller, *Feud: Hatfields, McCoys, and Social Change in Appalachia, 1860–1900* (Chapel Hill: Univ. of North Carolina Press, 1988); John Ed Pearce, *Days of Darkness: The Feuds of Eastern Kentucky* (Lexington: Univ. Press of Kentucky, 1994); Henry D. Shapiro, *Appalachia on Our Mind: The Southern Mountains and Mountaineers in the American Consciousness, 1870–1920* (Chapel Hill: Univ. of North Carolina Press, 1978); and Altina L. Waller, "Feuding in Appalachia: Evolution of a Cultural Stereotype," in *Appalachia in the Making: The Mountain South in the Nineteenth Century,* edited by Mary Beth Pudup, Dwight B. Billings, and Altina L. Waller (Chapel Hill: Univ. of North Carolina Press), 347–76.

INTRODUCTION

7. David Hackett Fischer, *Albion's Seed: Four British Folkways in America* (New York: Oxford Univ. Press, 1989); John C. Campbell, *The Southern Highlander and His Homeland* (New York: Russell Sage Foundation, 1921); and Horace Kephart, *Our Southern Highlanders* (New York: Outing, 1913).

8. Several historians have also begun to complicate our understanding of moonshiner violence in the post–Civil War South. See Gordon B. McKinney, "Moonshiners, Law Enforcement, and Violence: Legitimacy and Community in Western North Carolina, 1862–1882" (paper presented at the annual meeting of the Southern Historical Association, New Orleans, Nov. 1995); Wilbur R. Miller, *Revenuers and Moonshiners: Enforcing Federal Liquor Law in the Mountain South, 1865–1900* (Chapel Hill: Univ. of North Carolina Press, 1991); and William F. Holmes, "Moonshining and Collective Violence: Georgia, 1889–1895," *Journal of American History* 67 (Dec. 1980): 589–611.

9. In 1878, Redmond stated that he was born on October 24, 1855. R. A. Cobb also claimed that Redmond was born in 1855. See *Charleston News and Courier*, July 2, 1878; and R. A. Cobb, *The True Life of Maj. Lewis Richard Redmond*, 5.

10. *1850 United States Federal Census*, Militia District 536, Rabun County, Georgia, Roll M432-81, p. 329.

11. *1840 United States Federal Census*, Pickens District, Pickens County, South Carolina, Roll 514, p. 332; *1850 United States Federal Census*, Militia District 536, Rabun County, Georgia, Roll M432-81, p. 329; Tinsley, *The Land of Waterfalls*, 157; *1860 United States Federal Census*, Davidson's River Township, Henderson County, North Carolina, Roll M653-901, p. 458.

12. Recent scholarship has demonstrated that most Appalachian farming households were neither completely self-sufficient nor isolated from the outside world. See Richard A. Straw and H. Tyler Blethen, eds., *High Mountains Rising: Appalachia in Time and Place* (Urbana: Univ. of Illinois Press, 2004); Robert S. Weise, *Grasping at Independence: Debt, Male Authority, and Mineral Rights in Appalachian Kentucky, 1850–1915* (Knoxville: Univ. of Tennessee Press, 2001); Dwight B. Billing and Kathleen M. Blee, *The Road to Poverty: The Making of Wealth and Hardship in Appalachia* (New York: Cambridge Univ. Press, 2000); Donald L. Winters, *Tennessee Farming, Tennessee Farmers: Antebellum Agriculture in the Upper South* (Knoxville: Univ. of Tennessee Press, 1994); Paul Salstrom, *Appalachia's Path to Dependency: Rethinking a Region's Economic History, 1730–1940* (Lexington: Univ. Press of Kentucky, 1994); John C. Inscoe, *Mountain Masters, Slavery, and the Sectional Crisis in Western North Carolina* (Knoxville: Univ. of Tennessee Press, 1988); and Durwood Dunn, *Cades Cove: The Life and Death of a Southern Appalachian Community, 1818–1937* (Knoxville: Univ. of Tennessee Press, 1988).

13. For a detailed discussion on alcohol distilling in western North Carolina during the antebellum period, see Bruce E. Stewart, "'This Country Improves in Cultivation, Wickedness, Mills, and Still': Distilling and Drinking in Antebellum Western North Carolina," *North Carolina Historical Review* 83 (Oct. 2006): 447–78. For discussions on the importance of liquor manufacturing elsewhere in southern Appalachia, see Donald Edward Davis, *Where There Are Mountains: An Environmental History of the Southern Appalachians* (Athens: Univ. of Georgia Press, 2000); Miller, *Revenuers and*

Moonshiners; Joseph Earl Dabney, *Mountain Spirits: A Chronicle of Corn Whiskey from King James' Ulster Plantation to America's Appalachians and the Moonshine Life* (New York: Charles Scribner's Sons, 1974); David W. Maurer with the assistance of Quinn Pearl, *Kentucky Moonshine* (Lexington: Univ. Press of Kentucky, 1974); Jess Carr, *The Second Oldest Profession: An Informal History of Moonshining in America* (Englewood Cliffs, NJ: Prentice-Hall, 1972); Ester Kellner, *Moonshine: Its History and Folklore* (Indianapolis: Bobbs-Merrill Co., 1971); Harriette Simpson Arnow, *Flowering of the Cumberland* (New York: Macmillan Co., 1963); and Everett Dick, *The Dixie Frontier: A Social History of the Southern Frontier from the First Transmontane Beginnings to the Civil War* (New York: Alfred A. Knopf, 1948).

14. For a discussion on the Whiskey Rebellion of 1794, see Thomas P. Slaughter, *The Whiskey Rebellion: Frontier Epilogue to the American Revolution* (New York: Oxford Univ. Press, 1986).

15. Mary K. Bonsteel Tachau, "The Whiskey Rebellion in Kentucky: A Forgotten Episode of Civil Disobedience," *Journal of the Early Republic* 2 (Fall 1982): 239–59; Jeffrey J. Crow, "The Whiskey Rebellion in North Carolina," *North Carolina Historical Review* 66 (Jan. 1989): 1–28; and Kevin T. Barksdale, "Our Rebellious Neighbors: Virginia's Border Counties during Pennsylvania's Whiskey Rebellion," *Virginia Magazine of History and Biography* 111 (Jan. 2003): 5–32.

16. These brothers were Morgan "Jasper" and Robert M. Redmond. On July 19, 1862, both enlisted as privates in the Thomas Legion. On February 7, 1864, Union forces captured Robert, who spent the remainder of the war in Camp Chase prison. According to Lewis, Robert died in Camp Chase prison. Military records, however, fail to confirm or refute Lewis's claim. See *U.S. Civil War Soldiers, 1861–1865*, Jasper Redman and Robert M. Redman, Film Number M230, Roll 32; and *Selected Records of the War Department Relating to Confederate Prisoners of War, 1861–1865*, Robert M. Redman, Roll M598-84.

17. *Charleston News and Courier*, July 2, 1878. See also Tinsley, *The Land of Waterfalls*, 157.

18. For more on the Shelton Laurel massacre, see Phillip Shaw Paludan, *Victims: A True Story of the Civil War Era, 1860–1880* (Knoxville: Univ. of Tennessee Press, 1981).

19. For a discussion on guerilla warfare in western North Carolina during the Civil War, see John C. Inscoe and Gordon B. McKinney, *The Heart of Confederate Appalachia: Western North Carolina in the Civil War* (Chapel Hill: Univ. of North Carolina Press, 2000), 105–38, 232–65, 269–70.

20. The Commissioner of Internal Revenue oversaw a network of collection districts. A collector headed each district and "appointed subordinates to monitor the output of distilleries, breweries, and tobacco processors and to apprehend those who failed to pay taxes." See Wilbur R. Miller, "The Revenue: Federal Liquor Law Enforcement in the Mountain South, 1870–1900," *Journal of Southern History* 55 (May 1989): 197.

21. In 1868, the U.S. Congress lowered the liquor tax from two dollars a gallon to fifty cents. In 1872, the federal government raised the tax to seventy cents a gallon. Three years later, in 1875, it was increased to ninety cents a gallon.

INTRODUCTION

22. Miller, *Revenuers and Moonshiners*, 15.

23. George Wesley Atkinson, *After the Moonshiners, by One of the Raiders* (Wheeling, WV: Frew and Campbell, 1881), 13–14.

24. *Raleigh Daily Standard*, Oct. 20, 1869.

25. "Home rule" meant Democratic control of the state governments in the South.

26. R. M. Wallace, Deputy Marshal, to Commissioner of Internal Revenue C. Delano, Jan. 15, 1870, file no. 79S '70, Letters Received by the Adjutant General, Records of the Adjutant General's Office, Record Group 94, National Archives, Washington, DC; hereinafter cited as LR, RG 94.

27. S. A. Darnell to Attorney General Charles Devens, July 29, 1880, quoted in Miller, *Revenuers and Moonshiners*, 42.

28. *Report of the Joint Select Committee to Inquire into the Condition of Affairs in the Late Insurrectionary States*, 13 vols. (Washington: Government Printing Office, 1872), 42d Cong., 2d sess., H. Rept. 22, South Carolina, 37.

29. For description of moonshiner violence in southern Appalachia during Reconstruction, see Miller, *Revenuers and Moonshiners*; Bruce E. Stewart, "'When Darkness Reigns Then Is the Hour to Strike': Moonshining, Federal Liquor Taxation, and Klan Violence in Western North Carolina, 1868–1872," *North Carolina Historical Review* 80 (Oct. 2003): 453–74; Bruce E. Stewart, "Attacking 'Red-Legged Grasshoppers': Moonshiners, Violence, and the Politics of Federal Liquor Taxation in Western North Carolina, 1865–1876," *Appalachian Journal* 32 (Fall 2004): 26–48; and Stephen Cresswell, *Mormons and Cowboys, and Moonshiners and Klansmen: Federal Law Enforcement in the South and West, 1870–1893* (Tuscaloosa: Univ. of Alabama Press, 1991).

30. Miller, *Revenuers and Moonshiners*, 70, 72.

31. Radical Republicanism represented what southern Democrats believed were the evils of Reconstruction: African American equality, excessive taxation, and the expansion of federal authority. See Stewart, "Attacking 'Red-Legged Grasshoppers'"; and Miller, *Revenuers and Moonshiners*.

32. Quoted in Daniel J. Whitener, *Prohibition in North Carolina, 1715–1945* (Chapel Hill: Univ. of North Carolina Press, 1946), 79.

33. *Pickens Sentinel*, Sept. 14, 1876.

34. *Charleston News and Courier*, July 2, 1878.

35. *Keowee Courier*, Nov. 25, 1925, in Lewis Redmond Collection, South Caroliniana Library, Univ. of South Carolina, Columbia.

36. *Charleston News and Courier*, July 2, 1878.

37. See "Jury Inquest over A. F. Duckworth," *Coroner's Reports*, Mar. 2, 1876, Transylvania County, Clerk of Court Office, Brevard, NC, in Tinsley, *The Land of Waterfalls*, 157. See also Robert Douglas, U.S. Marshal, to Attorney General Charles Devens, Dec. 13, 1877, SCF, RG 60.

38. *1840 United States Federal Census*, Pickens District, Pickens County, South Carolina, Roll 514, p. 332.

39. *Charleston News and Courier*, Oct. 9, 1878; *Keowee Courier*, Oct. 17, 1878; and *Police National Gazette*, Oct. 19, 1878.

40. *Pickens Sentinel,* July 12, 1876.

41. Ibid., Sept. 28, 1876.

42. Hendricks recovered from his wounds. That February, however, an illicit distiller, Hubbard Garmany, shot Hendricks in the chest, killing him instantly. Garmany was tried for murder in the State Court but acquitted "on the grounds that Hendricks fired first." See *Pickens Sentinel,* Feb. 22, 1877; and R. M. Wallace, U.S. Marshal, to Attorney General Charles Devens, Dec. 31, 1877, Source Chronological Files, S. C., General Records of the Dept. of Justice, Record Group 60, National Archives, College Park, Maryland; hereinafter cited as SCF, RG 60.

43. L. Cass Carpenter to Hon. Green B. Raum, Jan. 17, 1877, quoted in "Enforcement of Internal Revenue Laws: . . . Report of the Commissioner of Internal Revenue . . . to Explain the Necessity For Employment of Armed Men . . ." *House Executive Document* 62, 46th Cong., 2nd sess. (1880), 175–76; hereinafter cited as "Enforcement of Internal Revenue Laws." See also *Pickens Sentinel,* Jan. 18, 1877; and *Charleston News and Courier,* Jan. 27, 1877.

44. L. Cass Carpenter to Hon. Green B. Raum, Jan. 18, 1877, quoted in "Enforcement of Internal Revenue Laws," 176–77.

45. L. Cass Carpenter to Hon. Green B. Raum, Jan. 22, 1877, quoted in "Enforcement of Internal Revenue Laws," 177. See also *Pickens Sentinel,* Jan. 25, 1877; R. M. Wallace, U.S. Marshal, to Attorney General Charles Devens, Dec. 31, 1877, SCF, RG 60.

46. L. Cass Carpenter to Hon. Green B. Raum, Jan. 17, 1877, quoted in "Enforcement of Internal Revenue Laws," 176; L. Cass Carpenter to Hon. Green B. Raum, Jan. 18, 1877, quoted in "Enforcement of Internal Revenue Laws," 176–77; and L. Cass Carpenter to Hon. Green B. Raum, Jan. 22, 1877, quoted in "Enforcement of Internal Revenue Laws, 177.

47. L. Cass Carpenter to Hon. Green B. Raum, Jan. 17, 1877, quoted in "Enforcement of Internal Revenue Laws," 176.

48. Green B. Raum to L. Cass Carpenter, Jan. 24, 1877, quoted in "Enforcement of Internal Revenue Laws," 178.

49. Ibid.

50. Orders No. 32 and No. 34, Apr. 23, 26, 1877, LR, RG 94. See also *New York Times,* Mar. 15, 1877.

51. W. A. Miller to the Post Adjutant, Apr. 26, 1877, LR, RG 94.

52. L. Cass Carpenter to Hon. Green B. Raum, Apr. 27, 1877, quoted in "Enforcement of Internal Revenue Laws," 179–80.

53. *New York Times,* June 6, 1877.

54. L. Cass Carpenter to Hon. Green B. Raum, Jan. 17, 1877, quoted in "Enforcement of Internal Revenue Laws," 176; and L. Cass Carpenter to Hon. Green B. Raum, June 13, 1877, quoted in "Enforcement of Internal Revenue Laws," 180.

55. R. M. Wallace, U.S. Marshal, to Attorney General Charles Devens, Sept. 13, 1877, SCF, RG 60.

56. *Pickens Sentinel,* Jan. 18, 1877.

57. *Charleston News and Courier,* Jan. 27, 1877.

INTRODUCTION

58. L. Cass Carpenter to Hon. Green B. Raum, Jan. 22, 1877, quoted in "Enforcement of Internal Revenue Laws," 177.

59. W. A. Miller to the Post Adjutant, Apr. 26, 1877, quoted in "Enforcement of Internal Revenue Laws," 179; and E. M. Brayton to Hon. Green B. Raum, Sept. 20, 1877, quoted in "Enforcement of Internal Revenue Laws," 184.

60. *New York Times,* June 6, 1877.

61. Green B. Raum to E. M. Brayton, Jan. 3, 1878, quoted in "Enforcement of Internal Revenue Laws," 186.

62. *Annual Report, Commissioner of Internal Revenue,* 1879, House Executive Document 4, 46th Cong., 2d sess., iv.

63. These civilian posses usually consisted of twelve to twenty well-armed and equipped men. A deputy collector, appointed by the collector of the district and paid a salary, led the posse. These men, whose base of operations were often in county seat towns, recruited local citizens to serve as special deputies. Each posse also had a deputy marshal, who issued warrants and could arrest without a warrant any moonshiner they caught in the act. See Miller, *Revenuers and Moonshiners,* 102–4.

64. E. M. Brayton to Hon. Green B. Raum, Mar. 2, 1878, quoted in "Enforcement of Internal Revenue Laws," 188. See also *Charleston News and Courier,* Jan. 8, 29, 1878.

65. E. M. Brayton to Hon. Green B. Raum, Mar. 17, 1878, quoted in "Enforcement of Internal Revenue Laws," 189–90.

66. *Keowee Courier,* Mar. 21, 1878.

67. *Pickens Sentinel,* Mar. 11, 1878.

68. E. M. Brayton to Hon. Green B. Raum, Mar. 17, 1878, quoted in "Enforcement of Internal Revenue Laws," 189–90.

69. E. G. Hoffman to Hon. E. M. Brayton, Mar. 13, 1878, quoted in "Enforcement of Internal Revenue Laws," 189.

70. Green B. Raum to E. M. Brayton, Mar. 12, 13, 26, 1878, quoted in "Enforcement of Internal Revenue Laws," 188–89.

71. E. M. Brayton to Hon. Green B. Raum, Mar. 17, 1878, quoted in "Enforcement of Internal Revenue Laws," 190.

72. E. M. Brayton to Hon. Green B. Raum, Apr. 4, 1878, quoted in ibid., 192; E. G. Hoffman to Hon. E. M. Brayton, Apr. 9, 1878, quoted in ibid., 193; and R. M. Wallace, U.S. Marshal, to U.S. Attorney General Charles Devens, Apr. 8, 1878, SCF RG 60.

73. E. G. Hoffman to E. M. Brayton, Apr. 29, 1878, quoted in "Enforcement of Internal Revenue Laws," 194. See also *Pickens Sentinel,* May 2, 1878; and *Washington Post,* May 8, 1878.

74. E. H. Hoffman to Hon. E. M. Brayton, Mar. 29, 1878, Box 1, Letters Received by the Commissioner, Records of the Internal Revenue Service, Record Group 58, National Archives, College Park, Maryland; hereinafter cited as LR, RG 58.

75. T. J. Mackey to His Excellency Wade Hampton, Mar. 21, 1878, quoted in *Pickens Sentinel,* Feb. 10, 1927; and E. H. Hoffman to Hon. E. M. Brayton, Mar. 29, 1878, Box 1, LR, RG 58.

76. *Keowee Courier,* Apr. 11, 1878.

77. R. E. Steele, Foreman, to His Honor, T. J. Mackey, Mar. Term, 1878, quoted in *Pickens Sentinel*, Feb. 10, 1927.

78. *Keowee Courier*, Mar. 28, 1878; and *Pickens Sentinel*, Apr. 4, 11, 18, 25, May 30, 1878.

79. *Keowee Courier*, Apr. 11, 1878.

80. R. M. Wallace, U.S. Marshal, to U.S. Attorney General Charles Devens, Apr. 8, 1878, SCF, RG 60.

81. R. M. Wallace, U.S. Marshal, to Attorney General Charles Devens, Apr. 22, 1878, SCF, RG 60. See also E. M. Brayton to Hon. Green B. Raum, Apr. 20, 1878, quoted in "Enforcement of Internal Revenue Laws," 193; H. H. Jillison, Deputy Collector, to R. M. Wallace, U.S. Marshal, Apr. 23, 1878, SCF, RG 60; and L. C. Northrop, S.C. Attorney General, to Attorney General Charles Devens, Apr. 25, 1878, SCF, RG 60.

82. Atkinson, *After the Moonshiners*, 112.

83. L. C. Northrop to Attorney General Charles Devens, June 14, 1878, SCF, RG 60. For a copy of the arrest warrant see, James O. Ladd to R. M. Wallace, Apr. 19, 1878, SCF, RG 60.

84. Hugh P. Kane, Special Deputy Collector, to E. M. Brayton, June 10, 1878, Box 1, LR, RG 58. See also Robert Scruggs, G. W. Moose, William Durham, and Hugh P. Kane to Attorney General [Charles Devens], June 10, 1878, SCF, RG 60.

85. *Pickens Sentinel*, June 13, 1878.

86. *Charleston News and Courier*, June 27, 1878, clipping in L. C. Northrop to Attorney General Charles Devens, June 27, 1878, SCF, RG 60.

87. *Greenville Enterprise and Mountaineer*, July 3, 1878.

88. W. E. Earle to Attorney General Charles Devens, June 15, 1878, SCF, RG 60.

89. E. M. Brayton to Hon. Green B. Raum, June 10, 1878, Box 887, LR, RG 58.

90. Hugh Kane, William Durham, and G. W. Moose to Attorney General Charles Devens, Aug. 5, 1878, SCF, RG 60; *Greenville Enterprise and Mountaineer*, July 3, 1878; *Charleston News and Courier*, July 17, 22, 27, 1878; L. C. Northrop to Attorney General Charles Devens, June 26, 1878, SCF, RG 60; L. C. Northrop to Attorney General Charles Devens, July 10, 1878, SCF, RG 60.

91. *Charleston News and Courier*, July 20, 27, 30, Aug. 3, 1878; *Greenville Enterprise and Mountaineer*, July 31, 1878; *Keowee Courier*, Aug. 15, 1878; *Pickens Sentinel*, Aug. 15, 1878; Attorney General Charles Devens to W. E. Earle, July 27, 1878, Aug. 8, 1878, Instructions from the Attorney General to U.S. District Attorneys and Marshals, bk. H, pp. 212–17, 241, RG 60.

92. Green B. Raum, Commissioner, to L. C. Northrop, June 17, 1880, SCF, RG 60; Court Proceedings, Dec. 7, 1881, SCF, RG 60; E. M. Brayton, Collector, to Hon. Green B. Raum, Aug. 15, 1881, Box 4, LR, RG 58; W. E. Earle to Attorney General, Apr. 4, 1882, SCF, RG 60. See also Miller, *Revenuers and Moonshiners*, 110–11.

93. *Charleston News and Courier*, Jan. 1, 8, June 6, 1878.

94. Ibid., July 2, 1878.

95. *New York Times*, Nov. 6, 1884.

96. *Charleston News and Courier*, July 4, 1878.

INTRODUCTION

97. Ibid., July 2, 3, 4, 1878.

98. *New York Times*, July 15, 1878; and *Police National Gazette*, July 20, 1878. In May 1877, an unknown person murdered Alfred McCreary, who worked as a guide and informer for the Bureau of Internal Revenue, while he plowed his field. Although revenue agents suspected that Redmond was involved, they were never able to find concrete proof of his involvement. More likely than not, Redmond (although he may have had knowledge of it) did not commit the murder. See R. M. Wallace, U.S. Marshal, to Attorney General Charles Devens, Dec. 31, 1877, SCF, RG 60; and *Pickens Sentinel*, May 30, 1877.

99. Quoted in *Pickens Sentinel*, July 18, 1878.

100. Ibid.

101. *Charleston News and Courier*, July 13, 17, 18, 19, 20, 29, 30, 31, 1878.

102. Ibid., July 13, 1878.

103. Ibid., July 18, 1878.

104. Quoted in *Charleston News and Courier*, July 29, 1878.

105. *Charleston News and Courier*, July 30, 1878.

106. E. M. Brayton to Hon. Green B. Raum, Mar. 17, 1878, quoted in "Enforcement of Internal Revenue Laws," 189–90; and *Greenville Enterprise and Mountaineer*, July 31, 1878.

107. *Keowee Courier*, Aug. 8, 1878.

108. Green B. Raum to W. H. Chapman, July 29, 1878, quoted in *Charleston News and Courier*, Aug. 3, 1878.

109. Green B. Raum to E. M. Brayton, Aug. 2, 1878, quoted in "Enforcement of Internal Revenue Laws," 196–97; and R. M. Wallace, U.S. Marshal, to Attorney General Charles Devens, Aug. 7, 1878, SCF, RG 60.

110. Quoted in *Charleston News and Courier*, Aug. 15, 1878. See also *Keowee Courier*, Aug. 15, 1878; and *Pickens Sentinel*, Aug. 22, 1878.

111. *Charleston News and Courier*, Aug. 10, 1878.

112. *Speight's Spartanburg Daily*, Aug., [?] 1878, clipping in E. M. Brayton to Hon. Green B. Raum, Nov. 8, 1878, Box 887, LR, RG 58.

113. *Keowee Courier*, Aug. 15, 1878.

114. *Pickens Sentinel*, Aug. 15, 1878.

115. R. M Wallace to Attorney General Charles Devens, Aug. 7, 1878, SCF, RG 60.

116. *Charleston News and Courier*, Aug. 10, 1878.

117. *Annual Report of the Attorney-General*, 1877, *House Executive Document* 7, 45th Cong., 2d sess., p. 24; and *Annual Report of the Attorney-General*, 1879, *House Executive Document* 8, 46th Cong., 2d sess., p. 25.

118. *Annual Report, Commissioner of Internal Revenue*, 1876, *House Executive Document* 4, 44th Cong., 2d sess., p. iv; and *Annual Report, Commissioner of Internal Revenue*, 1879, *House Executive Document* 4, 46th Cong., 2d sess., p. xxi.

119. *Charleston News and Courier*, Aug. 21, 1878.

120. Green B. Raum to Hon. W. E. Earle, Aug. 17, 1878, quoted in *New York Times*, Aug. 20, 1878.

121. *Washington Post,* Aug. 12, 1878; *Charleston News and Courier,* Aug. 6, 20, 22, 1878; and *New York Times,* Aug. 12, 23, 1878.

122. *New York Times,* Aug. 23, 1878. See also *Charleston News and Courier,* Aug. 20, 1878.

123. L. C. Northrop to Attorney General Charles Devens, Aug. 30, 1878, SCF, RG 60; and L. C. Northrop to Attorney General Charles Devens, Aug. 24, 1878, SCF, RG 60.

124. Jno. E. Gyles, Special Deputy Collector, to Hon. E. M. Brayton, Sept. 1, 1878, quoted in "Enforcement of Internal Revenue Laws," 197.

125. E. G. Hoffman, Special Deputy Collector, to Hon. E. M. Brayton, Sept. 2, 1878, quoted in "Enforcement of Internal Revenue Laws," 197–98.

126. Green B. Raum to E. M. Brayton, Sept. 7, 1878, quoted in "Enforcement of Internal Revenue Laws," 198.

127. E. M. Brayton to Hon. Green B. Raum, quoted in *New York Times,* Dec. 25, 1878; *Keowee Courier,* Feb. 5, 13, 1879; and L. C. Northrop to Attorney General Charles Devens, Mar. 4, 1879, SCF, RG 60.

128. *New York Times,* Jan. 10, 1879.

129. John L. Thornley, U.S. Commissioner to Hon. L. C. Northrop, Feb. 24, 1879, SCF RG 60; and John L. Thornley, U.S. Commissioner to Hon. L. C. Northrop, Feb. 27, 1879, SCF RG 60.

130. L. C. Northrop to Attorney General Charles Devens, Mar. 4, 1879, SCF, RG 60; E. M. Brayton to Hon. Green B. Raum, Feb. 10, 1879, quoted in "Enforcement of Internal Revenue Laws," 199; and E. M. Brayton to Hon. Green B. Raum, Apr. 17, 1879, quoted in "Enforcement of Internal Revenue Laws," 200.

131. *1880 United States Federal Census,* Nantahala, Swain County, North Carolina, Roll T9-983. In July, the *New York Times* reported that Redmond was in Transylvania County. See *New York Times,* July 4, 1879.

132. Cobb, *The True Like of Maj. Lewis Richard Redmond,* 21–22.

133. *Asheville Citizen,* Oct. 9, 1879. See also *Keowee Courier,* Oct. 23, 1879.

134. Edward B. Crittenden, *The Entwined Lives of Miss Gabrielle Austin, Daughter of the Late Rev. Ellis C. Austin, and of Redmond, the Outlaw, Leader of the North Carolina "Moonshiners"* (Philadelphia: Barclay & Co., 1879), 58, 63.

135. Crittenden, *Entwined Lives,* 66, 67.

136. Atlanta *Constitution,* Aug. 18, 1886.

137. Atkinson, *After the Moonshiners,* 113.

138. Cobb, *The True Life of Maj. Lewis Richard Redmond,* iv.

139. *Pickens Sentinel,* Mar. 24, 1927.

140. Robert Dick, to Attorney General Charles Devens, Feb. 19, 1881, SCF, RG 60; *Police News,* May 7, 1881, quoted in Cobb, *The True Like of Maj. Lewis Richard Redmond,* 7–9; and *Galveston Daily News,* Apr. 19, 1881.

141. Cobb, *The True Life of Maj. Lewis Richard Redmond,* 24–25; and *National Police Gazette,* May 21, 1881.

142. *National Police Gazette,* May 21, 1881.

143. Cobb, *The True Life of Maj. Lewis Richard Redmond,* 26.

INTRODUCTION

144. *Galveston Daily News,* Apr. 19, 1881; *New York Times,* Apr. 17, 1881; *National Police Gazette,* May 21, 1881; and *Police News,* May 7, 1881, quoted in Cobb, *The True Life of Maj. Lewis Rickard Redmond,* 7–9.

145. Cobb, *The True Life of Maj. Lewis Richard Redmond,* 26.

146. *Keowee Courier,* Nov. 25, 1925, in Lewis Redmond Collection.

147. *New York Times,* Aug. 6, 1881. For an account of the rumored rescue, see Arthur, *Western North Carolina,* 305.

148. *Atlanta Daily Constitution,* Aug. 12, 1881.

149. *Keowee Courier,* Aug. 18, 1881.

150. *New York Times,* Sept. 1, 1881.

151. Ibid.

152. *Greenville Daily News,* Aug. 30, 1881, quoted in Tinsley, *The Land of Waterfalls,* 164; and District Attorney Samuel W. Melton to Attorney General McVeagh, Aug. 25, 1881, SCF, RG 60.

153. Records of the U.S. District Court, Western South Carolina, Record Group 21, National Archives, Atlanta Branch, Box 11, case nos., 1261, 1264–68, 1284–85.

154. See Hendersonville *Independent Herald,* Aug. 26, 1881; *New York Times,* Aug. 26, 1881; *Washington Post,* Aug. 26, 1881; *Galveston Daily News,* Aug. 27, 1881; *Raleigh News and Observer,* Aug. 27, 1881; and *Frank Leslie's Illustrated Newspaper,* Sept. 10, 1881.

155. *New York Times,* Aug. 26, 1881.

156. *Washington Post,* Aug. 26, 1881.

157. *Pickens Sentinel,* Sept. 1, 1881.

158. Miller, *Revenuers and Moonshiners,* 145, 148–49; and Bruce E. Stewart, "Distillers and Prohibitionists: Social Conflict and the Rise of Anti-Alcohol Reform in Appalachian Western North Carolina, 1790–1908" (Ph.D. diss., Univ. of Georgia, 2007), chaps. 5 and 8.

159. *Statistics of the Wealth and Industry of the United States . . . Ninth Census: 1870* (Washington: Government Printing Office, 1872), 568; and *Report on the Manufacturers of the United States . . . Tenth Census: 1880* (Washington: Government Printing Office, 1883), 353–55. For a discussion on railroad construction in South Carolina, see Scott Reynolds Nelson, *Iron Confederacies: Southern Railways, Klan Violence, and Reconstruction* (Chapel Hill: Univ. of North Carolina Press, 1999).

160. *Statistics of the Population of the United States . . . Ninth Census: 1870* (Washington: Government Printing Office, 1872), 258–60.

161. *Statistics of the Population of the United States . . . Tenth Census: 1880* (Washington: Government Printing Office, 1883).

162. For more on the New South, see Galvin Wright, *Old South, New South: Revolutions in the Southern Economy since the Civil War* (New York: Basic Books, 1986); James C. Cobb, *Industrialization and Southern Society, 1877–1984* (Lexington: Univ. Press of Kentucky, 1984); Dwight B. Billings, *Planters and the Making of the "New South": Class, Politics, and Development in North Carolina, 1865–1900* (Chapel Hill: Univ. of North Carolina Press, 1979); Paul M. Gaston, *The New South Creed: A Study in Southern Mythmaking* (New York: Alfred A. Knopf, 1970); and C. Vann Woodward, *Origins of the New South, 1877–1913* (Baton Rouge: Louisiana State Univ. Press, 1951).

163. *Keowee Courier,* June 3, 1880.

164. Jane Boroughs Morris, *Pickens: The Town and the First Baptist Church* (Pickens, SC: Pickens First Baptist Church, 1991), 67; Frederick M. Heath and Harriett H. Kinard, "Prohibition in South Carolina, 1880–1940: An Overview," *Proceedings of the South Carolina Historical Association* (1980): 119; Leonard S. Blakey, *The Sale of Liquor in the South: The History of a Normal Social Restraint in Southern Commonwealths* (New York: Columbia Univ. Press, 1912, plates 2 and 3; *Charleston News and Courier,* Mar. 3, 1880; *Pickens Sentinel,* June 9, July 21, Oct. 6, 1881; *Keowee Courier,* Feb. 19, Mar. 25, May 6, May 13, June 3, June 10, July 22, Aug. 19, 1880, Apr. 7, Apr. 28, June 2, Dec. 22, 1881; *Christian Union,* July 28, 1880; *Western Christian Advocate,* Jan. 5, 1881, Sept. 7, 1882; *New York Times,* July 18, 1880, Jan. 2, 1881, Nov. 16, Dec. 3, 1883, Jan. 27, Sept. 21, 1884; and *Atlanta Daily Constitution,* Feb. 8, Dec. 4, 1884.

165. *Keowee Courier,* June 2, 1881.

166. For descriptions of Brayton's murder, see *New York Times,* July 21, 24, 1881.

167. *Charleston News and Courier,* Aug. 3, 1881, quoted in *New York Times,* Aug. 6, 1881.

168. *Greenville News,* July 21, 1881, quoted in *New York Times,* July 24, 1881.

169. *Keowee Courier,* July 28, Aug. 4, 1881.

170. Miller, *Revenuers and Moonshiners,* 144.

171. *Pickens Sentinel,* Aug. 18, 1881.

172. *Annual Report, Commissioner of Internal Revenue,* 1882, House Executive Document 4, 47th Cong., 2d sess., p. xv. See also E. M. Brayton to Hon. Green B. Raum, June 7, 1882, Box 4, LR, RG 58

173. Sally Elmore Taylor Diary, 170–74, South Caroliniana Library, Univ. of South Carolina, Columbia.

174. [Greenville petitioners] to Hon. Benjamin Harris Brewster, Mar. 1884, SCF, RG 60.

175. Sam W. Melton to Hon. Benjamin Harris Brewster, Marsh 24, 1884, SCF, RG 60; and *New York Times,* Apr. 6, 12, 1884.

176. *Atlanta Daily Constitution,* May 23, 1884; and *New York Times,* May 29, 1884.

177. Sally Elmore Taylor Diary, 172–73.

178. Tinsley, *The Land of Waterfalls,* 164–65.

179. Sally Elmore Taylor Diary, 171, 173–74.

180. *New York Times,* May 29, 1884. See also *Washington Post,* June 2, 1884.

181. Quoted in *New York Times,* Nov. 6, 1884. See also *Boston Daily Advertiser,* Nov. 8, 1884.

182. In 1890, Redmond cut Jim Smith with a knife during a fight. Smith survived and Redmond was fined $750. See Edwin Parker McCravy, *Memories* (Greenville, SC: Observer Printing Co., 1941), 100; and *Pickens Sentinel,* July 3, 1890, Mar. 24, 1927.

183. *Pickens Sentinel,* June 17, 1886.

184. Ibid., Mar. 24, 1927.

185. *Keowee Courier,* Nov. 25, 1925, in Lewis Redmond Collection.

186. McCravy, *Memories,* 100.

187. Ibid., 102, 103.

INTRODUCTION

188. *Keowee Courier,* Apr. 18, 1906, quoted in Jerry Hughes, *Once Upon a Time in Pickens County: The Amos Ladd and Lewis R. Redmond Story* (Pickens, SC: Jerry Hughes, 1993), 41.

189. For discussions on the "Lost Cause movement," see W. Scott Poole, *Never Surrender: Confederate Memory and Conservatism in the South Carolina Upcountry* (Athens: Univ. of Georgia Press, 2004); Gary W. Gallagher and Allan T. Nolan, eds., *The Myth of the Lost Cause and Civil War History* (Bloomington: Indiana Univ. Press, 2000); Gaines M. Foster, *Ghosts of the Confederacy: Defeat, the Lost Cause and the Emergence of the New South* (Oxford: Oxford Univ. Press, 1997); Thomas L. Connelly and Barbara L. Bellows, *God and General Longstreet: The Lost Cause and the Southern Mind* (Baton Rouge: Louisiana State Univ. Press, 1982); and Charles R. Wilson, *Baptized in Blood: The Religion of the Lost Cause, 1865–1920* (Athens: Univ. of Georgia Press, 1980).

190. Anthony Harkins, *Hillbilly: A Cultural History of an American Icon* (Oxford: Oxford Univ. Press, 2004), 29.

191. Shapiro, *Appalachia on Our Mind*; and Allen W. Batteau, *The Invention of Appalachia* (Tucson: Univ. of Arizona Press, 1990).

192. For a discussion on feuding and the creation of violent Appalachia, see Shapiro, *Appalachia on Our Mind*; Batteau, *The Invention of Appalachia*; and Waller, "Feuding in Appalachia," in *Appalachia in the Making,* 347–76.

193. J. W. Williamson and Anthony Harkins have shown the role that moonshining played in the making of the term "hillbilly." Both, however, focus mostly on media images of illicit distillers in the twentieth century. See J. W. Williamson, *Hillbillyland: What the Movies Did to the Mountains and What the Mountains Did to the Movies* (Chapel Hill: Univ. of North Carolina Press, 1995); and Harkins, *Hillbilly.*

194. For more on the local color writing, see Shapiro, *Appalachia on Our Mind*; Anne Rowe, *The Enchanted Country: Northern Writers in the South, 1865–1910* (Baton Rouge: Louisiana State Univ. Press, 1978); David E. Whisnant, *All That Is Native and Fine: The Politics of Culture in an American Region* (Chapel Hill: Univ. of North Carolina Press, 1983); and Kevin E. O'Donnell and Helen Hollingsworth, eds., *Seekers of Scenery: Travel Writing from Southern Appalachia, 1840–1900* (Knoxville: Univ. of Tennessee Press, 2004). On the rise of American literary magazines following the Civil War, see Shapiro, *Appalachia on Our Mind*; and Richard Ohmann, *Selling Culture: Magazines, Markets, and Class at the Turn of the Century* (New York: Verso, 1996).

195. Before Redmond's interview in 1878, literary magazines had published only one exposé on moonshiners in southern Appalachia. See "The Moonshine Man: A Peep into His Haunts and Hiding Places," *Harper's Weekly* 21 (Oct. 20, 1877): 821–22.

196. Constance Fenimore Woolson, "Up in the Blue Ridge," *Appleton's Journal* 5 (Nov. 1878): 104–25.

197. "Law and Moonshine in Western North Carolina," *Harper's Weekly* 24 (Aug. 23, 1879): 667. See also "Moonshiners," *Harper's Weekly* 22 (Nov. 2, 1878): 875; and "Moonshiners," *Harper's New Monthly Magazine* 59 (Mar. 1879): 380–90.

198. Louise Coffin Jones, "In the Highlands of North Carolina," *Lippincott's Monthly Magazine* 32 (Oct. 1883): 385.

199. "Studies in the South," *Atlantic Monthly* 50 (Jan. 1882): 90.

200. Donald Baines, "Among the Moonshiners," *Dixie* 1 (Aug. 1885): 10.

201. See also Rebecca Harding Davis, "By-Paths in the Mountains, III," *Harper's New Monthly Magazine* 61 (Sept. 1880): 532–47; Sherwood Bonner, "Jack and the Mountain Pink," *Harper's Weekly* 25 (Jan. 29, 1881): 75–77; Sherwood Bonner, "The Case of Eliza Bleylock," *Harper's Weekly* 25 (Mar. 5, 1881): 155–57; Atkinson, *After the Moonshiners;* Charles Dudley Warner, "On Horseback," *Atlantic Monthly* 56 (July 1885): 195–96; Morgan Bates, *A Mountain Pink: Realistic Description among the Moonshiners of North Carolina, a Romantic Drama* (Milwaukee: Riverside Printing Co., 1885); "Home of the Moonshiners," *Harper's Weekly* 30 (Oct. 23, 1886): 687–88; and Charles Dudley Warner, "Comments on Kentucky," *Harper's New Monthly Magazine* 78 (Jan. 1889): 269–71.

202. James Lane Allen, "Through Cumberland Gap on Horseback," *Harper's New Monthly Magazine* 81 (Sept. 1886): 60.

203. See Atkinson, *After the Moonshiners,* 15, 28, 32; Davis, "By-Paths in the Mountains, III," 533; "Home of the Moonshiners," 687–88; "Studies in the South," 91; Warner, "Comments on Kentucky," 270–71; and Allen, "Through Cumberland Gap on Horseback," 66.

204. Baines, "Among the Moonshiners," 14.

205. For more on Robert A. Cobb, see Edward William Phifer Jr., *Burke: The History of a North Carolina County, 1777–1920, with a Glimpse Beyond* (Morganton, NC: privately published, 1977), 195, 226, 250.

206. Cobb, *The True Life of Maj. Lewis Redmond,* 29.

C. MCKINLEY'S INTERVIEW OF REDMOND.

Redmond's Strange Story.
A TALK WITH THE OUTLAW IN THE HEART OF THE RIDGE.

Arranging for an Interview—The Journey—Face to Face—The Surprise—Beginning an Eventful History—Life on the Farm and at the Still—Death of His Parents—The Killing of Duckworth—How It Came About—A Narrow Escape for Redmond

Pickens C. H., June 28. It is not necessary that I should be at my pains to introduce the subject of this sketch to any well informed man, woman or child in South Carolina, or perhaps in any State of the Union. That kind office has been pretty well discharged for me and for him, on many occasions within the past few years, by his many friends and admirers of the United States Internal Revenue Service, and there is but little that I can now add, save in the way of truth, to what has been already said concerning "the great criminal," "the notorious desperado," "the bloated brigand of the Blue Ridge," "the infamous outlaw," "the red-handed rover"—Lewis R. Redmond! This is he that has turned two States upside down; set all law, human and Divine, at naught; defied the power of the best government the world ever saw; chased its officers pell-mell across a county; committed highway robbery; ambushed the faithful in the discharge of their duty; released criminals from jail; frightened women and children and eke grown men into fits, and who, finally, if the truth were known, was doubtless at the bottom of the disturbance in the Bald Mountain. Are not these things so, beside many others like not here set down! The proof is not far to seek since his enemies declare it, and the law has confirmed it by setting

Published in the *Charleston News and Courier* July 2, 3, 4, 1878.

a price on his young head, and in giving authority to his fellowmen "to bring his body into court—alive or dead!"

At The Bar of Public Opinion.

This last thing has been rather difficult, not to say impossible, of performance it seems, and has remained undone until accomplished by the *News and Courier,* in the person of its humble representative, by whom the redoubtable has been captured alive and who now produced the prisoner in court; that great court of public opinion where he shall be called upon to answer to the charges preferred against him! I happened in this wise. A week or ten days ago, I was commissioned by the *News and Courier* 'to go and find Redmond,' if possible, and to obtain from him a personal narrative of his eventful career.

A Fruitless Quest.

The quest was not very satisfactory, as I learned that its object had left the country, and no man knew of his whereabouts, concerning which I was further informed that they were changed with every sun. At the end of the second day I was compelled to abandon the search [and] return to the village whence I had started, no whit wiser than when I left it. Through the kindness and superior knowledge of the gentleman who accompanied me, however, I had been placed in communication with two of the outlaw's most trusted friends, and had left with them, to be forwarded to some unknown post office, a note addressed to him, in which I requested an interview at any time and place he might designate and under any restrictions he should choose to impose upon me. His verbal reply granting my request was received Monday morning, and for instructions and guidance I was directed simply to accompany Mr. W. G. Field, of Pickens C. H., whithersoever he might lead me.[1] Reporting to this gentleman without delay, an understanding was quickly had, and our plan of proceeding agreed upon to be carried into effect the same night.

The Rendezvous.

By this time, and in spite of great precaution, the fact of my first visit to the mountain had become known and its true object suspected. (The good people of Pickens have learned to be suspicious of strangers, and their every movement is watched with fond solicitude.) It was therefore necessary to move with caution for Redmond's sake, as well as for that of the success of my endeavor, and I have since learned that our pains were not taken altogether in vain, as one or more interested and would-be-captors of the fugitive were on the qui vive to learn the way we went and other information which might lead to his capture. The 24th day of June seemed longer by several hours than the 21st, but it finally came to a close, and about dusk I walked quietly out of town alone into the adjacent woods and by a circuitous route reached the rendezvous appointed for the night. After a few hours of rest here we started for the mountains, which could be dimly seen by the light of dawn far off to the northward, and avoiding the town and more frequented ways by a detour of several miles drove rapidly until afternoon.

A Hard Road to Travel.

The country through which we passed and the incidents of the journey furnished abundant material for an interesting letter, but I am not at liberty, under promise, to indicate our route, and am therefore regretfully compelled to keep silent, to my readers' positive loss. The road was all that a road, even a mountain road, ought not to be—but I forbear again. At the end of it we stopped at a cottage in the hills, and after a kind reception and excellent dinner, (leaving our buggies behind as being of no particular use,) we were joined by another guide and resumed on foot the journey that was to conduct us to the presence of the as yet unseen chief. My first companion did not now know whither we were bound, and our guide knew little more than that we were to follow a certain trail until haled by "the Major" (for so Redmond is called) at such a point at he might choose to await our coming. The trail seemed to lead directly upward to some veritable land of the sky, and at times took a direct 'cut' as it were in that direction by 'leading up a tree,' as such paths are said to do when they disappear in the undergrowth, or at the foot of an inaccessible cliff. My companion, Mr. Field and myself were soon exhausted with the unaccustomed labor of climbing, and paused to rest while our unknown guide pushed on ahead to find Redmond and inform him of our near presence. We were nearly already two hours behind the appointed time and it was feared he might weary of waiting for us and leave the mountains.

Found at Last.

After a short rest we, who were behind, followed as best we might in the direction our guide had gone, and had become nearly broken down again as we toiled upward, when my fainting spirits were suddenly startled into quickened life and my rapidly beating heart sent into my throat with a mighty bound by the sudden exclamation of my comrade in advance, who whispered back to me, without turning his head, "Yonder he is." "He always keeps his word." Looking up quickly, I saw, a hundred yards beyond and above us, two men sitting at the foot of a pine, one of whom I recognized as the guide, the other of course was Redmond! He was yet at some distance from me, and I had several minutes for reflection before I reached him. What my feelings were may better be imagined than described. I had nothing to fear, of that I was well assured from the unvarying good report I had received from his friends of the true character of the man; but the experience was a novel one, to say the least. I was presently to be confronted by one whose name had been long associated in my hearing with all manner of treachery and crime, and at whose mercy I had now placed myself, with no other guarantee of safety than his good pleasure. I was of course unarmed, (which fact had been assured by a careful search of my person at the foot of the mountain, to which ceremony I submitted as a matter of right and reasonable precaution,) and there I was at last—face to face with "the dreaded outlaw."

Face to Face With Redmond.

The dreaded outlaw rose up to meet me with extended hand and a pleasant smile as I advanced, and after a cheery "Good morning" from him, and a similar salutation in return on my part, we were introduced in due form. Shaking my hand cordially, he invited me to a seat beside him, on the rock, with a smiling apology for the absence of better accommodations.

"This gentleman has come three hundred miles to see you Major," said Mr. Field, "He represents the best newspaper in the State, and has come to give you an opportunity to say something in your own behalf in answer to the charges which have been made against you."

"I am very glad to see you," he replied, addressing me, "but I am afraid it was hardly worth the trouble for you to come so far to see me."

I do not remember what I said in response to this modest speech so modestly delivered. My amazed attention was wholly taken up with the unexpected appearance of the youth whom I saw before me.

Neither Hoofs Nor Horns.

I am not at liberty again to describe him because of a promise made to his friends, before seeing him, that I would not do so. I can only say, therefore, that he looked to be indeed little more than a boy in years; (he has seen only twenty three winters, and seems youthful for even that age.) He is of slender "build," and one of the handsomest men I ever saw. I can scarcely refrain from supporting this statement by presenting my readers with a pen portrait at least of his face and graceful, active form; but must forbear, lest I should thereby make myself the unwilling instrument of betraying him into danger. I may say, however, that at my earnest request he permitted me to sketch his features before our parting. The portrait was pronounced a faithful likeness by those who were present at our interview, and my judgment above expressed has been confirmed by the few to which I have shown it.

One of the Best Fellows In The World.

His frank open manner, innocent looking eyes, and more than all his honest sun-browned face and pleasant smile, which no man could wear and yet be a villain, inspired me at once with perfect confidence, and placed me so much at ease that I hazarded a very personal remark. I said: "You don't look like a very bad man, sir." "I don't believe I am one," he replied. "I have only been badly treated, and accused of many things which I never did." ("He is one of the very best fellows in the world," said the guide.)

It is claimed for him that he can always discern between a friend and a foe, at sight, by looking in one's eyes. Himself says he believes he can read a man's thoughts. I had not been long in his presence accordingly before I noticed that he was observing my face intently. Possessing in an eminent degree, so far as he was concerned at least, a *"mens conscia recti,"* I hesitated not to look him squarely in the eyes, and turning my own lustrous orbs full upon him, he was enabled to gaze down into their liquid unfathomable depths and read "friend" at their very bottom. The search satisfied him apparently—there is no resisting guilelessness like mine—he banishes suspicion and treated me thenceforth with something more than confidence so long as I remained with him.

A Refreshing Stream.

After a few minutes' rest we arose and, Redmond showing the way, climbed around the mountain side until we came to a particular steep place down which we stumbled and fell and scrambled and slid after him, and got up and scrambled and stumbled and fell again and again, until we reached the bottom of a glen where foot of man or beast hath never or rarely been, and where certainly deputies cease from troubling and even a moonshiner may be at rest. We halted on the brink of a falling foaming stream, whose waters, clear as air, revealed the rocky bottom at any depth, and cold almost as snow, presented us with a drink sparkling as champagne and pure as heaven's own dew. Mixed with mountain dew, colored like a rose with the tonic juice of wild cherries, it constituted a draught which might have been likened to a nectar flowing down from some illicit still run in the private interest of the gods up there on the blue wooded Olympus above. It was a singularly wild and beautiful spot even for a mountain glen, and any element of romance that might have been waning was fully supplied by the presence of the outlaw in our midst, whose somewhat picturesque garb was not out of keeping with the character of the scene. Amid such surroundings the hunted outlaw told his story while we sat and listened until the setting of the sun behind the mountain's crest and the approach of darkness admonished us to return to the outer world while as yet the devious path might be safely traced.

The Outlaw's Tale.

The outlaw's tale was a long one, and was not completed in the first interview. It will not be possible to repeat it in the limits of one letter. It was taken down almost verbatim, in short hand, in a note book on my knee as I sat by his side, and will be given as nearly as possible in his own words. Leaning his gun against a tree, but retaining his formidable sidearms and keeping a bright eye on guard the while he began his story:

"I was born in Georgia,"

he began, "but we removed to this State when I was quite young. My father was old and infirm, and my mother was bedridden. I have had to take care of them, and of several sisters—one of whom was a cripple, and could not move without the aid of crutches—since I was a child. I am now twenty three years of age, and will be twenty four on the 24th of next October—if I live."[2] This condition was added with a smile that was sadder than a sigh, and reminded us that the speaker's life was at the mercy of any man who chooses to take it, by day or night, on the highway or at home, or in the rocky lair to which he has been driven like a hunted wolf. "The revenue officers want to capture me," he continued, "for the sake of the rewards which have been offered for me—it is easier for them to make their money in that way than by working for it." (They may find themselves mistaken in this view.) "My father owned a still all his life, as did all the farmers about here, before the revenue laws were passed, and I worked it for him. We were very poor, and he could do very little.[3] I worked on the farm all day and at the still at night to make a living for us. I have often worked all day ploughing and then run the still all night until breakfast. I would be so tired next day that I have gone to sleep in the corn row between the plough handles, and would wake up only when my horse stopped at the end of the furrow. This kind of life was too hard for me and soon broke me down, so that I got to working one night at the still and sleeping the next. I worked in the farm every day at the same time. They (the revenue officers) pressed me so close after awhile that I quit distilling and went to hauling whiskey and selling it in North Carolina. They found out that I was doing this, and a warrant was issued for my arrest.

The First Trouble.

I had with the revenue officers was all on my side, as they captured and destroyed for me one hundred and twenty three gallons of whiskey. I had paid one dollar per bushel for the corn that made it, besides eighteen dollars to a man who ran the still. The officers cut up and emptied three barrels of the whiskey, and kept two barrels for their own drinking. They kept these two barrels hid in the woods, and would come back and get it by the jug fill whenever their supply gave out. Among those who got some of it were Clem Cism (Chisolm?) and a fellow named Hampden. Several people have told me that they drank some of my whiskey that was captured at that time. Old man——told me the other day, that when they came for the last of it they arrested him and took him off, and all the officers stopped on the side of the road and filled their jugs with the whiskey which, they told him, was Redmond's. They carried off twenty-three gallons at this load.

Father and Mother Killed.

The next morning, it was Sunday, the officers rushed into my house and presented their guns at my father and captured him. He was seventy-eight years of age, and my mother who was confined to her bed with palsy, was nearly as old. Father begged them not to alarm her—she was badly frightened—and he would surrender. They asked for me, but I was at the spring when they came up and saw them, and so escaped. Father told them I was not far off, but I kept out of the way and they took him down to the church near by. They captured several other men in the church, and the preacher stopped in the midst of his sermon and sat down. My father and several gave bail—the rest they took away with them. My mother was badly frightened by it all and died in a few days afterwards. My father had to go to Asheville.[4] The journey and exposures made him ill, and he, too, died a few weeks later.

After the Funeral.

Both of them died before I could get back to them. I was then keeping out of the way, as the revenue officers were watching for me every time I went to see either of them. I did not see my mother buried, but when my father died too, and my sisters were left alone in the house, I determined to go home and attend his funeral and see after them at any risk. On the road from the house to the grave, when we were following his body to burial, we met a revenue officer. He looked at me very hard; but he was alone, and seeing that I had some of my friends with me, he passed on, and arrested several of the neighbors who had dug the grave and were resting on the roadside.

After the funeral I still kept out of the way, and as my sisters were alone and helpless, I had to dodge in and out and try to take care of them as best I could. This was the beginning of my troubles."

The foregoing story was told as quietly as though none of the circumstances narrated were matters of any special wonder in a mountain district, and my two companions seemed to listen to it in like spirit as to a thrice told tale. I have no comments to make and have refrained from even the feeble emphasis of italics. After an interval spent in conversation on indifferent subjects, I led Redmond back to the matter in hand by asking what was his next "trouble." He replied that it was

The Killing of Duckworth

and concerning this well known affair he gave the following account:

"When Deputy Marshal Lee was discharged from the revenue service he had in his possession a warrant against me, which he turned over to Frank Case.[5] This warrant Alfred Duckworth, who had been recently appointed on the revenue force, tried to get from Case, who refused to let him have it.[6] Duckworth then swore he 'would take me, warrant or no warrant, or would kill me in the attempt.' 'He had taken one highflyer,' he said, 'and by God he intended to take another.' Duckworth had been almost raised with me from childhood, and we knew each other well. He was very bigoted, and was always bragging and doing rash things. He rode one day by his own grandfather's house, where there was a picture of Gen. Washington hanging against the wall of a room, and he shot several balls into it through the open door or window from where he sat on his horse. The holes may be seen in the picture and wall now. People told me what he had threatened against me, but I only said, 'surely he has better sense than to try to take me without a warrant.' I said I would meet 'Alf,' as I always called him, and try to laugh him out of it. He will give me the same chance he gives other people. A few days later I had to haul a wagon load of corn and went over to get it. The driver was sitting by me and on the road we saw a crowd coming. I said, 'There comes the revenue officers now.' The driver asked, what will they do? I said, 'Nothing, they have no warrant for me.' I knew that Case had it. They came up to us and stopped and we talked together about one hour and a half.

Duckworth Sulky.

I asked Duckworth about old times, but saw that he looked sulky and there was something wrong. At last he said, 'Major, did you know that I had a warrant for you?' I said 'No.' He said, 'Do you want to hear it read?' I said, 'Yes, if you have one.' He got off his horse and drew from his pocket a batch of warrants. I saw that he had one for a man named Southerly, but none for me, and I thought he was joking. He read the warrant and called my name in place of Southerly's. I still thought he was only joking, and asked him to let me see the warrant. He said, 'No, by God, there's no use in it.' I replied, 'If you don't want me to handle the warrant, let some of these fellows see it—that is all I want. I don't want to tear it up.' He says, 'I suppose you don't intend to submit to it?' I replied, 'I am willing to submit if you will make me certain it is for me. I can give you security.' He said, 'There is no use in that; you have got to walk before me to Brevard tonight.' I said, 'I don't know that I will see Brevard tonight.[7] I have other business. You ought to give me the same chance you give other men.' He then went to his horse to get his pistols.

Going For His Pistols.

I knew what he was going for as soon as he started. His horse was several steps from him, and I could have killed him before he got hold of them. I did not want to kill him, however, (this was said earnestly and feelingly), although I knew that he had threatened repeatedly to kill me or take me. I said to him that I had not come prepared to fight him, but he only replied, 'That didn't make any difference!' So he went up to the side of his horse and took two pistols from the holsters, and pointed one of them in my face. I saw the five balls in the chambers. Several men were sitting around and Jim Paxton now came up.[8] He had been with them and had heard what they were going to do. He spoke to me and drove on. He, too, knew they had no warrant for me, and thought I wouldn't be taken without one. So he rode on, as he didn't want to see any fuss. Duckworth's pistol was aimed at me, and I said, 'Look here, Alfred, I don't want any man to draw a pistol on me.' He said, 'Get out of that wagon.' I told him again to put up his pistol, and said, 'I have given you no occasion to draw weapons on me, and I want no fuss.' He then dropped his pistol from my face to my breast. I was sitting in the wagon whittling a stick. I had no weapon, but my driver had a pistol, a Derringer, belonging to me, and which I had given him to carry. I had killed a rabbit with it as we came on. When I bade Duckworth a second time to put up his weapon, I said, 'Alfred, I want you to understand that I want no trouble with you.'

The Fatal Shot.

I then dropped my hand into the wagoner's pocket and took the pistol and cocked it, and said again, the third time, 'Alfred, I want no fuss with you—I want only a gentleman's chance.' He replied, 'Get out of that wagon!' His pistol was cocked and aimed at me. I drew mine and fired on him. As I did so, and when the ball struck him, his pistol went off and the ball struck under the wagon wheel. I suppose his finger contracted when he was hit and fired off his weapon. He fell against the fence. Landford was behind the wagon and had two pistols in his hands.[9] A man can think pretty fast in such a moment, and I thought the best thing I can do is to run around and 'take' Landford's pistols from him. Then, I thought that would be a risk, as he might kill me. I started up the road and had gone thirty yards, when Landford shot at me and kept shooting until he had shot four times. He missed me every time, and I thought if that is the best you can do I will go back and kill you with a rock! Then I thought, as he had two pistols, he might kill me, so I crossed the fence and went on up the hill. I waited for my wagon to come on, but a man met it and turned it back.

A Visit to South Carolina.

I came over into South Carolina, and the next day the news came to me that they thought it was all right with Duckworth—the doctor had attended him and dressed his wound, (it was in the throat), and said he would get well if they didn't move him. They moved him, the wound bled afresh, and he died that night. They examined him and found that he had no warrant for me. Three men, however, jumped on their horses and went to Frank Case's to get the warrant, and he wouldn't give it up. Case soon after sent me word that if I would come and give him two dollars and a half (costs) he would give me the warrant. I thought it would do me no good and so I didn't go for it. He has it yet. The names of those who were present and saw the killing were Peter Lince, his son, William Lince, and Joe and Bass Glassby.[10] They could prove all I have said. * * * Duckworth's father told Jim Cantrell the other day that his son was high strung and had done wrong. That when he was first killed he wanted them to get me, but since I had been so persecuted he would do anything he could to help me. He hoped he said, that I would get out of the way. He said, at the same time, that he supposed Redmond would kill him, too, now, if he got a chance; but I would not hurt him or any other man, unless they force me to do so. Cantrell told him as much, and that I would come laughing, and if I had anything to drink he would get it. He would be just as good to you as he would to me.

Willing to Surrender.

"The feeling against me on account of Duckworth's killing has died out in North Carolina," said Redmond in concluding this portion of his story, "and I would be perfectly willing to go there and surrender myself any day for trial if my case could be tried in the State Courts. I am not willing to stand a trial in a United States Court, where the revenue officers would have it all their own way and could swear what they please against me, or pay some one else to do it."

THE DAREDEVIL REDMOND.
ANOTHER CHAPTER OF THE STORY OF THE MODERN ROBIN HOOD.

Redmond's Capture, and How He Escaped—Trying to Rescue Ladd—The "Cops" on the Run—Wounding of Barton, Hendricks and Gary—Capture of Barton—Redmond's Kindness to Mrs. Barton, &c., &c.

Pickens C. H., June 28: "The next trouble I got into," continued Redmond, resuming the narration which was suspended in the *News and Courier* yesterday, "took place some time after that one in which Duckworth was killed and it resulted in my capture." "I escaped, however," he added with a laugh of merriment over the recollection. Omitting many interesting particulars which might be considered irrelevant, and would extend this letter to a greater length than permissible, I commence in the middle of his story.

The Whiskey Business.
A large reward had been offered in North Carolina for his apprehension, and having his sisters to support and knowing, moreover, that arrest at that time meant trial in a United States Court and very speedy conviction, Redmond transferred the scene of his operations into South Carolina, where he drove a thriving trade almost in the midst of the 'Revenues,' who tried in vain to catch him. 'I bought and sold only the best whiskey,' he said, 'and could always get $1.50 per gallon for my stock where other traders could only command $1. 'Redmond Whiskey' soon became well known and was sought after by everybody, even the Revenues. I was always very liberal with my customers and have frequently set out a ten gallon keg for a 'treat,' and seen them drink every drop in a few hours. I have no doubt that I have 'treated' away fully 1,500 gallons in this way since I begun. I did not mind treating my friends, but I did hate to treat a rascal, as I have often done, though I never said a word. The fact is, he added, there is very little profit in the business, and what with losses and captures, and the risk of arrest and imprisonment a man necessarily runs, it does not pay to follow it. I have not distilled a drop for three years, and have not sold any for over six months.

Redmond Betrayed.
Among others with whom I used to trade was a man named Van Hendricks.[11] I met him one day and he told me that he wanted to buy a quantity. We finally

agreed to meet at a certain house that night where I was to deliver the whiskey and receive the money. He wanted it on credit, but I could not afford to let him have it, so he promised to come and bring the money. He was to meet me at 1 o'clock that night, and after dark I drew of what he wanted (I had to make the faucet out of a sweet potato) and carried it to an outhouse, where I waited for him. Amos Ladd, my wagon driver, was with me, and we kindled a big fire on the hearth and laid down to sleep. About half past 12 Hendricks and Jamison came in, and I drew a pint bottle full and 'treated' them both. I then laid down again with my coat and boots off and we commenced talking. I had my pistols by me, one in sight and one under my pillow, and Hendricks asked me to let him see what kind I used. He picked up one and examined it and then asked me to let him see the other. This made me suspicious, and I replied that I never allowed any man to handle all my weapons at one time.

The Capture.

Just then a crowd of men, who had been waiting outside, burst open the door and rushed in on me and surrounded me. There was a big light in the fireplace, and I saw a dozen guns were cocked and pointed right at me. They were hollering, 'Surrender! Surrender!' as fast as they could and Amos Ladd said, 'I surrender.' I said nothing, and turned over to get my pistol from under my pillow, and saw that Hendricks had run around behind me and had my pistol within a few inches of my head. Several of them jumped upon me at once, and held me down and pinioned my arms, and then they turned me over on my back and Barton and Gary tied my wrists, close together.[12] It was all done in a moment, but when they jumped on me, I thought to myself, 'if there were only two of you, how quick I could turn you under.' If I had done so, however, they would have riddled me with buckshot and balls, so I thought I would wait.

Brutal Treatment.

When they were tying me they used a small strong rope, and they pulled mighty hard on it. I had a 'rising' on one wrist and they hurt me pretty badly; they broke the rising and cured it. Here is the scar now, he said, laughing, but if they had torn my arm off I wouldn't have said a word. When I was tied, Barton asked me if I was Major Redmond? I said, yes! He said 'Yes, G-d d-n you, you are the man who wanted to kill me.' I replied, 'I have not wanted to kill you; I could easily have done so if I had wanted.' He ordered me to get up, but pulled so hard on the end of the rope he had me tied with that I couldn't get up. It is no easy thing to rise when you are on your back with your hands tied. I tried to do so, but couldn't get up quick enough to please him, and then, said the outlaw, his eyes flashing at the recollection of the indignity, 'then he kicked at me, his boot grazing my side! If he had kicked me squarely he would have hurt me, though I don't think he could have hurt me much, that night, whatever he did but that was enough. I felt like I was as strong as three men, and sprang up I don't know how. I kept quiet, however, and they held me, and Barton ran his hand into my pocket and took out my pocketbook. I had one hundred and eighty-six dollars. He asked me if it was mine? I said 'yes, put it back in my pocket you have no right to take my money. He said 'you have no right to it,' and kept it. I then said, 'Look here, I want my boots.'

A Dash For Freedom.

Barton dropped the end of the rope he had been holding and started past me to get the boots which were lying by my pallet. I was mad because he had kicked me, and felt as tall as if I were three feet above the floor. I turned my hands in the rope and 'whopped' my arms into Gary's breast and knocked him down. I knocked Moore down in the same way on the other side; the others were all standing two deep between me and the door.[13] I kicked at Charley White, who gave way; the rest scattered, and I jumped out of the door like I had been greased. My wagon was in front of the door, fortunately; so I ran around it, gathering up as I ran the rope with which I was tied to keep it from tripping me. (I knew they would catch me if I fell.) They dashed out after me. Bang, bang! went their guns. The balls stuck all around me and knocked up the snow. I heard one of them say, 'By G-d, I know we have killed him;' but I knew they hadn't, and kept on. I was still tied so tight I couldn't get loose, though I kept tugging at the rope as I ran. I had one pistol in my pocket and got it out, but dropped it in jumping a big chestnut log.

First Catch Your Hare.

There was a fence in the way, but I went over it without any trouble. I think I flew over, I got over so easily. The officers turned back; they were afraid to follow me very far, and then I stopped and untied the rope with my teeth, and knew I was safe. The snow was thick on the ground, and I was without hat or coat and in my stocking feet. I knew they had my pistols, but as they had Amos, too. I determined to rescue him or die. I thought they wouldn't stay long about there after I was loose so I ran across the fields in my stocking feet to a neighbor's house. I won't tell his name but when I got there the soles of my stocking were cut to pieces by the ice, and the legs were clinging around my ankles. I knocked and he let me in, and I told him those 'hell-fired devils' had captured me and my driver, and I intended to take him away from them. He gave me a hat and coat and shoes and a gun and ammunition. I then went back to the road, which I knew they would have to travel, and waited for them. I heard them getting ready to start with Amos, and all were talking and shouting together. They had captured a high strung black mare of mine, and when they hitched her to the wagon to start one of them whipped her, and she began to kick things to pieces generally. Barton was anxious to get away, so Amos told me afterwards, and stood by with his gun aiming at every noise he heard in the bushes. They got started finally; the bay mare did all the pulling, as the black was mad; and I heard them coming up the road. Amos was crying; he was nothing but a boy, then, and I can't tell you how I felt.

Attempted Rescue of Amos Ladd.

I just seemed to swell. I felt so big but I couldn't help from crying myself. I knew my own wagon by the black mare, which I could see against the snow bank. Their's was a one-horse concern and was in front, and just as soon as it came within reach I leveled my gun and fired! I heard some one holler, 'Run! Run! Run!' and heard Barton say, 'What's the matter?' I thought to myself, you wait a minute and I will show you what's the matter. Then some one in the foremost wagon fired at me two or three times and they all fell out of the wagon, and as they ran up the snow bank into the bushes I fired again. My gun was loaded with buckshot, and then I heard some one groaning and I thought 'I have got meat this time,' I shot six more times, but the banks were so high that I overshot them and didn't get anybody.

Charley White's Terror.

One of them, Charley White, had caught a shot in his thigh, and as Amos who was then dodging behind the barrels told me afterwards, tried his best to get under or into Amos for protection.[14] Amos told him 'to get out and take his share;' and he replied, 'I have got my share already.'

To do him justice, I may say here that the 'Major' did not seem to think that, under the circumstances, there was anything particularly wrong in his single handed attacked upon the dozen Revenues. He certainly enjoyed telling how poor Charley White had tried to crawl into Amos, and how his faithful black mare had 'fanned timber, with her indignant heels.' The officers took Amos into their midst and drove off rapidly, and Redmond ceased firing for fear of killing his friend.

Awaiting Another Chance.

'I hadn't got Amos out yet,' he continued, 'so as they drove on I ran on down the fence by their side until they got to the next house, (Mr. Pepper's) which was not far off, and then I heard them holler 'whoa!' and call for old man Pepper.[15]

Mr. Pepper started to bring out a light, but Barton ordered him not to bring it there. I was standing a few feet from him in the darkness watching for a chance to rescue Amos, but could not tell him from the others. He had untied himself in the wagon, however, while we were fighting and suddenly I heard some one holler, 'He's gone! He's gone!' and then several shots were fired; but I knew he had got off safely. I then thought I would rush in and cut the traces and recapture my horses, but thought they might hit me, so I stood still. They all went into the house, and I went off and whistled for Amos, who came to me and told me I had wounded Barton and Hendricks. We went back together to watch the house, and I looked through the window and saw them all sitting before the fire. I could have killed Barton or any of them, they were not ten feet from me; but I wouldn't shoot any one down in another man's house.

The Way the Revenues Run.

The next morning I saw them again in the road in the one horse wagon and wanted to shoot Jamison, but Amos begged me not to do it, and I wouldn't. Presently the others came along and Gary was riding on my horse by the side of Dr. Earle who had been attending the wounded.[16] It made me mad to see him on my horse, after all that had happened, but I would not shoot at him for fear of wounding Earle, who was between us. Gary had gotten him to ride by him. At last I saw Earle go a little ahead, and I saw my chance and fired and hit him, Earle helped him back on my horse, and then I never saw men run so in my life. I thought I would stop them so I shot my own horse; he commenced staggering, but he was game and kept going, and I followed on after them as fast as they and I could run. They crossed a creek and stopped and Gary hollered back to me, 'Come over here and I will kill you.' I had only one pistol, but I started towards him. I had to cross the creek on a small log, and loaded as I went. Before I could get across they commenced running again, and I called out to them to 'wait and I would kill every one of them.' 'That is the way you do,' I said, 'you steal all a man has and then run!' I then turned and went back. Gary had dropped his hat in the road, and I found it and tore it all to pieces. He had my overcoats, a shawl I had paid twenty-eight dollars for, and also my hat and boots and a fine dress coat. They gave the hat and boots and coat to negroes living on the roadside. I heard of it and gave out word that I would kill them all if they didn't bring them back. They brought them that same night, and I found them hanging on the wagon next morning. The revenue officers carried off my shawl and overcoat and kept them for their own use. (It was for attempting to recover this stolen property that Judge Mackey issued a bench warrant for him for committing highway robbery.)

A Moonshiners Raid.

'The next day,' continued Redmond, 'I sent word to Barton that if he would return my horses and money and have my wagon mended, I would call all square between us and be done with it. He refused to do it, so a few days later I raised a company of about twelve men from———creek and went to call on him. We rode all that night. It was very dark and we missed the way, and I rode into a cut in the railroad. It was very deep and I had a hard fall. My horse fell on me and knocked my leg out of joint. I thought it was broken it hurt so, but I called to the boys to halt or they would ride in too. One of them was so close that as he wheeled his horse's hind legs slipped over the edge and threw dirt down on me. I heard one of them say, 'He's killed, let's go back home.' I found my horse was not hurt much so I got on him and rode down the track until I could get out, and went back to them. My leg was hurting very badly, so I called one of the boys to me and told him to catch hold and pull as hard as he could. He did so, and my leg slipped back with a pop which I thought could have been heard a hundred yards off. I did not say anything about it. We had no light except matches, and burned about five boxes of them in trying to find our way. We got to Easley Station that night, and some of the boys wanted to go on at once to Barton's house.

I said no, let us wait until day and go like men; I am no robber or horse thief, and what I do I propose to do by day light. 'They go in like dogs—don't let us do like them!' We stayed at the station until daylight, and a man asked me where I was going. I replied, 'Bird hunting!' That was what the officers had said when they started after me. I got some ammunition at Easley and we started down the road. One of the boys tried to prime his old flint and steel rifle as he galloped along, and he left a black trail of powder for half a mile!' (The reader will doubtless have remarked that our autobiographer has a grim sense of humor, and nothing ridiculous escapes him under even the most serious circumstances.)

The Raid on Barton.

When we got nearly to Barton's house we saw a negro run in, and as we closed around the house I saw Barton steal out and crawl under it. Mrs. Barton came out wringing her hands and screaming, but I told her not to be alarmed as I didn't want to hurt anybody. I asked where her husband was and she said he was in Greenville. I told her he was under the house and asked her to call him out. She said I had come to kill him, but I told her no, I only came to get my horses and money. She asked if I would give her my hand on that? I did so and she called Barton, who came crawling out on his hands and knees. It had been raining and he was very muddy; he came forward, arm in arm with his wife and said to me, 'Redmond, I know you have come to kill me, and I want to die right here at home with my wife.' I told him that I only came for my property—my horses and wagons—and he replied that they were in Greenville, but that he would go there and get them, or I could send one of the boys for them. I told him I hadn't come for any foolishness, and would have them or his hide!

Redmond Demands His Own.

He asked for a chair and started off to get one, but I ordered him to stand where he was. He then asked me for a dry pair of socks, and I let him send and get them. I then told him I wanted my money. He asked how much it was. I said you know how much you stole from me—go and get it. (It was $186.) He said I have a check on the bank for $100. You can have that; it is all the money I have, and you can take my horses. I said I don't want your horses. I want my own, and I won't have your check. You took my money away from me; pay it back and I will go. He offered to send Mrs. Barton to Easley to get the money and I said all right. He then said I could go to his stable and take his horses. I replied that I was no horse thief, and did not propose to go near his stable; he could go and bring them and give them to me in the presence of those witnesses if he desired to pay me for what he took from me wrongfully. He took two negroes with him, and I told them not to touch the horses. He brought them out, and all who saw them said that neither of them was as good as mine, but it was the last chance, so I took them. He called a man who lived near him to witness that he gave up the horses freely, as I had told him that I wouldn't take them on any other terms. I told him he had to pay Amos also six dollars he had taken from him the night of our capture, and he said he had no money to pay him with. Mrs. Barton said there was some loose silver in the house and she wanted to get it, and counted out five dollars and gave it to Amos. He had lost his wages in my service, so I paid him the remaining dollar afterwards out of my pocket. Barton then brought out a jug of whiskey and offered to treat the crowd. Both Mr. and Mrs. Barton drank a little to show that it was all right, and one or two of the boys drank with. I could not drink his whiskey after all that had passed between us, but I had some of my own and the rest of the boys drank it with me.

The Visit to Easley.

Mrs. Barton then went on to Easley station with us, and she and I talked together all the way. She is a good woman and I was never so sorry for any one in my life as I was for her. She said they were broken up completely, and had nothing to live on or to work with. When we got to Easley she had the check cashed and gave me one hundred dollars. I had been thinking of what she told me on the road, so I told her never mind about the eight six dollars: she might have that. It was not the money that I had cared for, I only didn't want to be robbed and abused. A crowd had collected at the station by this time, and she was afraid to go home by herself. I sent one of my friends to keep her company, and told her to keep the horse to help make bread for her and her children. She did not want to take it, as she said I would come back on her husband for it. I told her that I would not, but that I didn't want to hear for him on any more raids. She was satisfied and went off.

A Kind Invitation.

I bought 5 gallons of whiskey at Easley Station and treated the whole crowd that had collected there. It looked like a regiment, and I didn't know there were half that number of men at the station. While they were drinking, I saw Moore, one of the men who had helped to capture me, standing at a corner, and some one asked me to treat him too. I called him and invited him to join us. I said 'Hello Lieutenant come up and drink with me.' He said he wouldn't come, and I told him I would bring him, and turned my horse to go after him. He said 'All right, I will come.' I said 'I paid my own money for this whiskey, it is not stolen, come and drink with me.' He refused again, but I made him take two drinks. Amos Ladd said to him, 'You were the man who tied me. Do you remember what you said when you did it?' Moore said 'No, I don't remember.' Amos replied, 'You said to me you have got the best man hold of you you ever saw, and yet you were the first man to run!' This turned the laugh on Moore, and soon after we rode off. Barton went on one raid after this; Moore never went on another.'

Bohemian and Brigand.
A Moving Plea for the Outlaw—
"Give Redmond a Chance!"

The Raid on Gary and Hendricks—The Pickens Jail Delivery—Chevy Chase with no Chasers—A Revenue Scapegoat—Mackey on the War-Path—Bench Warrants and Bench Warrants—Beating up a Neighborhood—A Night Interview—An Escaped Prisoner—A Boy Soldier—Redmond's Appeal to Hampton.

Pickens C.H., June 29. Redmond's second and last raid was made against his own wishes, was contrary to his judgment, and, as he declares, is the only thing he has done for which he condemns himself. The circumstances under which he told his brief story concerning it deserve to be mentioned for many reasons which will presently appear.

An Unexpected Sensation.

At the close of our first interview, on Tuesday afternoon, he accompanied my companion and myself to the foot of the mountain. Before we had reached that point, however, and while we were sauntering quietly along the 'trail,' we were suddenly saluted with the summons 'Halt and surrender! I am a revenue officer,' which proceeded from the bushes on our right. At the same moment the sound of horses afeet was heard in the road in our front, and for a moment I thought I was about to have an experience I had not bargained for. The voice was that of one friend, however, and the horse which quickly came into sight was bestrode by another, wherefore I was spared any further sensation than the numerous unpleasant ones I had just felt in my mind in view of an anticipated skirmish. The newcomers brought the information that a squad of thirteen 'Revenues' had just passed down the road, a mile or two distant, with a prisoner, a friend of Redmond's, in charge; that they were in search of Redmond himself, and that they were divided for the purpose of 'heating up' the neighborhood. Some of them might be expected any moment at the house nearest to us, (where I had left my buggy), they said, and it was advisable for us to keep a sharp lookout. A sharp lookout was accordingly kept, but Redmond accompanied us to the house and remained with us, and night had set in before he left us, and returned by another route than that by which we had come, to the mountain. I was quite ill by this time, in consequence of exposure to the hot sun, and of the unwonted and excessive exercise I had undergone in climbing, but after supper I started again to find him.

Who Can Stand This Sort of Life?

It was so dark under the trees and in the hollow of the hills that I could not see my hand held within an inch of my face. My guides seemed to know the way by instinct, however, and one of them taking my arm they led me by a devious path which seemed endless, and only to lead into deeper and deeper darkness until we came to the appointed rendezvous. Here one struck a match and lighted a small hand lamp, and I learned for the first time that Redmond had joined us somewhere on the way. We found seats on the ground or on rocks and roots of trees as best we might, and sat in silence around the flickering light while Redmond hastily ate the supper we had provided for him. I had brought a kettle of coffee at the risk of my neck, but he barely tasted it. It was very seldom that he ever touched it. He appeared very thoughtful and spoke but once or twice during the repast. Once he said to me. 'Who can stand this sort of life? It is enough to drive an honest man to do wrong.'

The Scene Was Impressive

and gloomy enough. We sat within a narrow circle of dim light, hedged in by a thick darkness that might have concealed an hundred enemies within as many feet from the lamp. The trees seemed to be whispering secrets to each other or warnings to us, and the leaves looked strangely as they reflected the light from their under sides. The air was heavy and oppressive, and seemed fraught with danger, and we looked in each other's faces with feelings not unlike what we might have experienced had all instead of one only been under ban and expecting betrayal and a death-dealing volley out of the night at any moment! It could not have been worse had we been on the frontier and surrounded by hostile Indians. Nor were these feelings confined to that little group out there in the forest. It was shared in kind by every household for miles around us. One of our party said: 'There is not one man in ten in this neighborhood, be he guilty or innocent, who will sleep in his house tonight!' 'And you say true,' echoed every vote but mine, within his hearing. I, too, learned its truth in part before many hours had passed.

The Raid After Gary.

I reminded Redmond of my errand, and his promise to tell me of his 'raid' after Gary. 'It was not my doing,' he said. 'I did not lead the party, and at first refused to go with them. They said they had gone with me when I needed them, and now I refused to help them when they needed me. So I went. Gary had broken up a still and behaved badly, and the man the still belonged to collected the crowd and went to thrash him. I said to them, 'He has done nothing to be killed for—this thing of killing a man won't do, but I will go with you, if you wish me, to get satisfaction for cutting up the still.' They said they did not intend to kill him, but only to 'put the withe on him,' (i.e., whip him). This was distinctly understood before we started. We did not chase any revenue officers, but went directly to Gary's house at Liberty. He was not there and we returned home. We started one Monday afternoon about 1 o'clock next morning. There would not have been anything said about this raid but for what was done at Hendricks' house. He was a brother of 'Van,' and the boys hearing that the overcoat and shawl which they had stolen from me were in the house determined to take them away.

Visiting Hendricks.

They found an overcoat, which several said was mine, but I did not think so, and would not take it. They tried to persuade me to do so, but I told them I would not wear another man's coat as long as I could buy one for myself. The shawl was not there, and one of the party was about to seize a saddle blanket in place of it, but I stopped him, and made him leave it where he found it. I told them that the officers had not stolen anything of the kind from me, and I would have nothing but what I knew was mine. I kept them from taking away several other things, and took nothing at all myself. The court met a few days after this, and a bench warrant was issued for me for stealing the two overcoats!'

Judge Mackey's Part.

I have been informed by an officer of the Court of Pickens county that when the charge was preferred in court against Redmond of having the overcoats, the grand jury examined the witnesses and, finding no proof against him to either matter, returned to the court room and handed in a verdict of 'No Bill!' Judge [T. J.] Mackey at once sent them back with other witnesses, and again they returned with the same verdict. He sent them back a third time with the remark, 'I suppose, gentlemen, you have not had enough witnesses,' and seeing that he was determined to have it, they returned at last with an indictment. The proceedings in a grand jury room are, of course, secret, but it is said in Pickens county that the evidence upon which this one based its final verdict was two fold, to wit: First, that two overcoats were taken by a party of men from Hendricks' house; second, that Redmond was seen at Pickens Court House next day with the same party! On this alleged evidence 'the Court' issued its bench warrant, ordering Redmond to be brought into its precincts dead or alive. A posse was accordingly sent after him, they found him at work in his field, and ordered him to halt and surrender. Not knowing who they were or what they wanted, Redmond refused to obey, and they fired upon him and continued firing until he obtained shelter in the woods. Possibly being just men they did not try to hit him—we may hope not, at any rate.

The Pickens Jail Delivery.

The Pickens jail delivery had taken place on the Saturday, the 9th, preceding the ineffectual raid after Gary, which took place Monday, the 11th, and of course Redmond, who did not lead the Gary raid, led the jail breakers also. Of course he did no such thing. In point of fact, he was across the line in North Carolina when the jail was broken, and knew nothing of it until he was informed of the occurrence. There are plenty of witnesses to prove that he was in North Carolina at the time, and if this is not enough Sheriff [Joab] Mauldin is ready to testify that he was not in the party who rescued the prisoners from his keeping. But the timorous revenue officers declared that 'Redmond and his gang of forty or fifty men' had chased them across the country for two days and until they found them safely within the walls of Easley Station; some one had evidently stolen their sacred overcoats from the (sometimes) inviolate sanctuary of a private dwelling; Judge Mackey and all the mighty revenue departments were excited for the fat of the country, and an example must be made of somebody! Who so suitable for the sacrifice as Redmond—the official revenue scapegoat—the raging ram presently to be caught in the thicket!

The Batch of Warrants.

I understand that at the same time the aforesaid bench warrant was issued for Redmond four others were issued for certain revenue officers who were also charged with sundry crimes and misdemeanors. That one against Redmond, as we have seen, was very nearly put into fatal execution, and still hangs over his head, the others, I am informed, were recalled before the court adjourned. Why were they issued, and why and when recalled? I do not know.

Another Bit of History.

And while I am off my subject, let me inform the public of another bit of revenue history. I do not propose to defend those who broke into Pickens jail, but it may be as well to know, for the first time, whom it was they turned loose on that occasion. The rescued prisoners were 3 in number; one a man named Beasley, who was caught in an illicit still house, the other two were a father and son named Stansill.[17] The father was 60 years of age, and the son 16. Both were arrested at their homes, handcuffed, carried to Pickens and there lodged in jail to await trial. Their neighbors released them and they returned to their homes and resumed their daily labor on the little farm from which they had been torn and marched off in disgrace. Re-arrested a little later by the county officer they were carried before the commissioner and discharged, there being no evidence against them. So much for the Pickens jail delivery, of which one crime at least, gentlemen, I charge you to acquit the prisoner, Lewis R. Redmond.

Judge Mackey.

One word of explanation in regard to Judge Mackey. I recognize the fact that it is scarcely within my province to criticize his action in the matters above referred to, or to that of any Judge of his ability in any matter. But I feel free to say, nevertheless, that I am honestly of opinion that he acted with more zeal than discretion in this one instance, and would have accomplished much more good had he followed up Redmond less closely and the revenue officers more so. To do him justice, however, he did order the recently reported investigation, and would no doubt make good use of it if opportunity were presented. To return to Redmond. I have promised to end his story with this letter, and though I hope no one of my readers have wearied of him as yet, I shall try to keep my word.

A False Alarm.

Feeling really ill from the effects of fatigue, as I have said before, I was compelled to close my second interview with him a little before midnight; when he again accompanied me to the house of our mutual friend, my host. There I bade him good-night, and went to bed, while he and my host took blankets and walked off to sleep in the woods. I quickly fell into an uneasy semi-conscious state, from which I was startled an hour later by the subdued voice of our kind young hostess, whispering to my companion, Mr. Field, to "get up, please, and strike a light; the Revenues are all around the house!" The frightened wife was clad in her night dress only, and seemed beside herself with anxiety and alarm. "I have heard some one walking in the yard," she said, "and they always come about this time of night!" Mr. Field arose and striking a match (how hard they were to find!) went to the window and called, "who is there?"

A voice answered, a whispered consultation followed, and at last my companion came back and whispered to me that not the revenues but the prisoner they had captured the day before was without! I congratulated him in my heart on his escape, and Mrs.———rummaged around and got him a supper. I did not see him, but my hostess and my companion told me they never saw a man eat so much in their respective lives. Then he pushed on over the hills and far away to the home from which he had been taken the morning before, and where, no doubt, he was welcomed as one risen from the dead. It was the old story of captors dozing, a sudden dash for liberty, a few bullets dodged, and freedom once more. How Redmond—nay, how the whole neighborhood rejoiced over the fact of his escape next morning! '*Peccavi,*' but I couldn't help it, nor could you had you been in my place.

Redmond's Benevolence.

Redmond breakfasted with us next morning, and our hostess waited upon us and could not do enough for him. The simple-hearted women of the mountains all admire if they do not love him, and neither his name nor his presence have any terrors for them. Why it was only last year, say they, that he paid off the taxes which were hanging over the heads of I am afraid to state how many poor families, and took his pay, when he got any, in "chips and whetstones" and other like valuables, among which was a veteran ram, which one old lady forced upon him, and which he never saw after the day of transfer. It preferred her yard to his, it seemed, and he never went back for it. And besides all this, did he not ride five consecutive days "working for Hampton" during the last campaign, and on election day did he not hitch up his own wagon and team and send eight or ten old men who couldn't walk and who hadn't voted for years, all the way from their homes to the poll at Eastatoe, where he dared not go himself? And, outlaw as he is, is he not now supporting his three sisters, who have no other dependence, and one of whom has been a cripple for eleven years? Certainly he has done and he is doing all these things, as everybody hereabouts will tell you.

Other Good Deeds.

It was not very long ago that a poor man, whose oxen and four sheep which he had taken to market were levied on for taxes at Pickens Court House, met "the Major" in the road and asked him for help and got it. It was a small sum, only $6.25, but it was a very large sum to the poor farmer and to the despised Samaritan, but it was given freely, and has never been returned or asked for. No, the money was neither stolen on the highway nor was it in the return of any unlawful sale; it was the price of produce grown on the outlaw's farm by hard labor, and which farm and home he dares not visit except at night and at long intervals, at the risk of his life. "The Revenues have been there after him very often," said one, a Revenue himself, to me today.

How Redmond Told His Tale.

I have made another digression I find, but do not think I need apologize for it. Not so much of good has ever been said concerning Lewis Redmond that I need silence the public voice of his praise on this the one single occasion of justification. I have written down in these letters every word which he has said against himself in speaking of his own misdeeds to me. I declare that the story was not told boastingly or evasively—but quietly and as I believe truthfully. He was careful to be correct throughout, and whatever other crimes have been charged against him no man has ever yet accused him of lying. "What he tells you you may rely on" is the testimony of all, and when Redmond gave Mrs. Barton his word that he would not harm his worst enemy, her husband, she knew her man, and called upon that husband to come out and face a dozen rifles in the hands of angry men who were eager to kill him on the spot. You may condemn some things he has done, and of which he has told you, if you will but for sweet justice's sake give me credit for the good that is in him, and of which other people tell you. What he has done we partly may compute himself only what he has resisted. "He will take more cursing than any man I ever saw," said a mountaineer to me. "I heard a man call him a G—d o—o liar, and he only laughed at him." He tries to keep the peace at all times, and never has a fuss with any one when he can help it. He is fair, and will hold his end of the bridle, but when he starts he is game. When he says 'that's enough' you may know it is a plenty. He is one of the most sensible men I know, and only needs an education to make him a leader in this country. This may be poor logic, but it presents no bad picture of the character of its subject.

The Last Interview.

After breakfast our party went once more upon the hillside where I held my third and last interview with the outlaw. The conversation was of a more general character than on former occasions, and his thoughts were directed at last to a review of his early life.

"You were not old enough to go into the war were you?" I asked.

"Yes," he said, "I ran away from home when I was thirteen years old, and went to join the company my brother belonged to.[18] When I first talked about going my father said if I went he would bring me back and whip me half to death. He sent me to feed the horses one night, and I took a pair of pants and a shirt and struck out for the nearest station, where my brother was, and got there just as the chickens were crowing for day. My brother and the other men told me to go back, but I would not. The company started off that day, and we had gone but nine miles when I saw father coming.

He met us at the forks of the road and stopped me. I couldn't help from shedding tears to save my life. He begged me to go back, and the men begged me, so I went. My brother came home afterwards on sick furlough, and when he returned to his company I went with him and stayed six months. He was shot and sent home, and they gave me a furlough at the same time to go with him. The Yankees captured him at home soon after, but I was so young they did not bother me. I never saw my brother again: he died in some Northern prison. Another brother, the oldest, came home a year before the surrender with his right hand shot off and one shoulder shattered, and was badly wounded in the foot. He had received seven balls in all.[19] I have another brother living in———(another State), but I never write to him now, and he does not know of my troubles. If I were to tell him it would only distress him, and he might come and get into a difficulty on my account."[20]

The Outlaw Weeps.

The outlaw paused, and looking up I saw that he was weeping and had buried his face in his hands. I had been intent on my note book while he was speaking, and though I detected a slight tremor in his voice, did not suspect the cause or look up until he ceased speaking. I was both surprised and shocked beyond measure at such a manifestation of emotion in such a man, and knew not what to say. He tried to control himself, and looking at me with a smiling, tear wet face, sobbed out in spite of all his efforts; "I can't help it—I can't help it. I am not a crying man, but when I think of these things and of my father and brothers, and how they fought, and were shot to pieces or died in prison, and then think how I have been served, I can't help crying. I ought not to do it, but I can't help it—I can't help it," he repeated sadly again and again, as if in shamed apology for a weakness he feared I would despise. I did not despise him, I was sorry for him. I am a poor tender-hearted fool myself, at best. One touch of nature will make me feel akin to anybody, even a revenue officer, and my best nature was touched. Bohemian and brigand, we were there together, sitting apart with the mountaineers looking wonderingly on, and it was all I could do to swallow something big and hard in my throat, and keep my own tears back. That's an honest confession, and any knave or fool is at liberty to poke fun at me if he likes.

Only Give Him A Chance!

Redmond, the outlaw, dried his sinful tears, and the smile he always wears came back again to his face, though his voice was very sad and came from his heart when he said on in his simple unaffected way: "It looks hard for me to have to go through all this. If I had done anything worthy of it I would not mind, but I have not done more than other people, and why should I have to bear it all? If they would only give me a chance (God help him!) like they give other men, I have settled my troubles with Barton and Hendricks, and this very week Gary sent me word that if I would let him alone he would quit the revenue service and go to work on his farm. I have nothing against him or any man. If they would let me alone I certainly would not trouble them. I sent word so to him. I wouldn't have any trouble now, but for this reward that has been offered for my capture, and they think they will get it if they kill me even. It was for the Pickens jail delivery and I was not there, and for the raid on Gary, with which I had nothing to do except what I have told you. I only want peace, so I can go back to my farm and work for myself and my sisters, without being shot at every day like a dog. They have shot at me twenty-six times already, and I think that ought to be enough. I am willing to surrender myself and stand my trial for killing Duckworth. I know they would acquit me. I have no money to pay a lawyer, but I suppose they would give me the reward if I surrendered myself, and he might take that! They say they are willing to give amnesty to all the other men, and I don't see why they should leave me out. Do you think they will?" he said suddenly.

"I do not know," I replied "but I will speak to Governor Hampton for you" (as I had promised him before this to do.)

The Message to Hampton.

"Tell Governor Hampton," he said earnestly in parting, "I am a poor man and have worked for my living all my life. I have not had a fair chance since this

Interview of Redmond

revenue party came in, and if he wants a recommendation of me—from my childhood up—I can give it to him. I would rather send him one than not. I will leave it to the citizens of the county, to Bradley and Bowen and Fields, and other county officers here and in North Carolina. The sheriffs of Pickens and Transylvania county will sign it, and every good citizen that knows me will sign it. Every man in Pickens will sign it, and I will send it to him if he wants it. Tell him I only want to go home and live at peace, and would be willing to stand trial even in the United States Courts if I thought I could get only a fair trial there. I am ready to surrender to-morrow, and can give $10,000 bail of good citizens, if allowed. Tell Governor Hampton all this for me," he said, "and see what you can do for me. I will wait for news from you. I know you are my friends now, and if you can do anything for me write or send me word, and I will go and surrender myself."[21]

Alas! What can I do for him? Nothing but to feebly write down his far off impassioned appeal to the executors of that stern law which has outlawed him, and then await the answer I must send. What shall it be? Will they give him a chance or not? I do not know.

C. McK.

NOTES

1. In 1876, W. G. Field became the judge of probate of Pickens County. That same year, he served on the Pickens County Executive Democratic Committee and was a member of the Hampton Rifle Club in Pickens County. See Morris, *Pickens*, 40, 41, 317.

2. Lewis had four brothers (Morgan, Robert, William, and Aaron) and five sisters (Martha, Margaret, Elizabeth, Mary, and Rebecca).

3. According to 1870 federal census records, Richard Redmond was poor. The average valuation of real and personal estate in Transylvania County was $752. Richard's real and personal estate amounted to $210. See *1870 United States Federal Census*, Castatoey Township, Transylvania County, North Carolina, Roll M593-1161, p. 423.

4. Asheville was the county seat of Buncombe County, North Carolina.

5. There are no records indicating that Lee and Frank Case were deputy marshals. More likely than not, Deputy Marshal R. M. Douglas had issued the warrant for Redmond's arrest. See Arthur, *Western North Carolina*, 304.

6. According to John Preston Arthur, Alfred was "a member of a large and influential family of Transylvania County." See Arthur, *Western North Carolina*, 304.

7. Brevard was the county seat of Transylvania County.

8. Jim Paxton was a farmer who resided in Cathey's Creek Township in Transylvania County. See *1880 United States Federal Census*, Cathey's Creek Township, Transylvania County, North Carolina, Roll T9-983, p. 247.

9. According to Alfred's brother in 1912, a Mr. Lankford was present at the time of the attempted arrest of Redmond. See Arthur, *Western North Carolina*, 304.

10. The 1870 and 1880 federal censuses do not list these men.

11. According to South Carolina Collector L. Cass Carpenter, Van B. Hendricks was posing as a potential customer. In February 1877, an illicit distiller, Hubbard Garmany, shot Hendricks in the chest, killing him instantly. Garmany was tried for murder in the state court but acquitted "on the grounds that Hendricks fired first." See L. Cass Carpenter to Hon. Green B. Raum, Jan. 17, 1877, quoted in "Enforcement of Internal Revenue Laws," 175–76; *Pickens Sentinel,* Feb. 22, 1877; and R. M. Wallace, U.S. Marshal, to Attorney General Charles Devens, Dec. 31, 1877, SCF, RG 60.

12. E. H. Barton and William F. Gary were deputy marshals and stanch Republicans. In 1876, Barton was the chairman for the Republican Executive Committee in Pickens County and ran for sheriff. Gary was a member of the Republican Executive Committee in Pickens County. See Morris, *Pickens,* 30, 41.

13. Bright Moore was a deputy marshal. In April 1877, he helped capture two members of "Redmond's band." As late as September 1878, Moore continued to search for Lewis Redmond. See W. A. Miller to the Post Adjutant, Apr. 26, 1877, quoted in "Enforcement of Internal Revenue Laws," 179; and E. G. Hoffman to Hon. E. M. Brayton, Sept. 2, 1878, quoted in "Enforcement of Internal Revenue Laws," 197–98.

14. According to South Carolina Collector L. Cass Carpenter, E. H. Barton was the deputy marshal who Lewis Redmond had shot in the thigh. See L. Cass Carpenter to Hon. Green B. Raum, Jan. 17, 1877, quoted in "Enforcement of Internal Revenue Laws," 175–76.

15. L. Cass Carpenter reported that Mr. Pepper, a Pickens County farmer, at first refused to let the revenue force enter his house. "Upon threatening to break down the door," however, "they were reluctantly admitted, but were insulted and abused and refused all comforts of every kind." Pepper also "refused to go for a surgeon to attend the wounded men, although one lived but two miles distant." "Enforcement of Internal Revenue Laws," 176.

16. Dr. George W. Earle lived in Pickens Court House Township with his wife and two children. He began practicing medicine in Pickens County in 1877 and was a deacon in the Pickens Presbyterian Church. In 1877, School Commissioner G. W. Singleton appointed Earle to serve on the County Board of Examiners. See *1880 United States Federal Census,* Pickens Court House Township, Pickens County, South Carolina, Roll T9-1238, p. 35; and Morris, *Pickens,* 48, 319, 321.

17. The full names of the three prisoners were Thomas Beasley, Milton Stansill, and James Stansill. Revenue agents recaptured Thomas Beasley in July 1878 in western North Carolina. See J. J. Mott to Hon. Green B. Raum, July 5, 1878, quoted in "Sixth District of North Carolina," 476.

18. Lewis was either lying or mistaken when making this statement. He would have been thirteen years old in 1867. By then, the Civil War had been over for nearly two years.

19. These brothers were Morgan "Jasper" and Robert M. Redmond. On July 19, 1862, both enlisted as privates in the famous Thomas Legion. On February 7, 1864, Union forces captured Robert, who spent the remainder of the war in Camp Chase prison.

Military records, however, fail to confirm or refute Lewis's claim that Robert died in captivity. See *U.S. Civil War Soldiers, 1861–1865,* Jasper Redman and Robert M. Redman, Film Number M230, Roll 32; and *Selected Records of the War Department Relating to Confederate Prisoners of War, 1861–1865,* Robert M. Redman, Roll M598-84.

20. Lewis is probably referring to his brother named William Kenzey.

21. Following the *News and Courier's* publication of this interview in July 1878, Gov. Wade Hampton withdrew a $200 reward that he had authorized following the Pickens County jailbreak for the capture of Redmond. See E. M. Brayton to Hon. Green B. Raum, Mar. 17, 1878, quoted in "Enforcement of Internal Revenue Laws," 189–90; and Greenville *Enterprise and Mountaineer,* July 31, 1878.

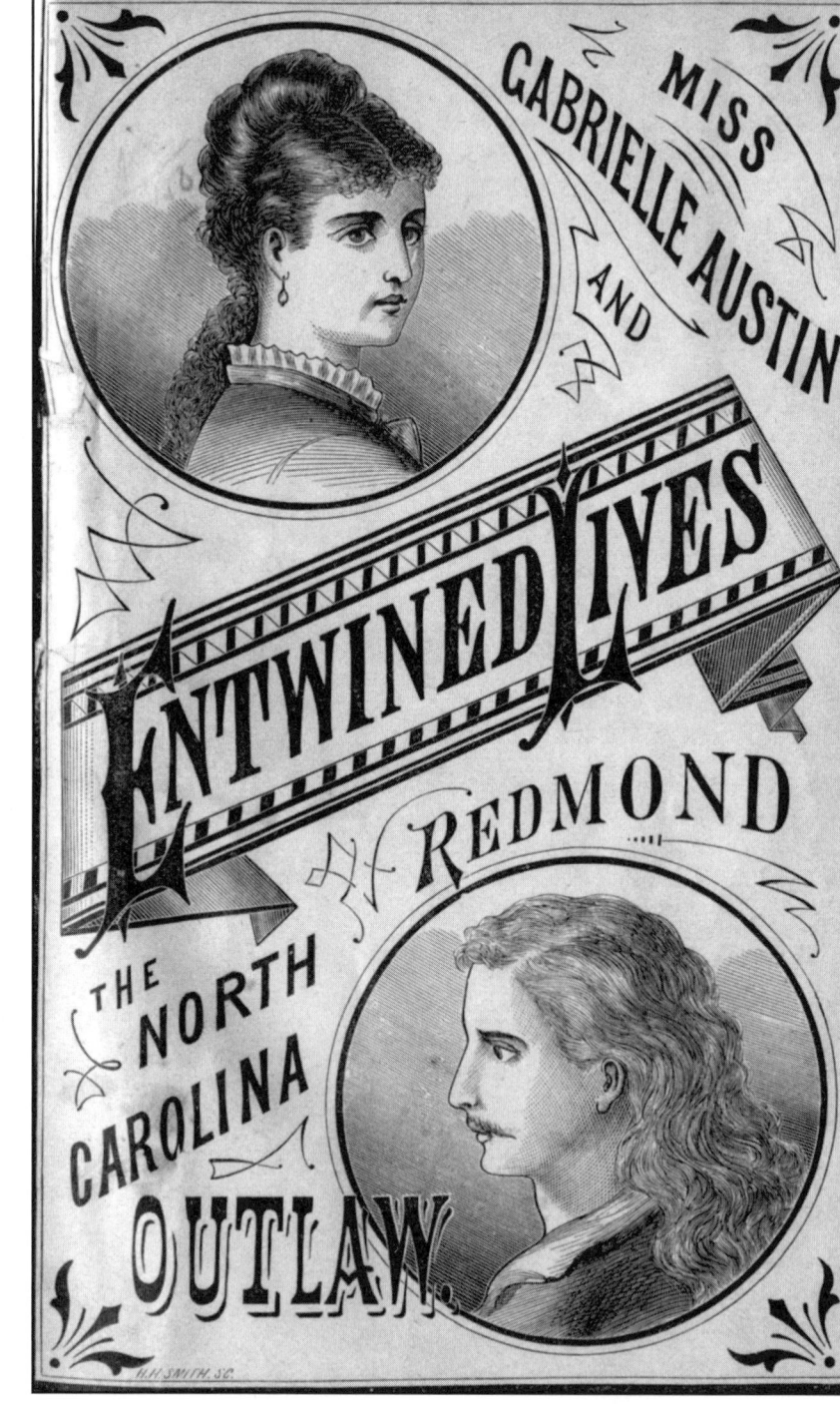

THE ENTWINED LIVES OF
MISS GABRIELLE AUSTIN,
DAUGHTER OF THE LATE REV. ELLIS C. AUSTIN.
—AND OF—
REDMOND, THE OUTLAW,
LEADER OF THE NORTH CAROLINA "MOONSHINERS."

WRITTEN BY
BISHOP CRITTENDEN,
OF NORTH CAROLINA.

The Bishop writes us:—"I emphatically endorse this narrative as true in every particular. Miss Austin I have known since she was an infant. Her very interesting story READS LIKE A NOVEL! THRILLS LIKE A ROMANCE! yet bears the honest stamp of truth in every line."
Edw. B. Crittenden.

PHILADELPHIA:
PUBLISHED BY BARCLAY & CO., 1879.

EDWARD B. CRITTENDEN

INTRODUCTION,

BY

BISHOP EDWARD B. CRITTENDEN, OF NORTH CAROLINA.

Charlotte, N.C., February 7th, 1879

Messrs. Barclay & Co., Publishers,

No. 21 North Seventh St., Philadelphia, Pa.

Gentlemen:

Your favor of January 9th, requesting me to give you for publication the facts in my possession concerning the remarkable adventures of one of the members of my church—Miss Gabrielle Austin, of Guilford Court House, N.C.—should have been answered many days ago; but when it was received I was absent, attending to the duties of my diocese, and since my return home I have been utterly prostrated with a severe attack of bronchitis. I take this, my first opportunity, to reply.

You ask, in your letter, if the story of Miss Austin's trials and triumphs is a "true one." I answer, emphatically, yes. Her father, the late Rev. Ellis C. Austin, was a schoolmate of mine, and a beloved and deeply lamented clergyman in the Methodist Episcopal Church, South, being at the time of his death, presiding elder of the Greensboro district. Her mother was the daughter of Judge Alexander Hoskins, of Lexington county, Kentucky, and her piety and Christianlike qualities made her the beloved friend of all who had the good fortune to meet her. Miss Austin early professed religion, and was admitted to membership in our church. I have known her since she was an infant, and have no hesitation in vouching for the truth of the enclosed narrative of her life. I have taken great pains to verify, by personal inquiry, every statement made by her, and in every instance the parties consulted have corroborated here to the veriest detail.

Trusting that, as you say, the publication of her life history may prove of interest to the world at large, and at the same time call public attention to that cruel relic of barbarism, THE WHIPPING-POST, the introduction of which in many sections, as a means of punishment for small misdemeanors, is a discredit to the civilization of the nineteenth century, and a decided refutation of our confident boast that the world is progressing,

Very faithfully yours,
Edward B. Crittenden

THE CRUEL TORTURES AND STARTLING ADVENTURES OF MISS GABRIELLE AUSTIN, OF NORTH CAROLINA.

Her Battle of Life Begun.
A Historic Birthplace—Early Orphanage—Determination to be Self-supporting—Departure for Virginia.

It devolves upon me in these pages, to relate a most wonderful and remarkably interesting story of the trials and triumphs of a pure and virtuous maiden; and, in a desire to do justice to the character of a martyr to the injustice and cruelty of our laws, I shall confine myself strictly to truthful facts. In the arrangement of the incidents of this truly wonderful history, I have adhered closely to conservatism, and if the reader stands amazed at the fearfully dramatic character of the situations, it will go to prove that "Verily truth is stranger than fiction."

The decisive battle of the war of the Revolution was fought at Guilford Court House, North Carolina, and resulted favorably to the cause of the colonial confederation. Of late years, the scene of the battle has been the Mecca of patriotic Americans. Not very far from the spot where the lines of the two armies met and clashed in deadly struggle, stands an unpretending frame cottage surrounded by a dense thicket of cedars, which screens it from the view of roadside passers, and fill the surrounding atmosphere with that balsamic odor peculiar to this class of verdure. You can step from the back door of the cottage upon the deep trench in which was buried the dead soldiers of Britain's army that fatal day.

To the right of the house stands the shattered stump of an oak, deep in the heart of which was found a few years since a solid shot, imbedded there by the British cannon. Even to this day, in tilling the fertile fields, human bones, gun-flints, buttons, rusty swords and bayonets, bullets, and other strange mementos of this celebrated battle are brought to light. In this house was born the heroine of this true story, Miss Gabrielle Austin, and nurtured in the midst of such patriotic surroundings, it is easy to believe that her thoughts early turned with pious adoration to that great Director of human events, Almighty God, who, in his wise providence, turned the tide of battle in favor of the struggling colonists, and enabled her to inherit the blessed privileges of freedom and equal rights, and escape the thraldom of that human tyranny, which we are taught to believe is distasteful to the Creator. Her father was one of God's ministers, her mother a pious sister of the church, and the early teachings of Gabrielle were of the purest and noblest character. In childhood she manifested a deep interest in religious subjects. At the age of eight years she experienced a change of heart, and was taken into the fold of the Methodist Episcopal Church, South, of which her father was a disciple and teacher, and to which great congregation she still belongs.

Before the war Elder Austin was considered a wealthy man—wealthy for that section of country. He owned a good plantation and the full complement of slaves necessary to its profitable cultivation. The war swept all this away, and left him at its close a poor man. In 1863, when Gabrielle was but two years of age, his beloved wife was called to Christ, leaving the bereaved husband and father the sole guardian of the tender infant. How well he fulfilled the great trust committed to his charge, is shown in the subsequent steadfast adherence of Gabrielle to the ways of right and virtue. The death of his wife, and his heavy pecuniary losses, tended to break down the naturally robust constitution of Gabrielle's father, and in 1876 he closed his eyes and went to sleep in the arms of the Redeemer, leaving his daughter as a heritage a good education and a strong heart. The young girl sincerely mourned the loss of her kind parent, but after time had in a measure assuaged her grief, she turned from vain spiritual repinings to a contemplation of her temporal affairs. Money she had none, and determined to be self-supporting, she besought her friends to assist her in securing a position that would enable her to earn her daily bread.

At last the courted opportunity presented itself. A teacher was wanted for the village school in Sanderson, Goochland county, Va., and on application Gabrielle was accepted by the school trustees to fill the place. Buoyed up with a firm confidence in her own ability to perform the duties of the position, and strong in the faith that God would assist her in her orphanage, she left the home of her childhood, with all its tender and holy associations, and started out to begin the great battle of life among strangers. A personal description of Gabrielle at this time may not be uninteresting to the reader.

Fancy then a girl nearly sixteen years of age, matured to womanhood, of slender figure, but with a resolute energy in her lithe movements that would at once prepossess a keen observer in favor of her ability to perform all the duties that pertain to the maturity shown in her well-turned limbs, plump figure and budding bosom. Her face was of a strongly marked Grecian type, her mouth tempting and rosy, eyes of that hard-to-define gray which can alike flash with the fire of anger or melt with the dew of pity, well-arched brows, and hair long, soft, and of a rich chestnut brown. She was of medium height, slender at the waist, broad at the hips, and from thence tapering to the shoulders, which were square and firmly planted on the body. She had small and perfectly-shaped hands, rose-tinted nails, round, white arms, dimpled at the elbows, a dainty foot, and tapered ankle. She had received a fine education, such an education as is given the noble women of the South. She could entertain in the parlor, or preside in the kitchen, and adorn both positions with grace and intelligence.

Goochland county is one of the back counties of Virginia, but many of its citizens own fine plantations, are intelligent and liberal-minded. The school trustees at Sanderson received the young teacher kindly. Her black dress and sad face touched their hearts, and they determined to bear patently with her faults, if any she had. School would begin in about a week after her arrival, and in the interim she confined herself closely to the house where she had secured board, busy with her thoughts and her books. Many of her scholars were her senior in years, but she won their hearts at once, and where others less magnetically gifted would have been obliged to use the rod, Gabrielle used kind words to rule the little dominion under her care. Her first day's experience in school favorably impressed her with the future. She grew confident in herself, and retired that night to revel in bright dreams born of the day's success.

Love's Young Dream.
Miss Austin's Hero—Her First Suitor—The Calm Before the Storm.

The young teacher secured board in the house of Mr. John P. Hashagen, one of the trustees and by all odds the wealthiest man in Goochland county. He was the owner of several fine plantations, and had the reputation of always being on the lookout for the main chance. He had an only son, on whom he lavished all the affection which he withheld from his fellow-men, denying him nothing.

At the time Gabrielle became an inmate of the Hashagen mansion, his son was nearing his majority, and in the interval which elapsed before the commencement of her school duties the two young people saw much of each other. Charlie Hashagen possessed the nature directly the opposite of his father. He was open and candid in his conversation, and generous to a fault. He was good-looking, and just a little vain of his muscular powers. He saw but little of female society, and this daily intercourse with a young lady, who possessed a beauty more alluring than any woman he had hitherto come in contact with, made a decided impression on him. Before, he had been able to sleep at night undisturbed by haunting visions. Now, however, he rolled and tossed in the delirium of ecstatic dreams. He lost appetite, took no interest in out-door matters, and suddenly developed a great fondness for reading. It so happened that Gabrielle read the same books, and the two often exchanged thoughts and opinions regarding their favorite authors. When the sun would sink to rest the earth became shrouded in that deliciously romantic twilight, about which poets write, and enthusiasts dream, Gabrielle and Charlie would put aside their books and stroll out upon the outskirts of the village, often remaining away until some time after nightfall. Charlie was heard to exclaim that he thought Gabrielle the dearest little woman it was ever his good fortune to meet, and it is presumed that Gabrielle was not adversely impressed with her handsome cavalier. Neither had as yet spoken of love, even in the vaguest connection. Nevertheless the winged god was silently at work, and before many days would impale each heart with the feathered barb of that all-consuming passion.

At last school began, and Gabrielle was busy all day with her boy and girl charges. Charlie chafed a great deal under the enforced separation, but accompanied Gabrielle every morning to the school-house door, and was there awaiting her when the noisy urchins were dismissed for the day. They still continued their delightful twilight strolls, which, taking advantage of zodiacal phenomena, were often prolonged until the lunar light of our great satellite bathed the earth in an aurora of silvery splendor. Thus three months passed away. Charlie was hopelessly in love with the young school-teacher, and if Gabrielle's tender heart had been subjected to rigid analysis some imprint of a similar passion would certainly have been found. As yet no love words had been exchanged between the two. They talked of books, and roamed at will amidst the great natural wonders spread about them in every direction; drawing inspiration for thought and expression from flowers and shrubs, from insect and bird, from star and moon, and all that magnificent and heterogeneous display which the God of Nature had prepared for our contemplation.

One night, when the full moon shone soft o'er all the world, the two, as usual, strolled out after tea, to commune in that entrancing style so peculiar when two young persons of the opposite sex are together, alone, in the midst of surroundings so full of romance as a full moon, balmy summer weather, and bright beaming stars. For some time the two talked of matters prosaic, but gradually the surroundings drew them into poesy, and they reveled in those delirious fancies which inspire poets. Then followed silence—a silence fatal to two young hearts. Cupid was in ecstasy, and fitted a fresh arrow to his bow. The two had been accustomed to walk together hand-in-hand like children, but now they unconsciously drew closer, a strong arm was slipped about a slender waist, a maiden heart fluttered wildly, and "eyes looked love to eyes that spake again." The winged god smiled triumphantly, drew his bow to his shoulder and two hearts were pierced with the barb of love.

"Darling," whispered Charlie, bending down to the sweet face lifted towards his, "darling, I love you."

A sob of joy shook the little frame clasped in his arms; a pretty mouth trembled and quivered; two dove-like eyes swam with tears, and then, with a sigh of relief, Gabrielle dropped her head on Charlie's shoulder and made glad his heart with this mute but eloquent confession of a reciprocal passion.

"You have made me the happiest of men," he said.

"And I am the happiest of women. Oh, Charlie, I love you so much."

"We will get married as soon as I come of age."

"What will your father say?"

"I don't know. He likes you; and he has never yet denied me what I asked for."

Gabrielle was silent several moments, busy with her thoughts; and then with a soberness that chilled poor Charlie's heart, said:

"Ah! Yes, Charlie; your father may like me very well when I am only a poor school-teacher, but I don't think he would be so favorably impressed did he know that his son desired me for a wife. You are rich, Charlie, and I am poor. I have a premonition of impending trouble."

"Nonsense!" replied Charlie, with a forced laugh. "Father knows that you are a lady, and can fill with credit any position. If I am rich, it don't matter. Father has never denied me anything that would promote my happiness, and I don't think he will commence at this late day."

"I hope not," said Gabrielle; but there was implied doubt in the intonation of her voice.

"There, there," said Charlie, folding her to his breast and kissing her passionately, "I love you, and you love me. I want you for a wife, and I'm going to have you."

Just then a noise as of some one passing through the bushes close by startled the lovers into a position more in accordance with propriety.

"Oh, Charlie, what was that?"

"A cow, I reckon, passing through the bushes. Shall we go home?"

"Yes."

The lovers retraced their steps in the direction of the village. As they passed around a bend in the road, a man stepped out from the bushes, and looked eagerly after the pair, his face distorted with rage.

"We shall see!" he cried, hoarsely. "We shall see!"

He raised his hat, as thought to cool his passion-racked brain, and stood revealed in the full moonlight.

It was Charlie's father!

A Villainous Scheme.

Gabrielle's Arch Enemy—A Scoundrel—
Attempts to Rob her of her Good Name.

To say that old John Hashagen was enraged at the discovery made by him of his son's love for the penniless school-teacher, would but feebly describe the mad passion which leaped and rioted in his parsimonious old heart. His son, heir to all his wealth, in love with a penniless girl. What nonsense! A dowerless bride would not suit his avaricious ideas. His son must marry money; more, if possible, than his father possessed. There should be no retrograding progress, increased wealth was all that would satisfy him. On the night of the discovery, he spent several hours coolly adjudicating the question of these two young persons' happiness. It was midnight before he arrived at a decision. What that decision was no one but himself knew. He kept his own secrets. That it was something underhanded and cruel, there could be no doubt. John Hashagen had the reputation of being a thoroughly unprincipled man. His behavior toward the two young people remained the same. To his son, he was tender and indulgent; to Gabrielle, scrupulously attentive and courteous.

One morning, about a week after the occurrence described in the previous chapter, the elder Hashagen turned to his son as the latter was leaving the breakfast-table, and said:

"Charlie, I want to see you in the library!"

"Yes, sir," replied the son. "Will it be time when I return from the school-house?"

"I suppose so!" was the elder man's reply.

Gabrielle had arisen from the table, and as she was leaving the room, the old man shot at her such a glance of vindictive hatred that his son, who was watching him closely, shuddered and turned pale with apprehension.

"I think I shall have trouble with father," he said to Gabrielle, as they walked toward the school-house; "but come what may, I shall ever love you, and always remain true."

"And I know I never could love another as I love you, Charlie," replied Gabrielle, as they parted at the school-house door.

Charlie hastened home, and found his father awaiting him in the library. It is not positively known what was the import of their interview, but the servants heard high words, angrily spoken, and when at last the door opened the two came out into the hall-way, the elder man was heard to exclaim:

"Well, well, Charlie; if you love her so much as that, I don't know why I should object, although I have always hoped you would marry Judge Boatright's daughter, Sallie."

"Sallie Boatright I could never love as I do Gabrielle," was the reply of the younger man.

"Since you are determined then," continued the father, "you have my consent; but I don't want you to marry for yet a while. Wait until you are of age. It will not be long now. A few months only, and in the meantime you can visit your Uncle Jacob, in North Carolina."

"Thank you, father;" said the young man, gratefully. "May I tell Gabrielle what you have told me?"

"Yes, yes; certainly. Tell her that I think it better for you two to separate a few months. I will make all necessary arrangements to-day, and you can leave to-morrow for Asheville."

When school was dismissed that night, Charlie was at the door, and as the lovers walked home, he told her the result of that morning's interview with Hashagen *père*.

"He was terribly mad at first," said Charlie, "and stormed and raved in a frightful way, but I was stubborn, and finding that his attempt to coerce me would fail, he tried cajolery, which was equally unsuccessful. I plead my cause so well that I finally won him over to my way of thinking. I told him that I would soon be of age, and would then be free to do as I pleased. I would please to marry you, my darling. Well, after a long argument he finally admitted that he was powerless to prevent our marriage, and gave his consent to our union as soon as I come of age. In the meantime, however, he thinks it expedient that I should go away, and has made arrangements for me to pay a visit to my Uncle Jacob, in North Carolina. I shall leave to-morrow morning."

"Oh, Charlie, don't leave me," cried Gabrielle.

"Why not?"

"I fear something will happen. If you go away I shall never see you again."

"Nonsense!" said Charlie, gayly. "Father is all right. He may seem a little rough, but he has a good heart, and will see that you come to no harm when I am away."

Thus assured, Gabrielle dismissed from her mind all gloomy thoughts of the future, and looked forward with expectant eyes to the bliss that would be hers when she should become Charlie Hashagen's wife.

The pair went out as usual, for a parting stroll that night, and, as they passed from the house, John Hashagen was walking up and down the piazza, smoking his vespertine cigar. He accosted the lovers jocularly, and with a smiling face; but as they passed through the gate and waved him an adieu, his face grew dark with malevolent thoughts, and, with a curse upon his lips, he threw from him the half-smoked cigar, and went into the house. He locked himself into the library, and gave vent to his villainous thoughts in a soliloquy like this:

"Curses rest upon them both! I will not be outwitted by a beardless boy and a simpering girl! He shall go to North Carolina, and she—well, I don't think my son will have much to do with her after my scheme has had time to develop itself."

At this moment one of the servants accounted Gideon Gannaway, and at a sign from his master admitted a man who will play an important part in this strange life-drama.

"Ah! Gideon," said John Hashagen, cordially, "I've got some work for you."

He led his visitor to a chair, and seating himself beside him, laid before his pliant tool a scheme of villainy most atrocious. In brief it was this: Gideon Gannaway was the village storekeeper. He was to secrete some article about the person of the young school-teacher the next time she visited his store. After she left, he was to discover his loss, and openly accuse Gabrielle of theft. She would, of course, indignantly deny the imputation. A search would be made, the missing article would be found on her person, she would be arrested, tried, found guilty, and punished. The shame of such a scandal would effectually break up the match between Gabrielle and Charlie.

"All right, Mr. Hashagen," said Gideon Gannaway at parting; "I'll fix her. Good-night."

"Good-night, Gid," said the older villain. "I don't reckon Charlie will marry a thief. Ha! Ha!"

In the Toils of the Enemy.
Miss Austin Falsely Accused—The Set of Jewelry—
Arrested as a Common Thief—The Villain's Exultation.

The next morning the lovers parted, Charlie to hasten on his journey to North Carolina, Gabrielle to remain in charge of her school. The final interview was a most affecting one. Poor Gabrielle sobbed and clung to the young man convulsively. The father watched them from the house porch and smiled sardonically.

"Write to me, Charlie, every day," said Gabrielle. "I shall miss you so much."

The young man promised, and with a last embrace, a parting kiss, dashed the gathering tears from his eyes and sprang into the carriage which was to convey him to the railroad depot.

"Good-bye darling," he cried as the carriage moved away.

Gabrielle waved her handkerchief, and then, overcome with a great dread of impending evil, sank down upon a low rustic seat near the gate, and buried her tear-washed face in her trembling hands.

"I shall never see him again," she moaned. "Oh! Charlie, why did you leave me?"

Several days elapsed. Mr. Hashagen still treated the young teacher with that old-time politeness for which the Virginians are famous, but his face, at times, wore a sinister expression that boded no good to the innocent young girl. One night after school hours, Gabrielle stopped at the store of Gideon Gannaway, to make some trifling purchase. She paid for the article, and was turning away, when some little feminine knick-knack in the show-case attracted her attention. Gideon was behind the counter himself, and was quick to perceive her admiring glance.

"They're nice; real beauties! Eh! Miss Gabrielle," he said, opening the show-case, and displaying the articles which had attracted her eye.

The young girl stepped to the counter to admire the pretty things, and began to turn over in her mind the possibility of being able to purchase one when she next received her school money.

"Shall I wrap one of 'em up for you?" inquired Gannaway.

"I would much like to purchase one, sir, but just at present I can't afford it."

She blushed, and turned away from the counter. As she did so, the crafty storekeeper lifted up one of the flittering baubles and softly dropped it into Gabrielle's pocket. The action was so quick that she did not detect him, and with a smile of satisfaction at the success of his little plot, Gideon replaced the jewelry in the show-case, and turned away to another part of the store. Gabrielle gathered up her purchases, and with a last glance of admiration at the treasures in the show-case, left the store, and walked quickly home. She had been gone but a few minutes when Gideon returned to the show-case containing the jewelry, which had attracted Gabrielle's attention. He looked into the case, and then turned sharply to his clerk.

"Have you sold one of these sets!" he said.

"No, sir," replied the young man, coming to his side.

"Then somebody has stolen one. I bought a half-dozen sets, and there are only five now."

To make assurance doubly sure he lifted out the tray and counted the contents again. The clerk did the same. But five sets remained.

"I just showed 'em to the school-teacher," said Gideon, with a cunning leer. "I'm pretty certain they were all there when she was looking at them. She went out suddenly, and Mrs. Gibson coming in, I put them back again without counting."

"You don't mean to say that Miss Gabrielle could have taken one?" cried the clerk, who, to tell the truth, had great admiration for the young teacher.

"Why not?" said Gideon. "You can't tell who to trust now-a-days. Anyway, it will do no harm to inquire. Perhaps she took it by mistake. I'll go over to Mr. Hashagen's and ask her about it."

He put on his hat, and started out. He did not go directly to John Hashagen's house, but stopped on the way, and told his loss to the village constable, a brutal and ignorant negro named Peter Andrews.

"I want you to come along with me, Pete," he said. "I don't say that this young woman took the jewelry, but she was the last one to whom I showed it, and the set is missing."

The pair went directly to John Hashagen's house, and Gideon Gannaway asked for Miss Austin. The servant was about directing him to the parlor, when the door opened, and the beautiful young girl stood before them.

"Did you wish to see me, sir?" she asked, looked inquiringly from Gideon to Peter.

Her appearance was so sudden and unexpected, that Gideon trembled with guilty fear, and could not articulate a word. The negro, less sentimental, stepped to the front, and said:

"Hit's jus' this, missy. Marse Gid says as how he's los' some jew'lry, and we kum hyar to see if you knowed anythin' 'bout hit."

"Lost some jewelry!" cried Gabrielle, in astonishment. "What do I know of his jewelry?"

"You were the last one that I showed it to," said Gideon, pompously, "and after you left I missed one set."

With flashing eyes, heightened color, and form drawn proudly erect, Gabrielle confronted the craven.

"Do you dare to charge me with the theft of your jewelry?" she cried.

"I don't charge you with anything," replied Gideon. "But the set can't be found, and you were the last person that I showed it to."

"Coward!" cried Gabrielle, white with indignation. "How dare you stand there and tell me that I am suspected of theft?"

She wheeled about and would have left the two men; but, at a signal from Gideon, the negro constable sprang forward and caught her by the arm.

"Hold on, missy," said Peter, "you may be innercent as a lam', but dat ain't 'cordin' to law. I'll hev to sarch you, honey."

One less hardened than he would have quailed before the fire of indignation that shot from the beautiful girl's eyes.

"Monster!" she shrieked, hoarsely, striving to break away from him.

"Search her pockets, Pete," cried Gideon Gannaway.

Thus commanded, the negro thrust his hand into the pocket of her dress, and pulled out, among other things, the missing set of jewelry.

"Hyar dey is, boss!" he said, holding up the ornaments.

"Now who's a thief?" was the exultant cry of Gideon Gannaway.

As for Gabrielle, she cast one swift and horrified glance at her accuser; looked piteously into the black face of Peter Andrews, and then, with a cry of agony that would have pierced a heart of adamant, sank to the floor in a dead faint. At the same instant, John Hashagen entered from a rear door, and stood for one minute guiltily staring at the innocent girl, whom his consummate villainy had thus humiliated.

"She ain't—she ain't dead, is she?" he ventured, huskily; and great beads of perspiration rolled down his forehead.

"Jus' fainted, boss," said the negro, who was bending over her.

The arch villain cast one swift glance of inquiry at his tool, and then, in well-simulated astonishment, inquired:

"What's the matter, Gideon?"

In a few words, Gideon Gannaway told his master what the latter already knew, and when he appeared incredulous and hypocritically uplifted his wicked old eyes, was corroborated by the constable, and confronted with the missing jewelry found in Gabrielle's pocket.

"I can hardly believe it," said Hashagen. "So young, and with such a bright future before her. Gabrielle a thief! No! No! It can't be. There must be a mistake."

Gabrielle had recovered from the swoon, and slowly risen to her feet. She looked about her in a dazed way, and then, taking a stop toward the father of her lover, said:

"Oh, sir, you don't think me guilty? You know that I would not steal. I, a thief! I, Gabrielle Austin, the daughter of one of God's ministers! No! No! Gentlemen. You are joking."

"Sorter serious for a joke," said the negro, with a brutal laugh. "Reckon I'll hev to take you to de jail-house, if de boss dar sez so."

Gideon Gannaway glanced covertly at his patron. The latter replied, with a significant shrug of his shoulders:

"Well, it's no more'n right that I should protect myself," he said, quickly. "But I reckon Mr. Hashagen here will go security for her."

Gabrielle turned to where John Hashagen had stood but a moment before. He was not there. She took a stop towards the library door; objects swam before her eyes, she staggered, and with a low, despairing cry sank into a chair and burst into tears.

"Take her to jail, Pete," said Gideon Gannaway, turning away.

The negro advanced to her side and touched her arm. She looked up quickly.

"Come, missy; I'se got to 'bey orders. Git your things on and come with me."

"To–," she faltered.

"Yes, missy; to jail!"

At these words Gabrielle seemed endowed with new resolution. She rose to her feet and facing the negro constable, raised her hand and said:

"The villain's plot was well laid, and with demoniac exultations he saw the innocent girl arrested for theft at his instigation." Courtesy of the North Carolina Collection, University of North Carolina at Chapel Hill.

"I am innocent of this foul charge; as the great God above knows, I am innocent! But I will go! Yes, even to jail!"

JUSTICE PERVERTED.
The Trial—Perjured Evidence—No Hope—Gabrielle's Agony of Mind— A Magistrate's Sympathy to no Avail—The Testimony Convicts Her.

Gabrielle was conducted by the negro constable to the jail-house, but the jailer, a compassionate man, whose children were the young girl's pupils and devotedly attached to her, refused to consider the young teacher a common felon, and gave her a room with his own daughter.

"It's a burning shame," he said to the constable. "That girl is no more a thief than I am myself. She's made an enemy of old Jack Hashagen, and he's determined to crush her. She shall be made comfortable while she's in my charge, anyway."

So thoroughly crushed was the poor girl's spirit, so cruelly humiliated was she, so much shame, and misery, and degradation had been heaped upon her by this dastardly blow, that Gabrielle appeared like another person. She offered no explanation; neither denied nor admitted the truth of the charge. It all seemed like a horrid dream. She could not eat, she could not talk, she could not sleep, but all that wary night sat crouched in a chair, shivering with the great dread that fettered the buoyant pulsations of her young heart.

Not until the next morning did the village folk know of the shame that had been heaped upon the bright-eyed young stranger who had, in the short time she had been among them, gained a strong hold upon their respect and love. Indignation at the outrage was general. No one could be brought to believe the young school-teacher guilty. At nine o'clock a large crowd collected at the town-hall where the trial was to take place. Sympathy for Gabrielle was universal. A young lawyer, who was hopelessly in love with the fair young prisoner, volunteered her defense. Under a recent law of the State her case would receive final adjudication before a magistrate, which officials had been given jurisdiction over all crimes of the petty character. So great was the excitement over the matter that nearly the whole town turned out to attend the trial. Conspicuous among the throng were the youthful faces of Gabrielle's pupils, clouded with grief for the sufferings of their beloved teacher. Not half the people could be accommodated in the court-room, and when the jailer approached the door with Gabrielle leaning on his arm, there was such a shout of genuine sympathy went up from the throats of those gathered about the door, that the young teacher's heart throbbed with joy and pride. All the world did not believe her guilty. John Hashagen, the negro constable, and the storekeeper Gideon Gannaway were all present, seated near the magistrate. Gabrielle was conducted to a seat within the railing, and when she raised her veil and looked about the room, with misty eyes and flushed cheeks, a murmur of indignation against her accusers arose, which the justice was powerless to quell. The storekeeper shifted himself uneasily on his chair and glanced apprehensively at John Hashagen. The latter, conscious of the power which wealth gave him, cared nothing for the sneers of his less fortunate fellow-citizens. He had plotted to ruin the character of the young school-teacher, and once undertaken, he was not the man to relinquish his perfidious persecution, because the world expressed indignation at his cruelty.

The case was opened by the magistrate, who adjusted his spectacles and inquired in a low voice what the young lady was charged with. Gideon Gannaway then told his story, and formally charged Gabrielle Austin, spinster, with the theft of one set of jewelry for female wear, valued at fifteen dollars.

"What say you to this charge, Miss Austin?" inquired the magistrate, kindly. "Are you guilty or not guilty?"

"I am not guilty!" was Gabrielle's reply in a firm voice.

"Have you a lawyer?" again asked the magistrate.

Gabrielle was about to reply that she had not, when the young barrister before mentioned arose and volunteered to conduct the defense. He was amply rewarded by the grateful look with which the beautiful young girl regarded him. He subjected Gideon Gannaway to a rigid cross-examination, but the oily villain had been well-drilled and clung firmly to his original story. The negro constable, the clerk and John Hashagen were in turn examined and cross-examined. Their combined testimony tended to corroborate the storekeeper's charge. Matters began to look dark for Gabrielle, and a smile of exultation flitted across the face of the arch-villain, John Hashagen. Gabrielle herself was put upon the stand last. With a manner that carried conviction of innocence to the minds of her hearers, and in a voice that at times trembled with the pathos of indignation, she declared her innocence.

The magistrate was in a quandary. He himself believed Gabrielle innocent. The evidence pointed to her guilt. He was sworn to abide by the law and the evidence. When Gabrielle had finished her story a dead silence fell upon the court-room. It was broken by the voice of the magistrate.

"Miss Austin," he said, "by virtue of my office I am placed in a most unpleasant situation. I believe you are innocent, and I think that conviction is general with the people here present."

"It is!" cried several voices.

Without noticing this corroborative interruption the magistrate continued:

"I believe you innocent. The evidence which has been given in this case conclusively points to your guilt. It is not in my power to go behind that evidence. I must believe you guilty, and pronounce the sentence of the law."

At these words a murmur of disapproval arose, which was with difficulty silenced by the court officers.

"The sentence of the court then is," said the magistrate in a voice that trembled with emotion, "that you be publicly whipped on the bare back nine and thirty times, by the officer appointed for that purpose, and, in accordance with the law governing the punishment of the whipping-post, the officer is directed to carry out the sentence of the court immediately."

During the delivery of this sentence, Gabrielle had risen to her feet and stood staring straight forward, with an appealing expression on her fair young face that touched even the stony heart of old John Hashagen. As the last words of the magistrate fell upon her ears, she clasped her white hands convulsively and raised her eyes to Heaven as though in appeal to her Heavenly Father for strength to sustain her during this terrible ordeal. Then she sank back in her seat and burst into tears.

"Shame! Shame!" cried several men in the crowd, jumping to their feet.

"Silence in the court!" sternly commanded the magistrate.

This sentence was so grossly unjust, that the better nature of the people revolted against it, and it looked doubtful if it were possible to execute the terrible sentence of the court in the face of such stubborn feeling against the indignity.

John Hashagen rose to his feet, and silence fell upon the crowded court-room. He was the richest man in the county, and although disliked personally, was respected and looked up to on account of his great wealth.

"Fellow-citizens," he began, in a cold, rasping voice, "we all feel for this unfortunate young lady—no one perhaps more deeply than I do. I have taken great interest in her. Since she came among us, she has been an inmate of my house. I myself believe her innocent. As the magistrate says, the evidence proves her guilt. We are all good citizens, I hope; and although it seems unjust, we must abide by the law."

He resumed his seat, and again there was silence. All saw the wisdom of his remarks, and all thought them disinterested; but behind his shaggy brows a pair of cold eyes flashed with cruel joy at the impression his words had made.

The magistrate beckoned to the negro constable, and said, in a low tone of voice:

"Perform your duty, officer!"

Peter Andrews approached Gabrielle, and touched her arm. She looked up and shuddered.

"Oh! My God!" she cried; "have mercy!"

"Must do it missy," said the negro, and taking her arm he assisted the trembling girl to arise, and led her sobbing and crying from the court-house, followed by the black looks and muttered threats of all who loved the young teacher and believed her innocent.

A Brave Man's Chivalry.

Miss Austin Condemned to be Publicly Whipped—Stripped to the Waist— Tied to the Whipping-Post—A Negro Constable to Apply the Lash!— An Exciting Scene—A Mysterious Knight of Modern Times—Who was he?

The State of Delaware is noted for its old-fashioned laws and old-time punishments for criminals. It still retains the whipping-post, the pillory and the stocks. Since the war, several of the Southern States have established that cruel torture of a barbaric age, the WHIPPING-POST. Virginia has it, South Carolina, Alabama and Missouri have lately adopted it. The present legislatures of North Carolina and Tennessee will probably enact a law punishing petty crimes in this manner. It had been a law in Virginia but a short time when Gabrielle Austin was so unjustly sentenced to undergo its punishment for a crime of which she was innocent. The whipping-post had just been set up in Sanderson, and this pure young girl was to be the first victim.

Tremblingly she was led to the instrument of torture. The crowd gathered about her in silence. Tears filled many eyes. The women in particular sobbed aloud. Even the magistrate cried behind his handkerchief. Two men only, except the brutal executioner, looked on coolly and unfeelingly—John Hashagen and his suppliant tool, the storekeeper Gannaway. A chair had been brought out, and in this the young girl was placed. An awkward break occurred. Finally the constable advanced, and placed his cruel hands on the neck of the young girl. She started back as though stung by a serpent, and a flush of scornful indignation tinged cheek and neck. Then, as though conscious of her weakness, she dropped her arms, which had been drawn up to protect her fair bosom, and the revolting and shameful outrage proceeded. Coarse men who had been attracted thither out of curiosity, could not look upon such a brutal and bestial desecration unmoved, and turned away their heads in shame. At last the horrid task was completed, and the lascivious eyes of Peter Andrews gloated over the beauty and grace of the pure bosom bared to the vulgar gaze. He placed his arm about her, and lifted her to the post. The round white arms were pinioned, and a sickening dread filled the hearts of those who watched the preparations for torture with breathless interest. The negro constable looked well to the fastenings of his poor helpless prisoner, and then took the whip from the hands of an assistant. The magistrate stood neat to count the strokes.

"Are you ready?" asked the magistrate.

"Yes, sah!" replied the negro, raising aloft the cruel thong.

Another moment, and the lash would bury itself in the quivering flesh of the poor girl. Strong men held their breath and closed their eyes. The women shrieked and screamed. All expectantly they awaited the fulfillment of the law's decision. The negro curved his arm and raised the lash above his head. Several times it circled round, then swiftly descended upon the white back of the innocent girl. A livid welt across the shoulders indelibly marked the law's degrading consummation of its sentence.

"One!" cried the magistrate under his breath; and the people shuddered as a low moan of anguish issued from the pale lips of poor Gabrielle.

Again the brutal executioner raised his heavy whip. Again the lash circled round his head. Before it could fall a second time, a man dashed through the crowd, and with one well-directed blow stretched the negro on the ground. Then whipping from his pocket a knife, he cut the thongs which bound Gabrielle's wrists and threw over her shoulders the articles of clothing which the brutal hand of Peter Andrews had torn from her pure body. Wheeling, then, he faced the crowd, and those nearest him saw the glitter of a pistol drawn quickly from the breast pocket of his coat.

"Are you men," cried the stranger, "that you stand here and permit this outrage to proceed?"

A cheer of approval greeted the daring man as he uttered these words, and several men sprang to his side with set and determined faces.

"No, we won't allow it!" cried one man, and the crowd took up the refrain.

"No, it must stop!" they shouted.

One man pushed his way to the front, and cried out, "Suppose we give Gid Gannaway what his perjured testimony would have inflicted on this poor girl."

"Yes, yes;" yelled the crowd. "Let's give the perjurer nine and thirty well laid on."

The cowardly storekeeper started to flee, but was caught and dragged up to the post. Angry hands were outstretched to tear away his clothing and lay bare his body. One man seized the whip, and despite the wretch's pleas for mercy, laid on the blows with all the force of a strong arm, and when nine and thirty had been counted, administered one more for good measure, as he said, which cut deeply into the flesh. Then they untied his hands, and he dropped to the ground in a dead faint, blood flowing from a score of gashes.

We all know what a southern "back country" mob is capable of when fully aroused. The constable sneaked away, and John Hashagen took refuge in the court-house. The magistrate in vain tried to quell the rising tumult. The crowd

"The horrors of the Whipping Post. Miss Austin sentenced to suffer for a crime of which she is perfectly innocent—stripped to the waist—publicly disgraced, and whipped by a negro constable." Courtesy of the North Carolina Collection, University of North Carolina at Chapel Hill.

was mad with indignant passion, and capable of going to any extreme. The kind-hearted jailer conducted Gabrielle to his house, and his wife and daughter placed her in bed. She lay in a state of semi-consciousness, silently brooding over the great indignity that had been heaped upon her. The crowd in the public square leaped and danced about the prostrate body of the miserable storekeeper with a fiendish glee. Some were in favor of hanging him even. They had no pity for the craven, but left him lying on the ground, and began to search for the young stranger, who had so bravely and chivalrously defended a woman's sacred honor.

He was not to be found!

No one saw him come, and no one saw him depart. No one knew him, and they only recollected that he had a handsome face, and a form like an Ajax.

An Accidental Meeting.

The United States Marshal—A Visit—A Rival in the Field—Love's Suspicions.

Sympathy for poor Gabrielle was unanimous among these kind-hearted people, and the jailer and his family nursed and tended her until she, in a measure, recovered from the shock of that terrible day's experience. As soon as she was able to travel, and despite the many kind invitations to remain, which poured in upon the unfortunate girl from all quarters, she made known her determination to leave a spot that from its associations had become hateful to her.

She anxiously expected a letter from Charlie, but as yet had received no answer to the many tender and loving messages she sent to him. In the hurry of his sudden departure she neglected to get from him the address of his uncle in North Carolina. She therefore inquired from John Hashagen. The old villain told her that this uncle lived at Charlotte. To Charlotte, therefore, she directed her letters. As Charlie's real destination was Asheville, of course he did not receive Gabrielle's letters. The poor girl could bear the shame and disgrace of her unjust trial, condemnation and happily prevented punishment without a murmur, but neglect of the man she loved so passionately weighed heavily upon her heart. She knew not what to think. She could not believe that Charlie—her Charlie—would so soon forget her.

In the neighborhood of Asheville, North Carolina, lived a married cousin of Gabrielle's, and to her the poor, heart-broken girl wrote, asking permission to pay her a visit until such time as she could arrange for the future. A prompt reply to her letter was received, and the invitation to come thither was given with such genuine hospitality, that Gabrielle lost no time in hurrying her departure. Her misfortunes had won for her many friends and when the stage which was to convey her to the railroad depot, at Belham, drew up at the door of the kind-hearted jailer's house, nearly the entire town turned out to bid her farewell. Such genuine and unmistakable affection, so touchingly shown, caused her heart to thrill with pride, and when the stage drove away, followed by the cheers of the male members of the crowd who had collected to see her off, she could only bury her face in her hands and sob with childish joy.

She reached Asheville without further adventure. The husband of her cousin was at the depot to receive her, and his greeting was so cordial, that Gabrielle fell in love with him immediately. He was a fine-looking young fellow, and spoke proudly of his wife and baby, both of whom he seemed to love devotedly.

"We're poor people, up here, Gabrielle," he said, "and can only give you a rough mountain welcome; but such as it is you are heartily welcome."

Gabrielle noticed that his clothes were of uniform blue, and that his coat was adorned with braid and brass buttons.

"Are you a soldier, sir?" she asked.

"Call me Dick, please," said the young man, laughing. "It's true we are not blood relations, but I mean always to regard you as such. No; I am not a soldier. This uniform is that of the internal revenue department. I am a deputy United States marshal, and a great many of the people here hate me for it."

He then explained to the beautiful girl the duties appertaining to his office. It was his business to assist the collectors of internal revenue, and to prevent violations of revenue laws. The mountainous section of several of the Southern States is the home and hiding-place of thousands of illicit distillers, who carry on their illegal business in the secrecy of mountain caverns, and put the government to much trouble. Although a large force of marshals, and whole regiments of soldiers are employed in breaking up the business of the "moonshiners" and "blockaders,"* the frequent raids and arrests made by them seem in no way to deter these bold outlaws. There are as many illicit distilleries in operation to-day in the Southern States as there were ten years ago, although many stills have been confiscated, thousands of gallons of liquor destroyed, and hundreds of distillers captured and thrown into prison. There seems only one way in which the government can hope to make these people law-abiding, and that is by removing the obnoxious tax upon distilled liquors.

Gabrielle, who speedily won her way into the affection of both her host and hostess, and was especially loved by the baby. She assisted her cousin in the performance of her household duties, and was a welcome companion when the husband was absent on a raid, he frequently being away for weeks at a time. In this quiet way the summer passed, and autumn—golden, mellow autumn—arrived, painting with the hand of Divinity the foliage of the primeval forests which covered the grand old mountains of that picturesque region from base to summit. This was the busy season for the illicit distillers. The new crop of corn and fruit was being harvested, and the mountains were alive with "moonshiners," industriously plying their dangerous business. Marshal Dick Allison was absent from his home now, nearly all the time. One night he came home, and after kissing the baby and his young wife, threw his tired body on the bed, and said:

"Lizzie, I'm going to Asheville to-morrow morning early. I've got three prisoners there in jail, and they'll have a hearing to-morrow before the commissioner. If you want to go down and make some purchases, I'll drive there in the wagon."

"I can't possibly go to-morrow, Dick," said his wife, "and I do need some necessary articles from the store that I wouldn't have a man to select for me. Suppose you go, Gabrielle?"

---

*The term "moonshiners" was given to illicit distillers in the mountains on account of their presumed partiality for moonlight nights, upon which to manufacture their liquor. "Blockaders" are the men who convey the illicit liquor to market. Dick Allison lived about five miles from Asheville, and although his home was but a humble four-roomed log house it was an earthly paradise.

"With pleasure," said Gabrielle; and so it was settled that she should go to Asheville the next day.

They were up and off betimes next morning, and when they reached Asheville, Marshal Allison proceeded to the jail, leaving Gabrielle to wander about the town, and select the articles desired by his wife. He promised to call for her at the hotel at noon.

It was nearly noon when Gabrielle completed her last purchase, and started for the hotel where Mr. Allison had left the team. She was walking along the street, busily intent on keeping the numerous bundles which she carried from falling to the ground, when, happening to glance across the street, she saw a face and figure deeply imprinted on her heart.

Walking up the street, on the opposite side, chatting gayly with a young lady, who clung familiarly to his arm, was Charlie Hashagen, the man who had promised to love her to eternity. Her dream of love was o'er. The presence of this lady companion explained his silence. He loved another!

It was a cruel blow, but she bore up under it with firmness. Ten minutes after this accidental meeting she could have confronted him face to face, as coolly as though he were a stranger. She might be indignant, furious; that would be natural, for

>"Hell knows no fury
>Like a woman scorned."

Thus do I Punish my Enemies.

In the Valley of the Shadow of Death—Redmond, the Outlaw, in Ambush—The United States Marshal Assassinated—A Discovery.

Gabrielle said nothing of her discovery to Mr. Allison. In fact she had not mentioned the name of her lover, or any of the circumstances surrounding her stay in Sanderson, to even her cousin. She locked the secret in her heart, and strove to hide the skeleton of her outraged love under a smiling face, and unnatural effervescence of spirits.

A few miles out from Asheville, the road leading to Dick Allison's plantation passed through a wild and gloomy stretch of mountain country. Tall cliffs darkened the road on either side, and great boulders hung threateningly over the roadway. When they reached this gruesome spot, both were in high spirits, laughing and chatting like magpies. When the shadow of the cliffs shut out the glad sunlight, Gabrielle stopped in the middle of a brilliant story which she was relating, and her face grew suddenly grave.

"What a gloomy spot!" she exclaimed, under her breath. "It reminds one of the Valley of the Shadow of Death!"

Were these words prophetic? The catastrophe of the next minute seemed to indicate as much. They had not proceeded two rods before this gorge became overcast with the shadow of death in reality. Hidden deep among the dense undergrowth which fringed the road on either side, were a dozen armed men, sworn enemies of the man driving on to doom all unsuspicious of danger. Suddenly a vivid flame lit up the fringe of bushes by the roadside: there was a sharp shock, and Marshal Dick Allison fell back into the body of the wagon, with a half-dozen bullet-holes through his body—dead!

The frightened horse reared and plunged, and the assassins leaped into the road, and grasped the animals before they could dash away in their mad fright. So suddenly had this tragedy begun, and so swiftly ended, that Gabrielle could only show her great terror in the frenzied look of horror which she cast upon the bearded men who crowded about the wagon. She did not hear their exclamations of admiration as they gazed upon her wondrous beauty. She only knew that a terrible murder had been committed; that her companion was the victim, and that the hands of these wild-looking men were red with blood. At last, she raised her head. The men who had first crowded around the wagon had stepped back, and one who seemed to be the leader approached her.

"Miss Austin said, 'It seemed like the "Valley of the Shadow of Death" when a vivid flame flashed across my eyes, and Allison, the U.S. Marshal, was a dead man—shot down at my very side.'" Courtesy of the North Carolina Collection, University of North Carolina at Chapel Hill.

"Don't be frightened, young lady," said the new-comer. "You shall not be harmed."

The voice was one of gentleness, and sounded strangely familiar to the frightened girl. She looked eagerly into the speaker's face, and a cry of amazement burst from her lips.

It was the daring stranger who had rescued her from the terrible punishment of the whipping-post!

Yes. It was he, standing there before her, accoutered in a wild and fanciful garb that set off his muscular form to great advantage. His beauty was not of that strong and florid type so much admired by women, and yet there was great beauty in his face. Under other circumstances, Gabrielle would have looked upon him with admiring eyes. Now it was with a sickening aversion in her heart, for this man's hands were as deeply dyed with blood as those of his associates. He was of medium height, but his frame was so well-knit, so finely proportioned, that he had the appearance of being taller than he really was. His eyes were blue, large, and expressive. His forehead was broad and white, and his nose and lips were as delicately shaped as a woman's. His chin was small and dimpled, and the carnation glow of perfect health tinged his sun-browned cheeks. A silky moustache adorned rather than concealed the proud curve of his upper lip. But the most striking feature was his hair. It was a golden mass that any woman would have been proud of. It rippled back from the broad brow, and fell far down on his shoulders in curls of spun gold. The hair and eyes and mouth and chin were decidedly feminine; what was it then that caused men to quail and tremble when this man's eye fell upon them? Was his face an index of his character? We answer, no! All who have met him are at first impressed that his will is as delicate as his features. All are mistaken. Those innocent blue eyes have looked upon the dying agonies of many brave men without one quiver of shrinking horror in their slumberous depths. Those slender, shapely hands are stained with human blood. Gabrielle was in the presence of that terrible desperado, the terror of the mountain South—REDMOND, THE OUTLAW!

Yes, it was he. This man with the woman's hair, and the baby-blue eyes was the acknowledged head of the most desperate band of outlaws of modern or ancient times. From the security of his mountain home this golden-haired man hurled defiance into the very teeth of his enemies, and set all law at naught. The dead man in the wagon beside her had told strange and startling tales of this man's wild career, a career that outrivals the wildest flights of romance. He had spoken of Redmond as an enemy to be dreaded. Only the day before he had said to her:

"Redmond has sworn to kill me if we ever meet."

The two men had met, and Redmond had kept his oath. Without warning, as one might kill a venomous reptile, or a dangerous animal, the outlaw had bushwhacked his victim.

She looked upon the face upturned to hers with horror, and yet she should have been fateful to him, for he had saved her from shameful humiliation. The outlaw was leaning carelessly on his carbine, yet smoking from the fatal discharge, and when he saw the look of horror which overspread the fair girl's face, his brow knotted itself into a dark frown, and the face that in repose seemed angelic was now demoniacal. He turned on his heel quickly and spoke to one of his band in a low tone of voice. The man thus addressed nodded to one of his companions, and the two approached the wagon.

"Come, miss!" said one, taking her arm. She made no resistance, and with the assistance of his mate, the outlaw lifted her from the wagon and led her into the bushes on the right-hand side of the road. She believed they meant to kill her, and a prayer to Heaven trembled on her lips. A short distance from the road were tethered the horses of the band. Here Gabrielle and her captors halted. Those who had been left behind in the road laid the body of the dead marshal in the bottom of the wagon, and turning the heads of the horses toward home, started them forward with their inanimate passenger. Then one of the band took a printed placard from his pocket and pinned it on the breast of the dead man. Below is given the *fac simile* of this terrible message of vengeance:

Redmond's Rocky Home.
In Captivity—Miss Austin's Dreadful Forebodings—
Awaiting the Chief's Return.

After completing their horrid task, the assassins joined their companions at the spot to which Gabrielle had been conducted. Redmond, however, did not put in an appearance. Acting under his directions, the prisoner was given a horse; and surrounded by the band, the whole party rode off rapidly in the direction of Mount Mitchell. Gabrielle received no intimation from her captors of what was to be her fate; and the shock of that terrible occurrence in the Valley of the Shadow of Death had so benumbed her faculties, that she was hardly conscious of what was passing around her. Toward night-fall the party reached the foot of the mountain; and arriving at a point where steep cliffs effectually barred their further progress, the horses were left in charge of two of the band, who led them away toward a neighboring thicket. The balance of the party continued the ascent of the mountain on foot. After an hour's hard marching up an incline not far from the perpendicular, climbing by means of jutting rocks and tray shrubs, they at last reached an open plateau level as a

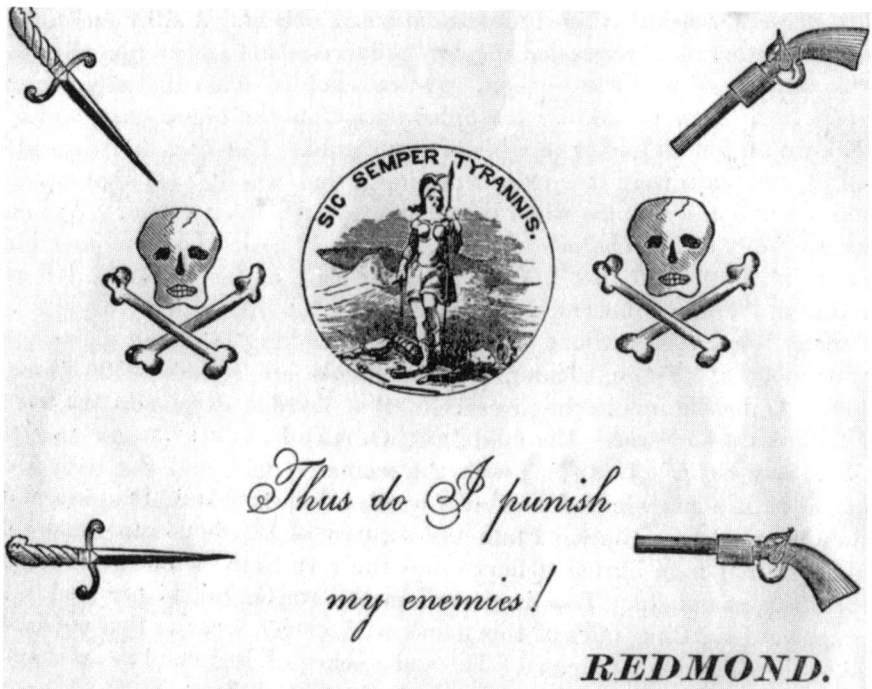

"Redmond's Placard." Courtesy of the North Carolina Collection, University of North Carolina at Chapel Hill.

floor, and with an area of about five hundred yards. This plain was guarded on one side—or rather on three sides, for it was of a crescent shape, being broadest in the centre—by a fringe of fir trees. The concave side was backed by a precipitous cliff, running up five hundred feet as smoothly as the front of a house. In the heart of this cliff was an immense cave, and in it lived the desperadoes, headed by Redmond, the outlaw. This house, with a floor and roof and walls of solid granite many feet thick, was entered through an arched door, placed nearly in the centre of the cliff. Into this strange abode Gabrielle was conducted. After passing through a long and narrow gallery, which curved gradually to the left, they came at last to a large chamber, which was the principal abode of the outlaws. This great room was lighted by day through apertures pierced in the roof. At night a large fire of resinous wood in the centre of the apartment cast weird and ghastly shadows around the wall of the room, but did not pierce the gloom which shrouded the arched dome above. When Gabrielle entered, twenty or thirty men were seated about the fire. They were variously engaged. Some were cleaning their guns, other repairing their clothes, one or two were reading. All were busy. The appearance of a young and pretty woman among them drew all eyes upon the frightened Gabrielle, who shrank back behind her captors. One of the men who had accompanied her, seeing that this rude attention affrighted his charge, spoke to one of those seated about the fire, who seemed to be in authority.

"The capting ordered we'uns to bring this gal woman along with us. He'll be hyar afore daylight, and will give us furder orders. She's to hev some supper, and a room to-night."

The man to whom he addressed these words arose from his seat before the fire, and came forward to where Gabrielle was standing.

"All right, Morgan; I'll take charge of her," he said. And then turning to Gabrielle, he took her hand and led her forward to the fire.

"We-uns are a rough lot, miss," he said, in a kindly, apologetic way; "but you needn't be skeared. You're as safe hyar as you would be in your own mammy's house."

This allusion to the mother, who died before she was old enough to miss her, opened the floodgates of the poor girl's heart, and sinking down upon the rude seat, which had been dragged up to the fire for her, she burst into tears, and great sobs of anguish shook her frame.

The stern faces of the rude men gathered about her softened and grew gentle, and in their homely way they tried to comfort her. She had passed through the frightful occurrences of that day tearless. Now came that blessed reaction, that loosing of the tense-drawn nerves which always leaves us better and stronger. Finding that their well-meant offers of sympathy and consolation had no effect upon the grief of that fair young creature, the outlaws left her alone with her sorrow, which finally spent itself, and she began to look about her with some curiosity.

Seeing that she had recovered somewhat from the first fierce transports of grief, the man who had led her to the fire again approached her, and inquired if she would like some supper. The poor girl had not eaten a morsel since morning; but her heart was too full of recent sorrow to allow her to eat; she simply shook her head.

"When you want to go to bed," said the outlaw, "Tom, thar," pointing to a negro on the other side of the fire, "will show you your room. Good-night."

He held out his broad brown hand, and Gabrielle just touched the palm with her white fingers. She could not help shuddering; for despite his kindly face, she believed this man's hands were dyed with human blood. Rising to her feet, she followed the negro across the room. She noticed then, for the first time, that several doors opened out of the main room. In front of one of these her sable conductor halted, and taking from his pocket a key unlocked the heavy door, and held it open for her to enter.

"You'll fin' matches an' a candle on de table, missy," he said, removing the key from the lock and fitting it on the inside of the door.

Gabrielle passed by him into the room, and by the light of the fire outside saw an apartment sixteen by twenty feet, hewn out of the solid rock, and furnished in a rude though comfortable fashion. Going forward to the table which stood at one end of the room, she lighted a candle, and then closed and locked the door. Two reed-bottom chairs, the table before referred to, a rough dressing-case, and a cot bed, comprised the furniture of the room. Some effort at comfort had been made by covering the stone floor with a home-made rag carpet. A case or frame was hung against the wall opposite the bed, and contained a bundle of magazines and illustrated papers, and several books. Two or three coarse pictures adorned the walls. One represented the "Hero Martyrs of the Confederacy;" another was "Scene at the death-bed of Stonewall Jackson," and a colored lithograph female head was entitled "The Mountain Rose."

The white bed looked inviting, and—first praying to the great Giver of all good, asking that mercy be shown friend and enemy alike, and that His protecting influence should abide with her for all future time—she disrobed and crept into bed.

Profound silence reigned about her, and it was not many minutes before sleep closed her eyes and shut out the dread phantasmagoria that had flitted through her mind since the terrible scene that morning in the Valley of the Shadow of Death.

The Lover to the Rescue.

Asheville Greatly Excited—Arrival of the Marshal's Body— No Volunteers for a Rescue—The Young Lover Goes Alone.

Leaving Gabrielle to complete her sleep in the rocky home of the outlaws, we will turn to other scenes. Asheville—in fact Buncombe county—was excited and indignant. The faithful horses of the murdered marshal, true to their instinct, had arrived safely at the stable door, and the placarded body was discovered by the young wife. The alarm was given, and the news spread like wildfire. Redmond had punished another enemy. Although the dead man had held a position which was inimical to the interests of a great majority of his neighbors, he was generally well liked, and now that he had been so foully murdered, not one could be found to speak of him unkindly.

Nearly half the male population of Asheville hastened to the scene of the murder as soon as the news was received, and many were the conjectures as to what disposition had been made of the young girl who was the marshal's companion. All pronounced the murder a brutal outrage, all were convinced that the murderers should be followed up and punished, but no one volunteered to lead a party against the outlaw chieftain. Many through fear, and after their first natural indignation had subsided, rather condoned the offence.

"He was a revenue officer, and would have killed a 'moonshiner' if he had had the chance," they said.

Among the crowd who gathered about the fatal spot was Charlie Hashagen. As yet he knew not that the beautiful young girl who had been carried away, and perhaps murdered, by the outlaws, was his own beloved Gabrielle. He had never ceased to think of her, not to wonder why she so cruelly neglected him. As soon as he arrived in Asheville he dispatched her a letter, and before an answer could possibly have time to reach him, sent off another. It is needless to remark that these two letters, and the many that subsequently were sent to Gabrielle's address in Sanderson, never reached their destination. They were intercepted and destroyed by the scheming old villain, John Hashagen. Fearful that the object of his love might be ill, Charlie wrote to his father for an explanation; and the old scoundrel replied, that Gabrielle had been detected in the act of stealing jewelry from the store of Gideon Gannaway; that she had been convicted of the offence charged, and punished for her crime at the whipping-post; and that, after remaining in town a few days, she had disappeared, whither no one knew.

The letter was worded skillfully, but it did not deceive the lover. Putting this and that circumstance together, he came to the conclusion that a gigantic plot had been engineered through by his father, to ruin his happiness and destroy the character of the woman he loved. He wrote to friends in Sanderson, making inquiries about the matter, but had as yet received no satisfactory clue to the whereabouts of Gabrielle.

He did not know that the young lady who had been captured by Redmond was his Gabrielle, and although he felt a natural and chivalric sympathy for the unfortunate girl who had been so mysteriously made away with, he was not reckless enough to volunteer her rescue from the toils of the man who was so generally feared as the golden-haired outlaw. After gratifying that natural curiosity which seems inherent in the American mind, the crowd dispersed.

Did it never occur to the reader, that the Americans are the most morbidly curious people in the world? For instance, none but an American crowd would stand for hours gazing at the spot where some startling occurrence had taken place, when, in ordinary, the spot did not possess interest enough to merit even a passing glance. Just after the robbery of the Stewart vault in St. Mark's churchyard, New York city, eager and excited crowds were clustered about the spot from early morning until late at night, gazing with all-absorbing curiosity at the hole in the ground, through which the grave-robbers effected an entrance into the vault!

Charlie Hashagen, in common with the friends who accompanied him from Asheville, had carefully scrutinized the trees and shrubs and rocks in the immediate vicinity of the spot where the murder took place, and his curiosity being gratified was turning away, when one of the onlookers exclaimed:

"Poor Miss Austin! It were better for her that she met death, than the fate in store for her, if she is yet alive!"

"Miss Austin!" cried Charlie, pushing his way to the side of the speaker. "Pray what was her first name, and where is she from?"

"It's a strange name," continued the first speaker, not noticing Charlie's agitation.

"Not Gab—!"

"Yes, that's it; Gabrielle Austin. Dick told me only a day or two ago, poor fellow. She's some kin of his wife's, and came here about three or four months ago from Goochland county, Virginia."

"My God!" cried Charlie, "Gabrielle! My Gabrielle in danger!"

"You knew her then?" asked the man.

"I loved her," moaned Charlie, while his face paled and his voice trembled. "She was to be my wife, and now—great God!—Why have I remained so long idle when she is in danger?"

"You can't do anything," continued the man. "Don't you know that Redmond, the outlaw, captured her?"

"What care I?" cried Charlie, with flashing eyes. "Redmond is but a man."

"He has killed fifty men."

"I care not if he has killed five hundred."

"You surely wouldn't dare to—"

"Dare! What will a man not dare for the woman he loves? Yes, I dare to hunt this terrible outlaw down. I dare to meet him on his own ground. I dare to demand at his hand the poor woman I love, or satisfaction."

"You're a fool!" said the man, turning away.

When it became known that the light-hearted, merry-faced young man, who had figured so prominently as a ladies' man at all the festive gatherings for miles around, a man considered capable of performing no greater deed of daring than flirting with a pretty married woman in the presence of her husband, was really bent on hunting down the king of the "moonshiners," an excited and apprehensive crowd gathered about him, and endeavored to dissuade him from so perilous an undertaking.

In vain! Charlie was determined to go. He secured the loan of a brace of pistols from one friend, a horse from another, and then, making diligent inquiry as to the probable location of the outlaw's den, he mounted his horse, and rode boldly off in the direction of Mount Mitchell.

"It's the last time we'll ever see him alive," said one of his friends. "Poor fellow!"

An Outlaw's Hospitality.
Gabrielle Treated with great Respect—A Modern Claude Duvalle—An Educated Outlaw.

We left Gabrielle Austin asleep in the room which had been assigned her in the rocky home of Redmond, the outlaw. She was awakened by hearing a heavy knock at the door. She listened a moment, and then asked:

"Who's there?"

"Me, missy," replied a voice which she recognized as belonging to the negro Tom. "Brek'fus is ready."

Her little room was quite light, irradiated from without through apertures cut through the roof of the cave. The shifting light falling aslant the crystal stalactites which hung from the roof and walls of the cave high above her head, sent out refractions of color which made the grotto a fairy-palace. Not neglecting to offer up thanks to God, on her bended knees, for his mercies and goodness, Gabrielle made her toilet and then seated herself at the table awaiting the pleasure of her captors. She selected at random one of the volumes from the shelf hung against the wall. It was Tom Moore's "Lalla Rookh." Surprised, she glanced at the titles of the other volumes. An odd copy of Dickens and Waverly, several of the poets, and "Murrell, the Land Pirate," comprised the collection. With the exception of the last-named, they were such books as a person of culture and refinement would be apt to read. One volume, in particular, attracted her attention. There was no title on the book, and opening it, she saw that it was Buckle's "Philosophy of English Civilization," and from its well-worn appearance, it had evidently been read carefully. The blank portion of the printed pages was crowded with annotations and comments, written in a fine, delicately shaded hand. Surely, a man—for although the chirography was feminine, Gabrielle could not believe that a woman's hand penned it—who read and annotated Buckle so learnedly, must be a strange character to head a band of desperate outlaws. On the fly-leaf of every book appeared the name "REDMOND," in the same delicate handwriting, and Gabrielle had undoubtedly been given the chamber in which the king of the "moonshiners" spent his moments of retirement and rest. She read a few random stanzas from the book which she had selected, when a knock at the door brought her to her feet.

"Missy," said the negro, "Marse Redmond sends his compliments. If you is dressed, he will send you brek'fus!"

Gabrielle replied that her toilet preparations were completed, and unlocked the door. In a few minutes the negro reappeared, bearing a tray, on which was a meal that might tempt an epicure. To it she did ample justice, and when the remains of the feast were removed, busied herself in tidying up the room. This task completed, she seated herself at the table, and again consulted that beautiful imagery which breathed in every line of barbaric Eastern splendor. So deeply absorbed was she in the glowing language of the poet, that the door opened unobserved, and when, in turning the pages, her eyes for a moment wandered from the book, she was astonished to see the king of the outlaws standing before her. She started, and dropped the book.

"I am sorry that I interrupted you, miss," said the outlaw, with a low bow, "but my time is not my own. I knocked several times for admittance, but you did not answer, and I ventured to open the door. You are fond of Moore?"

The outlaw dropped into a chair on the opposite side of the table, and leaned his face upon his small brown hand. The yellow curls fell about his neck like a crown of glory, and the great blue eyes beamed upon her with a sensitive sympathy in their slumberous depths. Gabrielle was so confused that she did not answer, and the outlaw continued in the same soft, delicately-modulated voice:

"This is my sanctum. We live in a rude fashion here; but it is in my power to provide you with any delicacy that you may desire. Any wish that you may have shall be gratified as soon as expressed."

Gabrielle assured him that she was comfortable, and she could hardly believe that this golden-haired, sensitive-faced man was in reality the terrible outlaw whose deeds of bloodshed had made his name famous throughout the land.

"Well, then, since you are satisfied," said Redmond, "I can only say that your privacy here is sacred. We are rough men, but you are my guest, and"—here the speaker's voice rose proudly, and his blue eyes flashed with unwonted fire—"I am king here!"

There was a silence of several minutes, during which Gabrielle studied the face of the outlaw carefully. Finally, Redmond spoke.

"Austin is your name, is it not, miss?"

"Yes, sir; Gabrielle Austin," was the reply; but she wondered how he possessed himself of the information.

"Gabrielle!" continued the outlaw, musingly. "A very peculiar, but a very pretty name. It does credit to the bearer."

This compliment caused the young girl to blush. The quick eye of Redmond detected the change of color, and a just faintly perceptible smile swept over his face.

"It is not my province to flatter," he said. "Pray believe that that complimentary allusion was meant in good faith—my sincere opinion."

Such frankness caused Gabrielle to blush even more deeply than before, and she raised the book to hide her confusion.

"I am Redmond," said the outlaw, with a suddenness that caused poor Gabrielle to pale with terror. He affected not to notice her agitation, and continued: "Men say that I am a desperado and an outlaw. Well, I care little for their opinion. You, Miss Austin, are the first person, male or female, who has ever been admitted to my stronghold. I don't know that I am exercising good policy in bringing you here. In fact, I don't know what made me order your removal to this place. I think it was because I saw horror written upon your face when I stood before you in the road. You looked upon me as a man who was incapable of anything good—"

"No, no!" interrupted Gabrielle; for she recollected the outlaw's interference in her behalf, when she was so cruelly tied to that terrible instrument of torture on the court-house green, in Sanderson. "No, no, sir! I know you to be a man who is capable of performing a noble action. Your interference a few months ago saved me from torture and shame."

"You recollect me, then?" said Redmond. "That was a shameful outrage. Those men claim to be law-abiding and peace-loving people. Thank God, I am different. I can never see a woman suffer. My mother would haunt me to eternity, did I permit such a cruel wrong to be done."

"For that interference I thank you," said Gabrielle, extending her hand. Redmond bent over the table and raised it to his lips.

"A partial atonement, Miss Austin, for my misdeeds. But I am wasting—it is true, very agreeably—time that should be given to other and sterner duties. Remember, Miss Austin, although you are my prisoner, you are none the less my guest. When you have exhausted the reading matter on yonder shelf, I will send you more. Good-morning."

He shook back the golden curls, bowed, and with a graceful gesture of farewell, left the room.

A Lieutenant's Perfidy.

*He Attempts Gabrielle's Honor—Sudden Appearance of Redmond—
No Mercy—Death the Reward of Perfidy—Saved—Redmond's Threat.*

The next day Gabrielle learned that Redmond, with a portion of his band, had departed on an expedition, the result of which would add further credit to his reputation as an outlaw, and strike terror to the ears of his enemies. One of his lieutenants, a young, fine-looking fellow, who was absent when Gabrielle was first brought to the cave, was left in command.

Since her imprisonment Gabrielle had remained in the room assigned her by Redmond, venturing out into the main apartment but once or twice. The afternoon of Redmond's departure, she determined to take a stroll on the plateau, and when the negro, Tom, brought in her dinner, she made known her desire, and the servant promised to attend her. He did, and conducted her through the long gallery to the level plain, which fronted the door of the cave. Desirous of being alone, the better to meditate, Gabrielle dismissed Tom from further attendance upon her, and selecting for her couch a moss-covered boulder, screened from the view of those coming to and going from the cave by the fir trees, she gave herself up to a review of all the startling and eventful occurrences which had marked her young life so far.

The crackling of a dry twig, crushed under the foot of some one walking in her rear, caused her to rise suddenly to her feet, and wheeling, she came face to face with the young lieutenant of the band.

The young man changed color, but with a self-possession, which might vulgarly be called "hardened cheek," came forward to where she was standing, and ventured some commonplace remark on the beauties of the view from the cliff-edge. Feeling that she was a prisoner, Gabrielle did not rebuke this unpardonable advance in a stranger, as she would have done under other circumstances; and emboldened by his reception, the young outlaw ventured another commonplace. Gabrielle made suitable reply, and from a simple monosyllabic dialogue—so far as she was concerned—became sufficiently interested in the subject to talk at some length. Expressing a desire, finally, to return to the cave, the lieutenant conducted her back, and left her only at her room door. The next day she met him again, and they had another long conversation. He was more intelligent than his fellows, though not so well-learned as Redmond; and proved himself quite an agreeable companion. Thus as week passed, and Redmond was still absent. The young lieutenant met her every day; and had she been sufficiently interested to study his face carefully, the beautiful girl would have seen that he was plotting against her honor, and only awaiting a favorable opportunity to attempt it.

One evening, when she was in her room reading from a volume of poems that had been furnished her by Redmond's orders, the door suddenly opened, and the young lieutenant, with a face unusually flushed and a manner unnaturally excited, entered the room, and closing the door behind him, came toward the table.

Gabrielle arose and faced him, but her lips refused to pronounce the words of condemnation which rose to her lips, at this unwarrantable intrusion upon her privacy. She did not dream what was contemplated.

With a cry of admiration the young man sprang to her side, and before she could prevent him, clasped her in his arms and kissed her passionately.

"Sir!" cried the indignant girl, struggling to release herself. "How dare you? Release me!"

"Not until you grant me the request I make," replied the outlaw, still holding her in his arms.

"Villain!" cried Gabrielle.

"You are in my power, now! I love you—love you madly! Redmond is absent, and if you will not consent to be mine, I will take you by force! I don't care if I die for it!" said the outlaw, while his breath came hot and fast.

"Help!" shrieked Gabrielle, redoubling her efforts to escape.

"It's no use. No one will hear you, and if they do, won't dare to interfere. You are mine, mine, mine!"

He held her fast, and with a last wild shriek for help, a last desperate struggle to escape, Gabrielle's head fell forward on her bosom and her senses forsook her. With lustful eyes he gloated over the beauty of the magnificent creature now in his power. Another moment, and Gabrielle had better been dead, but the great God who had watched over her, and with an all-wise and unseen power averted evil to her in the past, did not neglect her now.

The door suddenly opened. The outlaw raised himself guiltily, and stood facing his chief. The eyes of Redmond were bent upon him with a terrible meaning in their hidden depths. The face of the lieutenant grew ashen white, and his teeth chattered in his head.

"Have mercy!" he cried, falling on his knees.

Redmond did not speak, but advanced toward him. The coward, still groveling and begging, presented a piteous spectacle.

"Mercy!" hissed Redmond, while his face darkened, and his lip curled with contemptuous scorn. "Death!" he shrieked, and drawing a pistol he thrust it down close to the head of the wretch who sued for mercy.

"Bray!" he said, in a cold and icy voice. "I have trusted you; I have made you one of my lieutenants. You reward that trust by perfidy unpardonable!"

"Forgive me!" moaned Bray, catching the outlaw about the knees. "Forgive me!"

But Redmond spurned him as he would a serpent.

"Pray, pray!" he cried, while his eyes flashed with the fire of determination. "Pray, if you believe in a hereafter! Your doom is sealed! Your action this day has signed your death-warrant."

Still the outlaw groveled and wept, and besought pardon of the man he had so grievously offended.

"One!" cried Redmond.

"Mercy!" moaned the outlaw.

"Two!"

"Bray, Lieutenant of the Redmond Band, attempts Miss Austin's honor, and is shot dead by his Chieftain." Courtesy of the North Carolina Collection, University of North Carolina at Chapel Hill.

"Spare me!"

"Three!"

"Great Go—"

There was a flash, a loud report, which awoke echo upon echo in the stalactite-fretted dome of the cave, and the brains of the perfidious Bray were scattered about the apartment. At the same instant Gabrielle recovered from her swoon, and springing to her feet, rushed forward.

"You have been avenged, Miss Austin!" said Redmond, with a cold smile. And then he led her from the room.

The outlaws had gathered in force at the sound of the pistol-shot. They looked up inquiringly as Redmond entered the main apartment with the beautiful girl leaning on his arm.

"Throw the carcass of that dog yonder to the buzzards!" said Redmond, pointing through the open door of Gabrielle's room. "And, listen! This lady is my guest; he who dares offer her insult, dies!"

He gave order to have Gabrielle's effects removed to another room, and when this was speedily done, conducted her thither, and, with a courtly bow, left her to meditate over the terrible occurrence of the past few minutes.

When supper was brought her that night, Tom handed her a note in Redmond's handwriting. It read as follows:

"Miss A: Let the recollection of what you saw to-day be buried in your mind. Never allude to it, at least in my presence.

R."

She obeyed the injunction, and from what followed, would not have known that so terrible an occurrence had taken place. It was in her thoughts often, but Redmond and the remainder of the band seemed to have forgotten the fact that one of their comrades had suffered death at the hands of his chief.

Redmond's Proposition.

The Outlaw in Love—The Story of his Life—Pleading his Suit—
Miss Austin's Hesitation.

Several days elapsed before Gabrielle again saw Redmond. She read, and thought, and wrote. Two or three times, conducted by the negro Tom, she ventured out upon the plateau in front of the cave, and feasted her eyes upon the grand natural panorama unfolded to her view. The members of the band whom she met treated her with rough courtesy, and were it not for the realization that these men helped murder her dear friend, she might have made her stay in this picturesque place a very pleasant one. She spent many hours in silent thought, and tears would start involuntarily to her eyes, when in retrospect she reviewed the effect this terrible catastrophe would have on her poor cousin.

One morning Tom informed her that "Massa Redmond" would call upon her. The outlaw made his appearance shortly, and with well-bred skill opened an interesting conversation on books and their authors. Gabrielle was certainly impressed with the evident learning of her companion. He had read extensively and well, and seemed familiar with the later production of foreign and domestic *litterateurs*.

An hour passed in a very agreeable way, and when the outlaw at last rose to go, Gabrielle was sincerely sorry. She thought of him a great deal after he went away, and when these thoughts were analyzed, she found that pity for this golden-haired man had taken possession of her heart. She saw in him a lofty intellect, a noble mind, a chivalrous character, debased and degraded by the desperate career which had made his name infamous.

After this second visit, Redmond called upon her frequently. They became more familiar, and one day Gabrielle ventured to ask him what disposition he meant to make of her.

"Well, to tell the truth," he said, with a jocularity that he often assumed, "I have hardly decided yet. I cannot hope to win you over to my way of thinking about the laws of right and wrong; and now that you know so many of my secrets, it would hardly be good policy to restore you to your friends."

"Oh, sir," said Gabrielle, "if you only would allow me to go back and help comfort my poor cousin in her terrible affliction, I would bless you forever after, and your secrets would be as safe with me as though I did not know them."

"Philosophers tell us that a woman cannot keep a secret," said the outlaw, gravely. "Has your stay here been so unpleasant that you are desirous of leaving us so soon?"

"No! No! Not that," said Gabrielle, quickly. "But—but—"

"You are unhappy here?" interrupted Redmond.

"Not exactly unhappy, but I am not contented, and never can be."

"Since you have broached the subject," said Redmond, rising to leave the room, "I must give you my answer, for your stay or departure depends upon my decision. I will send it to you this night." He bowed and withdrew.

After supper that day, Tom brought a note from his master. The handwriting was the same she had noticed in the books which had been furnished her. Breaking the seal, she took the letter to the light, and read as follows:

"Head-Quarters Redmond's.

"My dear Miss Austin:

Agreeable to the promise made you this morning, in reference to my decision regarding your departure or stay, I herewith send it, but first allow me to lay before you a proposition that has troubled my mind for some days past.

EDWARD B. CRITTENDEN

Before referring to this matter, which interests both alike, I must speak of myself. You have several times expressed surprise that one so gifted as myself, should lead the life I do. Listen, then. Before the late terrible war swept over this country, I was the petted child of fond, indulgent, and wealthy parents. My father was prominently connected with the Confederacy, and the close of the war found him penniless. I had been well educated in the best universities in the country; and during the latter days of the war traveled in Europe, to gain that polish which contact with continental life and manners can alone give. My father's reverses brought me back again to North Carolina, and I arrive home in the spring of 1867.

At that time our State, owning to the mistaken policy of the Federal authorities, was in a condition bordering on anarchy. Being a Southern born girl, a native of my own State, you must have heard something of that protective organization started among the Southern people just at the close of the war, which has passed into history as the Ku Klux Klan. My father was prominently connected with this order. He sympathized with its aims, and assisted it to the extent of his ability in furthering its purposes. He was so prominently connected with the Klan, that when internal enemies betrayed it to the Federal authorities, he became a marked man. One night a body of Federal troops surrounded our house, and demanded my father's surrender. Like a brave man he refused, and gave up his life rather than sacrifice his liberty. The shock of that terrible night's occurrence killed my mother, and I, a boy in years and in experience with the rugged side of life's journey, was an orphan. Since then I have lived only for revenge, and how complete has been this revenge, you know better than I can tell you.

"Now I come to the proposition. You are young and pure, and the short time you have been my guest has been like an oasis in my wretched career. Contact with you has inoculated my mind with thoughts that a month ago I would have laughed at, had they found a place there. In brief, I love you. I am not rich, but I have enough to keep us comfortable for a year at least, in which time we could reach a part of the world where the name of Redmond is not known. I have no fear of the future. Inspired by the knowledge of your love, your decision will decide my future. If you refuse this proffered love, I pledge you my word of honor as a gentle-man, that you shall be returned to your friends. If you accept the offer, and thereby honor me more than I dare hope, we will together leave this place, and seek an asylum beyond the sea. I am not so selfish as to remind you of what may follow if you refuse. Of course, I shall continue in the career which destiny has marked out for me, and until some stray bullet ends my life, remain in your recollection, pleasantly, I hope; for I do crave and court your good opinion—what the world has been pleased to term me,

"Redmond, the Outlaw."

Gabrielle read this strange letter several times. Would the pity in her heart turn to love? She could not decide; and snatching up a sheet of paper she penned this line, which she dispatched to the outlaw chieftain:

"Sir:—Give me until to-morrow night. I will have my answer ready by that time. "G. A."

Why should she not accept, and become the wife of Redmond? Through the malignity of her enemies she had been disgraced and humiliated. The world did not reckon her innocent, now that the law had declared her guilty.

"Why not?" she asked, and revolving this question in her mind, fell asleep.

The Outlaw's Magnanimity.

Gabrielle Hesitates—The Outlaw's Prisoner—The Lovers Meet— Begging for the Life of the Man she Loves—Redmond Decides— "The Prisoner's Life shall be Spared!"

While Gabrielle was yet debating in her mind whether she should respond favorably to Redmond's offer, and seek with him as his wife an asylum in a strange land, or reject the offer and return to begin again the hard life-struggle against a fate that was manifestly adverse, Charlie Hashagen was riding up and down the mountain-passes of Buncombe, Yancey, and McDowell counties, industriously hunting for some clue that would lead him to the mountain-den of Redmond. On the same day and at nearly the hour when Gabrielle was reading Redmond's letter, he had possessed himself of information which caused him to turn his horse's head toward the black outline of Mount Mitchell, looming up against the distant horizon ten miles away. He camped that night at the foot of the mountain, and as soon as the eastern sky became tinged with the light of returning day, left his horse, and began the laborious ascent of the mountain. He knew that he was now nearing the goal to which he had so hopefully looked forward. Dread filled his heart, however, lest the loved object of his search should have come to harm.

It was hard work climbing that steep mountain-side, but love gave him strength and will. It was probably an accidental coincidence, but he followed the path usually taken by the outlaws, and ultimately reached the level, fir-bordered plateau. Tired with the heavy labor, he halted for a moment to rest, and seated himself on the edge of the plateau. He gazed out over the broad expanse of country open to view from that elevated position, drinking in with greedy eyes the glorious beauties of the ruddy-tinted forest, kissing the base of the mountain, and flowing away with graceful undulation as far as the eye could reach. A slight noise in his rear caused him to turn his head, but, alas! too late.

"Young Charlie Hashagen goes to Miss Austin's rescue and is himself made captive." Courtesy of the North Carolina Collection, University of North Carolina at Chapel Hill.

Before he could regain his feet and draw his pistol, a dozen men surrounded him; he was thrown to the ground, and his arms and legs were tightly bound.

"You're a cool 'un," said one of the outlaws, bending over him. "A powerful cool 'un!"

Then he was lifted up and carried into the cave. It so happened that just as the outlaws entered the cavern, Gabrielle stepped from her room, and accompanied by the negro Tom, was about proceeding to the plateau. She came face to face with Charlie Hashagen, just as the outlaws halted, and raised him to his feet. Their eyes met, and Charlie, but for the bonds which bound him tightly, would have sprung forward and clasped her in his arms. As it was, he could only cry:

"Oh, Gabrielle!"

And she, remembering only that this man once loved her, and that she had been happy in the knowledge of his love, rushed forward, and much to the wonder of the outlaws, clasped the prisoner in her arms and kissed him passionately. She looked about.

The lieutenant of the band, he who had taken charge of Gabrielle the night of her introduction to the outlaw's home, came forward and gently unclasped her arms from the prisoner's neck.

"Do you know this man, miss?" he asked.

"Yes!" faltered Gabrielle.

"I'm sorry," continued the lieutenant, "but he must go to the dungeon until the capting arrives."

So saying, he ordered some of the band to remove Charlie, and lifting him up, they bore him away, bound and helpless. Gabrielle returned to her room, but so excited was she that she could not remain, and hurried back into the main room to obtain permission from the lieutenant to visit Charlie.

"It's agin orders," responded the outlaw, when she made known her wish, "but the prisoner's thar, and I don't reckon you could help him to git away, so I expect I kin let you see him for a few minnits."

"Thank you, sir," said Gabrielle, and the lieutenant conducted her to a room, similar to her own, on the opposite side of the main apartment.

"You kin stay thar fifteen minnits," said the outlaw, as he opened the door. Gabrielle entered, and she heard the door shut, and lock behind her.

Charlie was lying on a rude pallet in one corner of the room. His bonds had been removed, and as Gabrielle entered, he rushed forward and clasped her in his arms.

"Oh, my darling!" he cried, "I have found you at last!"

Then, with their arms about each other's neck, they reviewed the events which had transpired since their parting in Goochland county, and mutual explanations were made.

"You still love me, Charlie?" said Gabrielle, blushing.

"As I love my God!" cried the young man, enthusiastically.

They were left together at least an hour, and when one of the band unlocked the door and bade Gabrielle come out, the reunited lovers embraced tenderly, and Gabrielle, happier than she had been for months, reluctantly tore herself away, and followed the outlaw into the main apartment.

"The capting has come back, miss," he said, after carefully locking the door, "and he has just decided what shall be the fate of your friend."

"And that decision, pray?" inquired Gabrielle, all unsuspicious of the terrible truth.

"Is death!" said the outlaw, solemnly.

"Death!" cried Gabrielle, while here dove-like eyes dilated with fear. "Death! Oh, no! You would not be so cruel!"

"The capting has said so, and his word is law!"

"I will appeal to him. I will pray to him on my bended knees. No, no; he would not be so cruel. Where is he? Take me to him!"

The outlaw thus solicited conducted her to the room occupied by the king of the "moonshiners," and trembling with alternate fear and hope, Gabrielle knocked for admittance.

"Come in!" said Redmond, and thus invited, Gabrielle opened the door, and rushing toward the outlaw, cast herself, all pale and trembling, at his feet.

"Oh, sir!" she cried, tears gushing from her eyes. "Spare him! Spare him! For my sake! It is he! It is Charlie! My Charlie!"

The face of Redmond grew cold and stern, and bending down, he raised the agonized girl to a chair, and she noticed that his hand trembled in hers.

"This man has penetrated to our stronghold," said Redmond, at last, "Our safety demands his life!"

"It was for love of me," sobbed Gabrielle.

"And do you love him?" said Redmond, in a low, sad voice.

"Yes, yes!" was the eager response.

"Then I can never hope—"

Gabrielle looked up quickly, for the words dropped from his lips like the wail of a lost soul. She knew what he meant, and her heart sank like a lump of lead.

"I loved him long ago!" moaned Gabrielle.

"And you love him yet!"

"Yes!" came faintly from the pale lips, which quivered with a terrible fear.

The outlaw was silent, and Gabrielle dared not raise her eyes. At last he spoke, and the words fell from his lips coldly and mechanically. It was the first time he had ever addressed her as Gabrielle, and she felt his hand tighten on hers, as though he would keep her always with him.

"Gabrielle," he said, "I doubt if this man loves you as I do. I know that you love him better than I can hope you would ever love me. It is my great love for you that has decided the fate of this man, whom I sincerely hate, because he has robbed me of the only person that could ever make me change the life I now lead. When I say this, you don't know how much the effort costs me. It tears my heart to shreds. The prisoner's life shall be spared. God bless you, my darling!"

He bent down, and clasping her in his arms, kissed her face upturned to his, bright with the joy which filled her heart.

Departure of the Lovers.

They are Initiated into the Secrets of the Cave—How Moonshine Whiskey is Made—Redmond's Last Request—They Leave for Asheville with an Escort of Outlaws.

Gabrielle's heart was so full of gratitude to the outlaw who had confessed his great love for her, she so fully realized the noble magnanimity which spared Charlie Hashagen's life, that she allowed him to hold her in his arms some moments.

"I must give you up," he said, stroking her hair. "Oh, Gabrielle, my darling! This day a dark cloud forever hides what I fondly looked forward to—happiness in the future with you. It is my destiny!"

He released her, and buried his face in his hands. A great grief had possession of his heart, and the baby blue eyes were moist with tears. Tears! Redmond cry! His strong will asserted itself, and passing his hand across his eyes, all traces of emotion vanished, and he rose to his feet—*Redmond, the Outlaw!*

"I shall not see you again, Miss Austin," he said, holding out his hand. "I will give order to have you both escorted to the vicinity of Asheville. I hope—you—I trust you may be happy. Good-bye."

Had she not studied the character of this man so thoroughly, it would have been hard to believe that the will alone could so effectually conceal his emotions.

She took the extended hand. There was nothing but friendly warmth in the pressure. She murmured the thanks that out of gratitude rose unbidden to her lips, and kissed the brown hand which lay in hers. Redmond started, and his face changed color; but he quickly recovered himself, and lifting one of her tresses, that had escaped from the band which confined her brown hair, he smiled, in that sympathetic, sensitive, womanish way of his, and said:

"I will probably never see you again. We part friends. Give me this tress to remember you in the future. I will cherish it religiously."

She lifted a pair of scissors from the table, and clipped off the slender braid. He twined the hair about his finger and turned away. A deep groan burst from his lips, and Gabrielle's eyes moistened with the dew of sympathy.

He turned towards the table, and resumed the writing which Gabrielle's entrance had interrupted. He did not look up again, and Gabrielle stole softly away. She hastened to her own room, and falling on her knees, prayed long and earnestly for the desperate man, whose heart was filled with noble qualities which might have made him a king among the world's people.

Charlie was released from confinement, and he and Gabrielle spent the day on the plateau talking over the bitter past, the glorious present, and the uncertain future. She told him the story of her persecution in Goochland county, and how, not hearing from him, she had thought herself forgotten; her accidental meeting with him in Asheville, and the confirmation, through what she then saw, of her worst fears; she dwelt with trembling voice on the terrible scene in the Valley of the Shadow of Death; and then, with shyly averted gaze, told of another's love for her, and the great sacrifices he had made because of that love.

"God bless him," said Charlie, fervently, when she had finished. "He has displayed a magnanimity more than human. I shall never forget him, and to-day would lay down my life in his defense."

After nightfall they returned to the cave, and in obedience to Redmond's directions, were shown through the stronghold, and taken deep down into an inner cavern where great copper cauldrons were hissing and seething, tended by half-naked men, who in the dull glare of the furnace fires looked like demons minding the fires of Hades. Then they were conducted back to the main room, and after supper fiddles and banjos were produced, and the granite walls of the cave re-echoed with wild barbaric melodies, such as these men sing.

The festivities continued until nearly midnight. As a large gong in the dome of the cave struck the hour of twelve, the entire band filed into the main room, and, headed by the lieutenant-commander, marched several times around the lovers, who stood speechless and amazed at this strange spectacle in the middle of room. When the band were ranged about the apartment, the lieutenant advanced, and producing a Bible, swore the two to eternal secrecy regarding what they had seen in the cave. The band then dispersed, and the lovers retired to their respective rooms.

At about ten o'clock, the lieutenant of the band informed Gabrielle that the escort was ready to conduct her and her lover to Asheville. Ten men would accompany them; and as the party left the cave, a ringing cheer from those who remained behind bade them God-speed. At the foot to the mountain horses were in waiting; and, mounting the cavalcade rode swiftly on toward Asheville. The sun was yet two hours high, when they halted within a mile of the town.

Conclusion

Asheville was startled and excited when the news reached the town that Marshal Dick Allison had been murdered by Redmond, and Miss Gabrielle Austin carried off into captivity, but Asheville was wild when Charlie Hashagen and the missing young lady walked down the main street of that quaint backwoods town, and mounted the steps of the principal hotel. Charlie's uncle had mourned him as lost, and after the first exuberance of greeting had subsided took him to one side, and in a solemn voice told him that while he was absent his father had suddenly died of paralysis.

This unexpected catastrophe necessitated Charlie's immediate departure for Virginia; good taste and respect for his father's memory alone prevented him from making Gabrielle his wife before his departure; but he promised to return in three months, when he would claim her as his bride. So he left, and Gabrielle found a home with her cousin Mrs. Allison, who had removed to the town.

About a week before Christmas Charlie returned to Asheville, and preparation were begun for their wedding, which was to take place on Christmas eve. The night of the suspicious event was clear and crisp, and a full moon flooded the earth with a soft and mellow radiance. The ceremony was performed in the Methodist church, the historian of this remarkable but none the less truthful story officiating, assisted by the pastor of the church, Rev. Moses W. McDowell.

But little remains to be told. Mr. and Mrs. Hashagen returned to Goochland county, and Gabrielle was welcomed by the whole town. Gideon Gannaway left Sanderson soon after the death of his patron, and was never seen again. The negro constable emigrated to Liberia. Redmond the outlaw still defies the authority of the law, daily commits crimes unparalleled in history, has startling adventures and hairbreadth escapes. Mount Mitchell still produces gallons of illicit liquor, which the authorities in vain attempt to capture before it is sold and consumed.

EDWARD B. CRITTENDEN

Charlotte March 3, 1879

Messrs. Barclay & Co
Philadelphia, Pa.

Gentlemen,

I emphatically endorse this narrative as true in every particular. Miss Austin I have known since she was an infant. Her very interesting story really reads like a Romance, and thrills like a Novel, yet bears the honest stamp of truth in every line.

Have just read a copy of your well gotten up little book and can heartily recommend it.

Very Truly Yours,
Edward B. Crittenden

REDMOND'S STORY OF HIS LIFE.

Introductory Note.

Head-quarters' Redmond,
October 23, 1878.

My Dear Miss Austin:

When a man becomes his own historian, he often falls into the grievous error of imagining trivial incidents heroic catastrophes. Unconsciously he glorifies himself to an extent that borders on egotism. You have manifested an interest in me, and have expressed great surprise that I should lead the life I do. It is in defense of the causes which impelled me to alienate myself from my fellow-men that I write this, and I have endeavored to justify myself in all acts that I may have committed in the past eleven years in opposition to laws that are oppressive and tyrannical. I have not aimed at embellishment, but rather to a strict adherence to fact and the truth.

Trusting you may be interested in the perusal of what follows, and that the reading of my narration may incline you toward me more charitably than the rest of the world, who judge me and my acts unknowingly, I remain, with great respect,

Yours Very Faithfully,
Redmond.

THE LIFE STORY.

I was born in close proximity to the birthplace of American liberty. My ancestors were among the foremost of those "blue and buff hornets"—as they were then jocularly termed—who met in old Mecklenburg county more than a year before the representatives of the thirteen colonies assembled in Independence Hall, Philadelphia, to protest against the tyranny of King George. I come by my love of liberty naturally, and my hatred of tyrannical and burdensome laws is inherited. I believe that all governments derive "their just power from the consent of the governed." My father believed this. This belief allied him to the cause of the Confederacy. When the war that followed secession deluged the Republic with the blood of brothers shed by brothers, I was at school in a Northern university. My strongly expressed sentiments drew down upon me the enmity of my fellow-students and the faculty of the college, who were all Northern born and especially intolerant toward the South.

Redmond Visits Europe.

I communicated with my father's representative in New York city, and acting under orders received from him, I was dispatched to Europe to complete my studies, while my father, at the head of a regiment of "hornets," manfully battled for the cause he deemed just, under the "bonnie blue-flag" of the Confederacy. War losses by the entire Southern people were enormous, but my father suffered in particular. When the ragged remnants of Lee's once great army laid down their muskets at Appomattox, my father, bowing to the inevitable, returned to his once prosperous and happy home, a ruined man. Then followed that period, when, in the lately conquered States, anarchy ruled supreme. It is not my intention to dwell upon this matter, or to discuss the question who was at fault. In vain the Southern people appealed to the Federal government for protection. Their cry was unheeded, and at last, driven to desperation, they organized a protective society which was given the name "Ku Klux Klan." My father was one of the leaders of the Klan in North Carolina, and did much to advance its interests. All this time I remained in Europe, ignorant of the great reverses which had befallen him. Pecuniarily unable to keep me there any longer, he bade me come home, and in 1867 I arrived in North Carolina. A few months after my return, internal enemies betrayed the leading members of the Klan to the Federal government, and excited Northern prejudice against the order, by gross and willful misrepresentation. From that day my father was a marked man, and on the night of October 13, 1867, a body of armed soldiers surrounded our house and demanded my father's surrender. Like a brave man, he refused, and in attempting to defend his honor and the sanctity of his home, was overpowered and brutally

Murdered Before My Mother's Eyes.

The shock which followed the witnessing of such a terrible outrage caused my poor mother's death a few days afterwards, and I was an orphan. On the night of the attack I was absent from home, visiting an old school-day friend in Charlotte. I was a boy in years and experience, but this terrible catastrophe made me a man. Without making known my intention to the friends who in vain attempted to console me for the loss of my parents, I disposed of the property left by my father, and bade adieu to the world. From that day I was an outlaw, and a price was set upon my head. I gathered about me a band of men, whose courageous and daring acts are a matter of common history. We have been the friend of the oppressed, and the enemy of the oppressors. If we have slain men it has been because they richly merited death. But, with this brief introduction, this succinct recital of the causes which led to my outlawry, I shall now proceed to a brief narration of the principal events in my life since that time.

North Carolina Customs.

The custom of distilling liquor from grain and fruit is one immemorial in the western portion of my native State. The people are a hardy, resolute body, and are continually warring with Nature for subsistence. A lack of communicative facilities with the outside world necessitates the conversion of our staple products into the smallest possible bulk. As is well known our principal products are fruit and corn. These are taken to market in the shape of distilled liquor. Before the war, there was no tax upon liquors, and when the Federal Congress imposed a duty as a means of affording revenue to pay the interest on the enormous war debt, the burden fell heavily on these hardy mountaineers. For reasons which I shall not here attempt to explain, it is impossible for the small farmers to pay the tax on distilled liquors with profit to themselves. But they must live, and they can only live as their fathers lived before them, by growing corn and fruit, distilling it into liquor, and selling it to the outside world, free of tax. I believe the law taxing liquor an unjust and tyrannical imposition. We have a right to protest against laws which injure us. If our protest is not heeded, the document which declared us a free and independent nation instructs us to exercise our right and duty, and "throw off such government," and the men who are associated with me believe that the law which forbids us to manufacture the products of our own land without first paying the government a tax thereon unjust. We believe that we are right in resisting this law, and to resist it we have mutually pledged to each other "our lives, our fortunes and our sacred honor."

He Determines to Resist Unjust Laws.

As I before stated, I was without experience when I determined upon the life I now lead, and when I left my ruined home and turned my face toward the setting sun, my purposes for the future were not well defined. I proceeded as far as Asheville, when learning that a party of United States troops had that very morning started out to hunt down a man accused of being connected with the Ku Klux, I determined to hasten to his assistance. Procuring a fresh horse, for the one I had ridden from Charlotte was well jaded, I purchased suitable arms and rode forward in the wake of the soldiers. The squad numbered sixteen men, and was commanded by a lieutenant and two deputy marshals, making nineteen in all. The point for which they were aiming was about twenty miles northeast of Asheville in the neighborhood of High Peak. The man who had rendered himself objectionable to the Federal authorities was a small farmer with a correspondingly large family. He was a man about sixty years of age, and by name John Prather. Mr. Prather's family was composed of five able-bodied men beside himself, making six in all. So we were nearly half as strong as the enemy, and undoubtedly the lack of numbers would be more than compensated for by the intrepidity and valor of the Prathers. He had been scout during the war, and had been ably assisted by his five grown sons.

The military rode forward slowly, confident that they would catch their man napping. I pushed my horse to his utmost limit of speed, and before the party had made half the distance found myself immediately in their rear. I had determined to act boldly, and without attracting attention made a detour and left the enemy in the rear. I reached Prather's house late in the afternoon, and found him at home. Two of his sons were absent on the mountain hunting, but were expected home at any minute. His wife prepared me a warm dinner, and after seeing that my horse was comfortably provided for, I entered in to consultation with Mr. Prather and the three sons who remained.

Redmond Plans to Defeat of Marshal Blacker and the Soldiers.

Our plan was soon matured, not of defence, but of offence. One of the marshals in the party, rapidly approaching the home of my host, had in his pocket a warrant for the arrest of the entire family, or that portion old enough to know right from wrong, and courageous enough to defend their opinion. If arrested they would be thrown into prison, where they might linger for years, while the wife and young children suffered. Without waiting for the return of the two hunters, we armed ourselves to the teeth, and proceeded down the road about half a mile, where a thick undergrowth fringed it on either side. We distributed our forces equally, or nearly so. The elder Prather and two of his sons concealed themselves on one side of the road, whilst one son and the writer took the other side. Then we patiently awaited the arrival of the enemy. An hour passed and the suspense was becoming intolerable. At last, our ears, alert and keen to catch the faintest rustle, detected the faint sound of horses' hoofs, resounding from the hard dirt-road. Soon the clanking of sabers and the voices of the men could be plainly heard, and in a minute the head of the column appeared in sight, the lieutenant leading. Unsuspicious of danger the horsemen came down the road, talking and laughing. We cocked and raised our rifles, and loosened our pistols in our belts. When the soldiers were fairly in front, I leaped to my feet, and gave the command, "Fire!"

Bushwhacked.

A vivid flame lit up the bushes on each side of the road; there was a sharp shock, and five of the enemy threw up their hands and fell from their saddles. Before the remainder of the command could return the unexpected fire, another volley belched forth; five more men fell into the dusty road, and then, drawing our pistols, we jumped into the road and continued the fight. It was an easy victory. Those of the soldiers who escaped death, or were not seriously injured, put spurs to their horses and fled through a perfect hail of bullets from our guns and pistols. One of the marshals was the notorious Jack Blacker, whose cruel persecution of my countrymen had rendered him an especial object of my hatred. I had good reason for believing that he led the band which murdered my father. I desired to capture him alive. Death by the bullet was too good for him. At the second fire, Blacker, who was a man of gigantic stature, dropped his bridle-rein, threw both hands to his breast, and reeled in the saddle. His horse, probably maddened by a bullet-wound, wheeled and dashed down the road with his powerless and wounded rider lying across his neck, and was soon lost to view in a cloud of dust. As the capture of Blacker was the principal object in my mind, I was much chagrined to have him disappear before my eyes, and accompanied by Prather and his sons, I at once started out in pursuit. A few miles down the road we found Blacker's horse quietly grazing by the roadside, but Blacker was nowhere to be seen. Fearing that my enemy had only been slightly wounded, and had slipped from his horse and taken shelter in the thick woods which stretched away for miles on both sides of the road, I requested my companions to carefully search for traces of the missing man. It was a difficult task, for the undergrowth was thick and matted, and after beating the woods carefully until dark, without success, we returned to Prather's house, leaving the dead bodies of thirteen of our enemies lying in the road where they fell. Such of the horses as remained in the neighborhood we caught and conveyed to Prather's stable. The arms and ammunition of the dead men were also confiscated, and what money and valuables they had on their persons. That night we entered into a formal organization, and Prather and his five sons formed the nucleus of "Redmond's Band."

Blacker's Terrible Death.

I was vexed because Blacker escaped my vengeance, but a Power mightier than I punished the villain with far greater severity than, wicked as he was, he deserved. A few months after the battle before referred to, a party of citizens were hunting in the vicinity, and came across the skeleton of a man in a little clearing in the woods. Portions of the dead man's clothes were scattered about, having been torn from the body by buzzards, who had literally picked the bones clean. Among the bones the hunters picked up great wads of hickory-bark, leaves and grass which had evidently been chewed and swallowed by the unfortunate man before his death, to appease a hunger that was terrible. One of the men picked up a note-book containing letters and papers, and from these they learned that the man who must have died in such horrible agony was the wounded deputy marshal, John Blacker. He must have lived eight or ten days after he was wounded, for he was a man of strong constitution, and literally died of starvation. In his note-book was found an entry in his own hand, giving an account of his terrible sufferings the first three days after his escape from us. He then, apparently, lost consciousness, and dragged out the weary days until death intervened and put an end to his sufferings—a gibbering maniac. He was, according to the account in the note-book, wounded in two places, through the right arm at the shoulder-joint, and through the left hip. He fell from his saddle and rolled into the bushes. He became unconscious, or rather delirious, and in this condition

Dragged Himself Farther into the Woods.

He recovered his mind next morning, and being consumed by a terrible thirst, he sought to allay it by sucking the dew from the leaves and grass about him. He thought himself on the right-hand side of the road, whereas he was on the left. Painfully he crawled through the bushes, buoyed up by the hope that he was nearing the road, where he could wait until some chance traveler assisted him. He called loudly for assistance, and listened with beating heart for an answer, only to be mocked by the echo of his own voice, as the sound-waves widened and receded from him. His wounds pained him, his throat was dry and parched, and his tongue swollen. He became weak and dizzy, and broke off pieces of bark and the tender hickory-twigs and ate them ravenously, so terrible was his hunger. He filled his stomach with these and grass, and felt stronger. He still shouted at frequent intervals, and continued his weary, painful march, in the direction in which he presumed the road lay. He could not stop at night, but kept dragging himself forward. It was not until the third day when he began to realize that he might be going from the road instead of toward it. When this horrible suspicion dawned upon his mind he appears to have given up hope, and the last words scratched in his book so feebly as to be almost illegible were these:

"I am Lost! God have mercy!"

You can imagine the rest. With reason bereft him, dying for water and food, wounded and helpless, he crawled through those dense thickets, alternately crying, singing, laughing, shouting, praying, as maniacs do, until death stiffened his limbs; and the buzzards, who had hovered expectantly over his head, flew down and began their ghoul-like feast, tearing with their sharp beaks his quivering flesh, and plucking out, as dainty tit-bits, his sightless eyes! Thus did Almighty God have vengeance upon one who had offended him—a vengeance more frightful in its lingering torture than the ingenuity of mortal man could conceive!

When Prather and his sons agreed to my terms of organization, and took an oath of eternal fidelity to me, he had in his store-house about nine hundred bushels of corn, and this we determined to manufacture into whiskey. Loading the horses with heavy packs of the precious grain, we conveyed it to this place, which had been discovered by one of the Prather boys while out hunting. It was a secure and not easily approached retreat, and we have, thanks to its inaccessible position, been able to defy the enemy for more than ten years. This cave is the head-quarters of the band and my home. We have scattered over this and the adjoining States of South Carolina, Virginia, Tennessee, and Georgia, branch distilleries, as securely hidden as the main establishment, and they annually produce thousands of gallons of liquor, which we have no difficulty in disposing of. The frequent raids which are made through the States mentioned do not affect us. The marshal capture only private establishments, run in a small way and very poorly protected.

The Business of Moonshining.

No business is managed with greater care than the distilleries under my charge. At the date of my writing, there are one hundred and twenty-seven branch distilleries in the States mentioned, and five hundred and thirty-eight men are required to manage them. Attached to the main establishment are two hundred and sixty-four men, making eight hundred and two the number of my followers. We annually manufacture, in the main and branch distilleries, about two hundred and seventy-five thousand gallons of liquor, which we dispose of at a profit of about twenty-cents on the gallon, netting us in the neighborhood of $50,000. Every man attached to the band is a shareholder in the profits of the distillery, and finds it a paying business. Their families, with such assistance as they can from time to time afford them, make a crop of corn; the company purchases it, and manufactures the grain into liquor, paying out of the money received from its sale all the expenses of running the establishments, with the profit above mentioned. Besides the corn-liquor, we also distill large quantities of fruit—apples and peaches—into brandy. The money received from the sale of this class of liquor is almost all profit, and is used as a sinking fund to assist needy members of the band and their families; to purchase arms, horses, clothing, etc.; to provide counsel for those unfortunate enough to be captured and thrown into prison, and to extend the business.

Redmond the King.

Over this vast business, with its eight hundred odd employees, I exercise absolute authority, and appoint from time to time subordinate officers to assist me, whose salaries are paid out of the common fund. I receive no regular salary, but a percentage of all liquor sold. From my head-quarters I direct the movements of all members of the band. I organize raids against the enemy, have full charge of the purchasing and selling of supplies and stock, both crude and manufactured, and decide all questions of equity or common law which may arise between members of the organization. My powers are dictatorial, and from my decision there is no appeal. We have a constitution, to which every member swears allegiance, and by-laws to govern our actions. When an offense is committed, the crime is specifically drawn up in writing and referred to me. I decide what shall be the punishment of the culprit. This applies to all offenses except treason. Any member of the band has power to punish this crime, which is always with death. We have a code of signals to communicate with each of the branch distilleries and the main establishment, when a dangerous enemy approaches. We have spies in all the principal towns, who watch the commissioners and marshals, and apprise us when a raid is projected, and in what direction. This hasty sketch will give you some idea of the magnitude of our business relations, and the perfect discipline which governs the band. But enough of this. I will now proceed to give you a brief *résumé* of my history, from the date of the organization of the band I command.

A Yankee Trick.

The nine hundred bushels of corn taken from Prather's store-house were speedily distilled, and as soon as a sufficient quantity was ready for market, I took it upon myself to "run the blockade." I could have delegated this perilous undertaking to one of my companions; but they were marked men, and I was as yet comparatively unknown to the authorities, and would run but little risk. So one fine morning I left our stronghold, driving a pair of stout mules, who were attached to a canvas-covered "Studebaker" wagon, in the body of which, hidden under a pile of "shucks," were five barrels filled with the precious fluid. My destination was Asheville, where I could find a customer for the liquor. The road was an ordinary mountain trail, and I drove all day without meeting any one. The sun was just sinking behind the mountains, when three men, whom I immediately recognized as deputy-marshals, came suddenly upon me at a cross-road. I was disguised with a beard and butternut clothes so effectually that my dearest friend would not have recognized me; and although my heart throbbed a little faster as the three horsemen approached, I was outwardly calm and collected, and regarded them curiously as they drew nearer. Their uniform was concealed under heavy cloaks; but their holsters contained pistols, and they had Winchester repeating rifles thrown over their shoulders. My wagon had nothing suspicious about it. The fly was up, and the shucks looked very innocent. When they reached me they drew their horses to one side, and the leader of the party, whose name was Crowder, accosted me as follows:

"Howdy, neighbor?"

"Howdy, gentlemen?" I replied, touching my hat. "Powerful fine weather we'uns are hevin!"

"Yes," said one of the marshals.

I reined up my mules, and Crowder again took up the conversation.

"Can you tell me," he said, "where we can get some whiskey? We are strangers in this section, and are dry as herrings."

"Gentlemen," I replied, still imitating the uncouth twang of the crackers, "whiskey is mitey hard to git. Thar's so many uv these hyar dep'ty marshals 'round that we'uns are 'fraid to tech the pesky stuff."

At this they all laughed, and Crowder continued:

"I believe the marshals do create considerable disturbance among you occasionally, but we don't want to buy much—just enough to fill our flasks."

"Well, now, gentlemen," I said, with a cunning leer, "you can't prove it by me that you'uns haint marshals!"

They laughed again, louder than before, and one of the marshals denied that they were revenue officers.

"You know all about these illicit distilleries," said Crowder, "and I believe you've got blockade liquor hidden under those shucks."

"Well, now, gentlemen," I said, with a look of surprise, "you'uns hev hit that nail right on the head. I hev got a little moonshine hyar, and I run a pow'rful risk in conveyin' hit; but hit's only a few gallons that I use for my stomach's sake. I more'n half believe that you are rev-nue officers; but you seem tolerbul clever, and hif you'uns will promise not to say anythin' about it, I'll let you hev a little."

This frank confession of mine rather staggered them, but I saw that it threw them off the scent, and still laughing, they produced their flasks. I had a jug containing about three gallons under the wagon seat, and taking this out I filled their bottles and handed them back. Crowder offered to pay for the liquor, but with assumed cunning I answered him that the acceptance of money for the liquor would lay me liable to arrest. At their invitation I drank with them, and then whipping up my mules drove on, having completely hoodwinked them by this shrewd trick. I sold my liquor in Asheville, made some necessary purchases and reached the mountain again without further adventure. Afterwards I made many similar trips, and always with success. That winter our band was increased by several new members, and we manufactured and sold many gallons of liquor.

Redmond Outlawed.

Early in the following spring a large force of marshals established themselves at Asheville, and assisted by a company of United States troops, began to raid through this section of country quite extensively. They watched the roads closely for blockaders, and it required considerable skill and ingenuity to get through their lines. I made the trip several times, however, and at last excited their suspicions. I now drove four mules, and concealed the liquor under a pile of miscellaneous "truck," shucks, chickens, eggs, butter, etc. I always went well-armed, and was prepared to make desperate resistance. I would drive slowly, and four members of the band always accompanied me, they making the journey on foot, and keeping concealed on each side of the road, in close proximity to my wagon. I made several trips in this manner without adventure; but one evening when but a few miles from Asheville, a squad of soldiers and two deputy marshals, one of whom was the man Crowder, before alluded to, sprang up from their place of concealment among the bushes, and made a rush for my wagon. I knew that prompt action was necessary, and drawing from my pockets a brace of revolvers I dropped the reins and taking cool and deliberate aim at the two marshals discharged shot after shot until the chambers of both pistols were empty. The smoke cleared away, and revealed both men prostrate in the road. My allies had not been idle, but had attacked the soldiers from both sides of the road. Not knowing our strength, and demoralized by the downfall of their leaders, and this raking cross-fire, they broke and fled. Without waiting to count the number of the slain, I turned my wagon toward the mountain and drove rapidly back, arriving there in safety. That was the last of my blockading.

It appeared afterwards that both of the marshals had been killed, five of the soldiers, and several badly wounded. Asheville and all the adjoining country was placarded with printed bills offering a reward of $1,000 for the murderers, "one Redmond," and his accomplices, and the startling adventure which followed this catastrophe gave me the name, "REDMOND, THE OUTLAW," which I have borne ever since.

The Chronology of a Desperate Career.

I have promised to write a faithful account of my life, and from my diary herewith present a recapitulation of my adventures and their results, arranged in chronological order:

Born in Mecklenburg county, North Carolina, December 15, 1844.

Entered Princeton College, New Jersey, spring term 1860.

Left college for Europe, May 14, 1861.

Returned to North Carolina, June 27, 1867.

Parents died October, 1867.

Reached Asheville, with the determination of becoming an outlaw, October 25, 1867.

Was concerned in the killing of Deputy United States Marshal John Blacker, Deputy Marshal Edward B. Claghorn, and twelve members of the Second U.S. Infantry, near High Park, North Carolina, October 25, 1867.

Killed Deputy Marshals Crowder and Chambers, April 1, 1868.

Killed a revenue informer named Harkleroad, on Big Yadkin river, June 5, 1868.

Assisted in the killing of Deputy United State Marshal Jesse Davis, First Lieutenant James Miller, of Second United States infantry, and nine private soldiers, October 11, 1868.

Was nearly captured by the negro revenue informer, Toby Small, near Seneca City, South Carolina, December 18, 1868.

Shot and mortally wounded Toby Small, in a bar-room at Westminster, Oconee county, South Carolina, December 20, 1868.

Reward of $10,000 offered for my capture, dead or alive, by the United States government, January 1, 1869.

Shot dead United States Commissioner Irwin C. McDowell, in the post-office, Asheville, North Carolina, May 26, 1869.

Was concerned in the killing of Deputy Marshal John P. Appleby, and four citizens, who were paid informers, August 9, 1869.

Had a narrow escape from capture at Morganton, North Carolina, March 17, 1870.

Shot Deputy Marshal Charles Chamberlain, September 25, 1871, at Dahlonega, Georgia.

Was concerned in the killing of Deputy Collector Peter Holtzclaw, and his secretary, Charles F. Waite, on the road from Asheville to Morganton, February 13, 1872.

Great efforts were made to capture me and break up my band from March, 1872, till December, 1874, during which time had many narrow escapes, and the total number of my enemies who lost their lives was thirty-seven, among whom was Deputy Marshal Edward Findley, considered to be the bravest and most reckless man in North Georgia, with whom I had a hand-to-hand conflict with pistol and bowie-knife, on the banks of the Chattahoochie river, near Gainesville, Hall county, Georgia, July 4, 1874. I was wounded in several places, and Findley was literally cut and shot to pieces. A large party of his friends started in my pursuit, and I kept concealed for several months.

In December, 1874, the troops were removed from my vicinity, and many of the marshals were dismissed from the service.

Mortally wounded Henry Boylin, a notorious revenue informer, April 14, 1875, at Asheville, North Carolina.

Killed Deputy Marshal Hermann Bradley near Mount Mitchell, North Carolina, August 26, 1875.

Was nearly captured at the house of James Welchell, near Big Laurel, North Carolina, by a detachment of the Second Infantry, October 11, 1875.

Seriously wounded Captain Nathan Price, of the Second Infantry, near Statesville, North Carolina, January 5, 1876.

From February, 1876, to January, 1878, but few raids were made by the United States marshals.

April 21, 1878, shot and instantly killed Judge Arthur Spates, as he was leaving the court-room in Franklin, Macon county, North Carolina.

May 4, 1878, the Governors of North and South Carolina combined to effect my capture, and a detachment of the City Guards from Charleston, South Carolina, and forty men from the Charlotte, North Carolina, "Grays," assisted by a large posse of United States marshals, and many citizens, entered on a campaign against my band.

June 15, 1878, an engagement between my band and the assaulting party took place near Mount Mitchell, North Carolina, resulting in the defeat of the military, with a loss of nine men and Deputy Marshals Fitzgerald and Murphy.

July 13, 1878, narrowly escaped capture by members of the Charlotte Grays, at the house of Mrs. Nancy Hambright, in Buncombe county, North Carolina.

In the encounter I wounded two men and killed a third, whose name I have not been able to learn.

September 15, 1878, assisted in the killing of Deputy Marshal Richard Allison, near Asheville, North Carolina, and took as a prisoner Miss Gabrielle Austin, who was his companion.

October 4, 1878, shot my lieutenant, Henry Bray, for treachery.

Recapitulation.

Number of men killed from September 15, 1867, to October 4, 1878, by the band of which I am a leader, 227.

Number of men killed in whose death I was directly concerned—54.

Number of United States marshals killed, 12.

[NOTE BY EDITOR.—This list, up to the date given, is a correct one; but in the past few months Redmond has shot, and either killed or seriously wounded many more. Up to the hour of publication he had not been captured. To give anything like a detailed account of Redmond's many adventures, narrated with great fidelity in the manuscript placed in Miss Austin's hands, would be impossible in a volume of this size; we have therefore selected some of the most prominent, and give them a condensed form.]

Redmond is Captured by the Negro Informer, Toby Small; Escapes, and two days afterwards Kills Small.

In the month of December, 1868, Redmond made a trip to Oconee county, South Carolina, to superintend the establishment of a branch distillery, and to more thoroughly organize his followers in that State. A citizen who was in sympathy with the Federal authorities recognized the outlaw as he was riding past his house, and gave the alarm to a notorious revenue informer, a negro of Herculean stature, named Toby Small. On receiving the information, Small mounted his horse and started out in pursuit. He rode on to Walhalla, the county-seat, and learned there that no such man had been seen to enter the town. Thinking perhaps that Redmond had taken the river road, a few miles from the town, and rode down to Seneca City, at the junction of the Blue Ridge & Air-Line Railroads, Small pushed on to that place, and was overjoyed to learn that Redmond was at that minute eating dinner at the hotel. Had Small been possessed of less avarice he would probably have succeeded in capturing Redmond, but he coveted the entire reward offered for his apprehension, and determined to attempt the capture of the desperate outlaw unaided.

He would not be allowed to enter the hotel dining-room on account of his color, so he contented himself with watching for the desperado, when he should issue from the house. He had not long to wait. Redmond soon finished his dinner and strolled out to seek the stable where he had left his horse. The negro followed him. Redmond had ordered his horse to be fed, and made ready for a further journey whilst he was at dinner, and the animal stood in front of the stable door, ready saddled and bridled, awaiting his pleasure. As he approached, the negro hostler came out of the stable and led the horse toward him. Redmond, with his accustomed liberality, rewarded the negro generously, and, placing his foot in the stirrup and his hand on the neck of his horse, was about to vault into the saddle, when Toby Small stepped suddenly behind, and seizing him by the arm presented a cocked pistol at his head, and called upon him to surrender.

Redmond wheeled quickly, and this frightened his horse, which trotted off toward Walhalla. There was a determined expression in the negro's eye, which caused the outlaw to hesitate about resisting and to obey the command, "Throw up your hands." Then, with his pistol still presented, the informer ordered the hostler to remove Redmond's weapons and bring them to him. The hostler hesitated, but Small threatened him with death if he disobeyed his command, and Redmond was soon disarmed and at the mercy of his captor.

Small then ordered Redmond to march in front of him to the hotel, and, with his arms still raised above his head, the outlaw did so. A crowd of course collected at the unusual spectacle of a fine-looking, well-dressed white man in the custody of a negro, and taking advantage of this excitement Redmond made a bold dash for liberty. The negro had dropped the muzzle of his pistol to reply to some question of a bystander, and he was so excited that he did not think to use it in the proper way, but instead, raised it aloft and hurled it at Redmond's head with all his strength.

The heavy missile went true to its aim and struck the retreating outlaw in the head. He staggered; blood gushed from the wound, and the negro bounded forward with a cry of joy; but Redmond was only stunned for a moment, and recovering himself he leaped forward, and ran toward the woods as only a man can who realizes that his life depends upon the effort. The negro, with a yell of rage, started after him, crying:

"Cotch him! Cotch him! I'll give one hun'ed dollahs to de man wha' cotches him!"

The promise of reward stimulated several to start in pursuit, but the fleeing man had gained so much and so steadily increased the distance—he ran like a deer—that they gave it up, leaving Toby Small to continue the pursuit.

Redmond struck the forest, on the right hand side of the Walhalla road, and at first ran at random, but finding a sharp lookout for his enemy. He reached the highway at last, and was overjoyed to perceive his horse quietly feeding by the roadside.

So admirably trained was the animal, that when Redmond approached he raised his head and came trotting toward him with a neigh of welcome. He suffered himself to be caught, and with the bridle over his arm, Redmond walked back into the pine forest a short distance, where he had crossed a small branch.

Here he washed his wounded head, which had bled considerably from an ugly gash just above the occipital bone, and binding it up with his handkerchief, mounted his horse and rode across the country to the point where the branch distillery had been established. This was December 18. The next day his head pained him considerably, and he made inquiries regarding the presumed whereabouts of the negro informer. On the morning of December 20, Redmond learned that Toby Small had been seen in Westminster, a small station on the Air-Line Railroad, about six miles below Seneca City, where he was busily engaged in drowning his mortification at the escape of his prisoner in deep potations of villainous whiskey, imported from the North. His informant told him that Small would probably remain there for several days.

Without making known his intention, Redmond mounted his horse, and with two good pistols pendant from his belt, rode off in the direction of Westminster. He reached that place about three o'clock in the afternoon, and learning that Small was in a low grocery near the railroad, frequented a great deal by negroes, he hastened to the spot and boldly entered.

Small was in the act of drinking a glass of liquor as the outlaw stepped over the threshold, and looked up. Recognizing him, he dropped the liquor and attempted to draw a pistol. Redmond was too quick for him, however, and discharged his pistol at the distance of about ten paces, aiming at Small's heart.

The negro fell forward on his face, with the cry:

"Oh, God, I'm hit!"

The astounded loungers did not raise a hand to detain the daring assassin, and, with his smoking pistol still in his hand, Redmond backed quickly from the room, mounted his horse and rode away.

Toby Small was not killed outright, but the wound was a mortal one, and after lingering in great agony for several days, he finally died.

Redmond shoots United States Commissioner Irwin C. McDowell in the Post Office, Asheville, N.C.

In April, 1869, several of Redmond's band were captured by deputy marshals and taken to the jail in Asheville. One of these outlaws was the superintendent of a branch distillery, and Redmond was his staunch friend. It appears that after they were placed in the dungeon of the jail, this outlaw taunted one of the marshals, a desperate and determined man named Findley, who was afterwards killed by Redmond. Findley was of an irascible and hasty temperament, and drawing his pistol, shot the outlaw dead.

For this crime he was arrested and brought before United States Commissioner Irwin C. McDowell. So much influence was brought to bear upon the case in Findley's favor, that McDowell discharged him, and by this manifestly unjust action brought down upon his head Redmond's enmity.

On the morning of May 26, 1869, Commissioner McDowell went to the post-office in Asheville to get his mail matter. The room was crowded with citizens, and he was in conversation with a friend, when some one touched him on the shoulder. He turned and faced a cocked and leveled pistol, in the hands of a young man, whom he at once recognized as the dreaded outlaw Redmond.

The commissioner cried out:

"This is Redmond, seize him!" and bravely stepped forward to arrest the desperado, when the pistol was discharged and the brace commissioner fell with a bullet through his heart, and expired almost instantly.

As soon as the fatal deed was accomplished, Redmond dashed from the building, brandishing his pistol, and despite the efforts made to detain him, ran across the public square and into a drinking saloon, in the rear of which stood a horse ready saddled and bridled.

Mounting the animal Redmond clapped spurs to his sides, and with a yell of defiance rode rapidly off in the direction of the mountains.

Redmond has a Desperate and Bloody Encounter with Deputy United States Marshal Edward Findley, at Shallow Ford, Ga., on the banks of the Chattahoochie River. He is wounded several times but finally kills Findley.

Redmond had sworn to kill Deputy Marshal Edward Findley, for the unprovoked and cowardly murder of one of his lieutenants in the jail at Asheville. Findley belonged in Hall county, Georgia, and had the reputation of being a brave and desperate man. After his discharge by Commissioner McDowell he returned to his home, and thither Redmond followed him, but did not succeed in meeting him. Five years passed away, and Findley had probably forgotten the whole matter. Redmond, however, still harbored revengeful feelings toward the deputy marshal, and swore that if he ever met him, he would have his life, or give up his own.

It so happened that the fourth day of July, 1874, was to be celebrated by residents of Gainesville, the seat of Hall county, Ga., in an unusually patriotic manner. Redmond was in the neighborhood and determined to join in the festivities. With this object in view he mounted his horse early in the morning, and rode toward the town. He crossed the Chattahoochie river at Shallow Ford, and was ascending the bank on the Gainesville side, when he espied Findley riding toward him. Drawing his pistol, Redmond awaited the approach of his enemy.

When he was in range he fired, and put spurs to his horse to dash forward. Findley returned the fire and also pushed forward his horse. Thus they approached each other, still firing. Redmond was wounded once in the left shoulder, but still kept firing. In this way they emptied the contents of their pistols and neither had been killed. By this time they were as close to each other as it was possible to force their panting and frightened horses.

"I've sworn to have your life!" cried Redmond, springing to the ground and drawing a huge bowie-knife.

"Take it then!" was Findley's defiant reply, also jumping to the ground.

Both were determined, and with flashing eyes and distended nostrils they confronted each other, knife in hand, and watched for an advantage.

"I am Redmond!" cried the outlaw.

"That don't frighten me!" sneeringly replied Findley, who was bleeding from a bullet-wound in his cheek. "Come on!"

Redmond sprang forward and the two men closed in a terrible conflict. Their bright knives flashed in the sunlight and anon dripped with blood. It was a frightful combat. At first neither man seemed to have the advantage. Finally an adroit thrust from Redmond broke Findley's guard, and the keen knife entered to the hilt in the deputy marshal's breast. It was a mortal wound, and with a gasp of despair Findley fell to the ground. Redmond sprang toward him and completed the act by drawing the keen edge of his knife across the wounded man's throat. He was wounded himself in many places, but managed to reach one of the branch distilleries, where he remained until his wounds healed.

Redmond shoots Hon. Arthur Spates, a Judge of the Circuit Court, in the Court-House door, at Franklin, Macon county, N.C.

Hon. Arthur Spates was elected Judge of the Circuit Court in North Carolina, in 1876. His district was composed of what is known as the "mountain counties." The position was new to him, and some of his decisions and sentences were unnecessarily severe.

In March, 1878, one of Redmond's band, named Kinney, visited his home in Macon county, to assist his wife and young children, who were all sick with the fever. It was charged that Kinney had been concerned in the murder of a farmer some time during the previous winter, and had fled to the home of the "moonshiners" for protection. The evidence against him was purely circumstantial. Some of the neighbors learned that the suspected man was at his home, and a party was organized to secure him. Kinney was nursing his sick wife and children, when the citizens reached his house, and their entry was so entirely unsuspected, that he was secured before he had an opportunity to defend himself. It was charged that his wife knew something of the murder, and she was taken along with her husband to Franklin, the county-seat of Macon. One of the party volunteered to take charge of the sick children, and sent his wife to Kinney's house. This was the 2d of April, and although spring had fairly set in, the night of the capture of Kinney was cold and wet. The distance from Kinney's house to Franklin was about ten miles, and the journey thither was made on horseback. The exposure and mental anxiety was too much for the sick wife. Both she and her husband were confined in the jail, but in a few days she was taken out to die.

At the spring term of the court, which was held the last two weeks in April, Kinney was arraigned, and pleaded not guilty to the charge of murder. The farmer of whose death it was charged that he was guilty was a man well-to-do and generally respected. Much indignation against the murderer was aroused, and when, after a two days' trail, the jury in the case returned a verdict of guilty, the public were clamorous that the death sentence be imposed. Judge Spates therefore sentenced Kinney to be hanged, and he was removed to the jail to wait until his execution. In delivering the sentence Judge Spates used language unusually severe and bitter for the bench, and very impoliticly expressed the belief that Kinney's captors would have been justified, had they hanged him the night of his capture.

The night after the sentence a mob forced an entrance to the jail, and, despite the efforts of the sheriff to protect the prisoner, dragged Kinney from his cell and hanged him on the court-house green.

When Redmond was apprised of this outrage, he became very bitter against Judge Spates, whom he blamed for inciting the mob to riot. He lost no time in hastening to Franklin, arriving there at noon on the 21st of April, 1878. Court had just adjourned as the daring outlaw rode boldly into town, and when he arrived opposite the court-house door, Judge Spates was descending the steps, on the way to his hotel.

When he appeared Redmond drew his pistol, and taking deliberate aim, discharged the weapon. Judge Spates fell to the ground, his heart having been pierced by the leaden messenger. The crowd about the court-house were horror-stricken at the terrible tragedy, and before any one could summon enough self-possession to attempt the arrest of Redmond, he had galloped away.

Redmond narrowly escapes capture by Members of the Charlotte Grays, a North Carolina Militia Organization.

The killing of Judge Spates created considerable excitement in North and South Carolina, and the public press demanded that some decisive action be taken to secure the daring desperado. Governor Hampton, of South Carolina, and Governor Vance, of North Carolina, corresponded at some length over the matter, and at last, on May 4th, a detachment of the Charleston City Guards and forty men from the Charlotte Grays, were dispatched to the mountains to capture Redmond, and break up his band. On June 15th an engagement took place between the militia and the outlaws, resulting in the defeat of the former. Several attempts were afterwards made to capture Redmond by isolated bodies from both commands, but no concerted effort was made to rid the country of the desperate man and his equally desperate followers.

On the morning of the 13th of July, Redmond stopped at the house of one the members of his band, named Hambright. Mrs. Hambright entertained the outlaw chieftain, and started to prepare him a warm breakfast. She had a young baby, and Redmond, who has a great fondness for children, lifted the little one from the cradle and took him to the door, where he sat dancing the child on his knee, laughing merrily at the funny antics of the wee bit of humanity. His carbine was resting in one corner of the room, but two pistols depended from his waist belt.

He was yet dancing the child, unconscious of danger, when a noise in front caused him to raise his head. The house was surrounded by men in the uniform of the Charlotte Grays. With a look over his shoulder into the room, Redmond tossed the prattling infant over his head onto the soft feather bed. Then drawing his pistols he dashed towards the soldiers, firing as he ran. Three men fell before his unerring aim, one of these with a mortal wound. They closed about him in great numbers, but he dashed down several who opposed him, and breaking through the line ran like a deer for the woods, amid a perfect hail of bullets. He reached the shelter of the woods in safety, and halting for a moment to hurl maledictions of defiance at his enemies, he disappeared in the forest, and the militia picked up their dead and wounded comrades, and returned sorrowfully to Asheville.

Redmond's Last Exploit.

We learn that a few weeks ago the redoubtable outlaw, whose life-history has been briefly sketched in these pages, performed, with the assistance of his desperate followers, a deed of daring that eclipses any of his precious exploits. It appears that after the departure of Miss Austin from his mountain retreat he formed the acquaintance of a young lady living in Asheville, the daughter of one of the wealthiest men in Western North Carolina. The meeting between the two was a romantic episode, and characteristic of human nature in its *finale*. This young lady, Miss Minnie Stevens, was wandering with a party of lady and gentlemen friends, among the picturesque beauties of that section of country, and got lost on the mountain. Suddenly, in her hurried scramble among the rocks, she reached an open plateau, hemmed in on three sides by gigantic boulders. A yellow panther, with bloodshot eyes, crouched in one corner of the plateau, ready for the fatal spring. Miss Stevens was paralyzed with fear, and the panther was creeping toward her with greedy eyes, when Redmond suddenly appeared and killed the brute by a shot from his carbine. He retuned Miss Stevens to her friends, and it appears that the young lady fell dead in love with the golden-haired outlaw. They met clandestinely, and she finally consented to become his wife. Her father in vain attempted to dissuade her from the step. The young lady was determined. Preparations were made for the wedding, and one day the bold outlaw summoned about him his hardy followers and apprised them of the coming event. With a body-guard of two hundred and fifty "moonshiners" Redmond rode into Asheville, on his wedding night. Before the authorities could divine what was the meaning of this sudden influx of armed men, Redmond had captured the town and trusted sentries were posted around the houses of the United States Commissioner and the Sheriff. The strange spectacle of a dreaded outlaw in possession of a populous town was thus presented. Every means to prevent a surprise was taken, and when every one who would possibly do injury to the King of the "Moonshiners" was covered by pistols that never missed fire, Redmond entered the house of his intended bride, and the two were made one. After the wedding festivities were over, the outlaw summoned his followers to his side, and with three rousing cheers for the newly-made wife, the band galloped off into the night.

Front cover of *The True Life of Redmond,* by R. A. Cobb. Courtesy of the North Carolina Collection, University of North Carolina at Chapel Hill.

THE TRUE LIFE
OF
MAJ. LEWIS RICHARD REDMOND,
THE NOTORIOUS
OUTLAW
AND FAMOUS
MOONSHINER,
OF
WESTERN NORTH CAROLINA,
WHO WAS
BORN IN SWAIN COUNTY, N.C., IN THE YEAR 1855, AND ARRESTED
APRIL 7TH, 1881

WRITTEN BY
R. A. COBB, DEPUTY COLLECTOR OF THE SIXTH DISTRICT OF
NORTH CAROLINA, MORGANTON, N.C.

RALEIGH:
EDWARDS, BROUGHTON & CO., STEAM PRINTERS AND BINDERS.
1881.

PREFACE.

Feeling that it is but just to the subject of this sketch to place him aright before the public, I have undertaken the task of compiling the account of his varied and adventurous career, which follows.

Redmond has been greatly slandered by printer's ink. He has committed murder, he has violated the Internal Revenue laws systematically and with defiance; but he never did either the good things or the bad things which the lives heretofore published of him make him do.

One of those so-called lives, published in Philadelphia under the attractive title of "The Entwined Lives of Miss Gabrielle Austin and of Redmond the Outlaw, written by Bishop Crittenden, of North Carolina," is a hoax, and a fraudulent hoax, throughout. It is sufficient to say in regard to it that there is no Bishop Crittenden in North Carolina and that Redmond has no female acquaintance by the name of Gabrielle Austin. So that the "entwining" aforesaid is a pure matter of moonshine, originating in the back streets of the Quaker City by some poor penman hungry for bread.

There are many sorts of lies, as we all know. Great writers have classified and illustrated the different species; but the lie of the dime novel, the lie written to feed a hungry belly by some starving hack, who harasses a diseased imagination for the substitute of facts—that type of the lie carries with it such a cry for charity that even good men smile, pity, and pass it by.

In this blood-and-thunder pamphlet Redmond kills a United States Commissioner, Irwin C. McDowell, in the post-office at Asheville, N.C., kills the Hon. Arthur Spates, a Judge of the Circuit Court, in the court-house at Franklin, Macon county, and has a Charleston company of infantry and the "Charlotte Grays" detailed by Governors Vance and Hampton to capture him.

Now there is a post-office at Asheville and there is a court-house at Franklin and the names of the Governors are right, the rest is a bad sort of lie badly told. In fact, there is a murder to the page of this little pamphlet, and when horrors have actually palled upon the composer, he quits with this amusing entry:

"Recapitulation.

Number of men killed from September 15, 1867, to October 4, 1878, by the band of which I am a leader, 227.
Number of men killed in whose death I am directly concerned—54.
Number of United States Marshals killed—12.

[Note by the Editor: This list, up to the date given, is a correct one; but in the past few months Redmond has shot, and either killed or seriously wounded many more. Up to the hour of publication he had not been captured. To give anything like a detailed account of Redmond's many adventures, narrated with great fidelity in the manuscript placed in Miss Austin's hands, would be impossible in a volume of this size; we have therefore selected some of the most prominent, and give them in a condensed form.]"

I have not time to speak more of this print, which grossly libels the people of my native mountains. It is the life of an outlaw, but not the kind of outlaw Major Redmond is, whose word I have for it that, while he may deserve the Albany penitentiary, he ought not to be paraded in print as a second Murrell.[1]

He has never baby farmed or advertised himself in the *Herald* as having studied abortion in Paris, followed by an appeal for patients. He never knew Mary Stinard, as her pastor and guide, and would really have given poor Jennie Crammer a helping hand on that dark night by the sea-beach.

His killing has been confined to men, and to men in open daylight with guns in their hands. He would beg his Philadelphia publishers to make him a remittance and to confine their enterprise for the future to that part of our broad domain which is more fruitful of matter for the uses of "Illustrated Covers," than the plain but proud Old North State can ever hope to be.

In conclusion, whatever is herein set down hath at least this merit: It is the tale as told me by Redmond himself. I give it as I got it.

The Author

THE TRUE LIFE OF MAJ. LEWIS R. REDMOND.

Major Lewis R. Redmond's Parentage—His Early Life,
Disposition, Habits and Marriage—Aspiration to be
Called a Bully by his Comrades.

While the lives of hundreds of men have been written and eagerly sought after by those who spend sleepless nights poring over the pages with as much zeal as the miser does in delving after hidden treasures, and after those books have been read and reread, we are at a loss to know whether there ever lived such a man as the hero, and whether the mighty deeds so vividly portrayed by word and illustration, are true or false. In presenting this work to my readers, I propose to give the truth, and not fiction.

Maj. Lewis Richard Redmond was born in the county of Macon, now Swain county, North Carolina.[2] His father's name was Richard Redmond, his mother's name was Rusk.[3] Major Redmond was born in the year 1855, making him at the time of his last capture twenty-six years old. His education is quite limited. In fact, a near relative of his informs me that he has known him from infancy; that he never went to school a day in his life; that he never manifested any fondness for books from childhood to the present, but that his mind always seemed to run in a different direction. His disposition has always been wild and roving. He has never been satisfied long at any one place.

Richard Redmond, the Major's father, lived in Swain county until Major Redmond was seven years old.[4] He then moved to Transylvania county, where he lived until the year 1870. About this time the Major's father and mother both died. He then courted a Miss Ladd, whom he afterwards married. His wife was born and reared in Transylvania county, North Carolina. Before they were married some suspicions arose in the neighborhood that Redmond and Miss Ladd were too intimate for people who were not married. Redmond, having some apprehension that the law might be enforced, went to South Carolina, where he and Miss Ladd were afterwards married. They have lived together ever since. Two children were born to them before marriage; they lived together from the time they were married in South Carolina until the year 1877, when they moved from South Carolina to Swain county, North Carolina.[5]

Major Redmond is six feet high, weighed when arrested 190 pounds, is of rather dark complexion, with black hair and moustache, blue eyes, with a pleasant countenance and a commanding appearance. He is one of those men who once seen is never forgotten. Redmond also possesses the tact of exerting a powerful influence over men, and especially young men, whose character is not formed, and whose habits are not fixed. He is fully aware of the famous reputation that has gone abroad about him, and seems to take pride in the name of "Redmond, the outlaw."

On all occasions he seems to exert himself to sustain his reputation as a bully among followers. It is his custom when any person manifests a desire to form his acquaintance, to introduce himself thus: "Sir, you say you want to form the acquaintance of Maj. Redmond, the outlaw. This is the man! I am Maj. Redmond, the famous outlaw of whom you have heard so much talk; the man who has killed so many men! Sir, take a good look at me, so you will know me the next time you see me." Men who are familiar with his life, say that when he introduces himself to a stranger or any person whom he would be likely to come in contact with at any time, he endeavors to expand his muscles and cause his personal appearance to present as formidable an aspect as possible.

Redmond has not only gained a well earned State reputation as the king of "moonshiners," but has a national reputation. Soon after the last capture and arrest of Maj. Redmond in Swain county, North Carolina, the following appeared in the *Police News,* a newspaper published in the city of New York, which I herewith quote to give the reader some idea of the reputation of the subject of this volume. When Redmond was arrested, comments were made and long articles appeared in nearly all the leading newspapers throughout the United States:

(Comments from the *Police News* of the 7th May, 1881.)

"Major Lewis R. Redmond, the Outlaw, Captured—The Famous Moonshiner, the American Robin Hood, at last in Jail, with six Bullet Wounds.

"Maj. Lewis R. Redmond, the notorious moonshiner and outlaw, who has so long and so successfully evaded arrest, has at last been captured. He was placed in Asheville jail on Monday the 25th April, being taken to that place from the mountains by a guard of six men. He fought like a tiger for this freedom, and carried in his body six bullet wounds, the result of his obstinate resistance. Redmond is really the king moonshiner of the United States. He is a Georgian by birth, and is only 27 years old. He and his father both have been engaged in Transylvania county, North Carolina, in the distillation of illicit whiskey. The old man attended to the distillery while Redmond Jr. traveled about and sold the proceeds of the old man's labor. The Major's first notorious crime was the murder near Brevard in Transylvania county, North Carolina, in the spring of 1875, of United States Deputy Marshal Duckworth.[6] Redmond agreed to surrender to Duckworth, and when the latter lowered his pistol, Redmond drew his pistol and shot him through the throat, producing death in a few hours. A price of 600 dollars was soon after put upon his head. His headquarters have been in South Carolina, in the heart of the Blue Ridge Mountains, near the junction of the White Waters and Toxaway rivers, where his log cabin could be approached only by two narrow mountain paths. Shortly after this change of base, over 500 able bodied mountaineers were organized in this wild country under the lead of Redmond's dare-devil spirit, who heralded every approach of the revenue officers by beacon fires at night, using signal horns by day. Spies have been mercilessly shot or hung. In the winter of 1876 Deputy Marshals Bastin, Moore and Gray, with two citizens, captured Redmond by an ambush, but he escaped from them, borrowed a gun, and shot Bastin and another man. Bastin was badly wounded, and before he recovered, Redmond visited his residence and proposed to hang him. He confiscated Bastin's horse and one hundred dollars in money, and was satisfied to depart after Bastin promised never to molest him again.[7] Capt. E. G. Hoffman had good success in bringing in some members of Redmond's gang, but the outlaw continued at large, although rewards aggregating fifteen hundred dollars were offered for him. Three years ago the State militia was called out to pursue him, but accomplished nothing. The full details of his escapes from revenue officers would fill a volume.

"In September, 1878, Redmond married Miss Bell Ladd, one of his numerous mistresses.[8] At the time of her marriage she was the mother of two children, of whom Redmond claims to be the father. Of the extent of Redmond's power and influence some opinion may be formed from the fact that 378 of his followers plead guilty to illicit distilling at one term of the Federal Court, and as many more were released on bond.

"The circumstances of Redmond's capture were as follows: He was at his house, when some revenue officers went to arrest him, they having concealed themselves in the bushes near by, but being soon detected by Redmond's dogs, Redmond took his gun and went to investigate the matter, when he was hailed by the party to halt. He immediately raised his gun to shoot, but was fired upon by the officers, some of whose balls took effect, and will in all probability result in his death. He said to Deputy Marshal Ray and his gang, who shot him: 'You have shot me. I have never surrendered, nor ever would have done so.' His capture took place in Swain county, where his house is on the banks of the picturesque Tennessee River, ingeniously ensconced among the cliffs. His front yard had this deep and rapid stream for a fence. On the south is a mountain, whose perpendicular side next to the house is entirely impassable. On the east and west are cliffs, which, while they are not so perpendicular nor so high, had never been trod by the foot of a human being, and these, closing in and projecting over the river, make the best natural fortification one can imagine. In this natural enclosure are about six acres of alluvial soil of remarkable fertility. Here, for the last three years Redmond has been farming and enjoying the sweets of domestic happiness, if such a wild and tameless spirit can be said to enjoy anything. No illicit stills were found anywhere on the premises by those who accomplished the arrest."

The Killing of Deputy Marshal Duckworth—The First Important Event of Redmond's Wonderful Life.

The first time we saw the name of Maj. Lewis R. Redmond heralded from fireside to cross-roads, from town to city, then over the telegraph wires throughout our great nation, was in consequence of his killing Deputy Marshal Duckworth, near Brevard, in Transylvania county. In the year 1876, Redmond, as has been said, was engaged in illicit distilling. He had frequently sent word to the officers that distilling whiskey was a privilege that he had a perfect right to, and that he intended to make whiskey at all hazards, and defied the officers to molest him under pain of death. Redmond, being guilty of illicit distilling and retailing whiskey, which was contrary both to the State and United States laws, a warrant was issued for his arrest and placed in the hands of Deputy Marshal Duckworth, who felt it to be his duty as an officer of the Government to execute the warrant and bring Redmond before a United States Commissioner to answer the charges against him. Consequently Duckworth proceeded to arrest Redmond, and in doing so he told Redmond he had a warrant for him charging illicit distilling, whereupon Redmond replied that it was all right—that he would go with him and give him no trouble, but that he (Duckworth) must not take his pistol away from him. The two men started off quietly together, and Redmond making such fair promises, Duckworth had confidence in his word, and was in the act of putting the warrant in his pocket and his pistol in its sheath, when Redmond drew his pistol in an instant and shot Duckworth through the neck, the ball striking Duckworth's collar button, and killing him instantly. There being no one near at this moment, Redmond made his escape to the mountains.

"The Killing of Duckworth." Courtesy of the North Carolina Collection, University of North Carolina at Chapel Hill.

From the Killing of Duckworth Redmond Gains Great Notoriety as a King Moonshiner and Notorious Outlaw.

After the killing of Duckworth Major Redmond gained great reputation as a desperate character. All men, after they form a character for bravery, and have success in their undertakings, whether good or bad, invariably have followers. This was the case with Major Redmond. The killing of Duckworth gave him a reputation for bravery among his brother mountaineers, who consequently regarded him as their leader, as in fact he was regarded by all the moonshiners of Western North Carolina and South Carolina. From that time on he enlisted under his banner a host of ruffians of like passions with himself, and these, organized into a band, made a formidable resistance to all officers of the law. When any attempt was made to interfere with the illicit distillation of whiskey in Western North Carolina, or the northern part of South Carolina, Redmond had only to sound the signal and his warriors were ready to march at a moment's notice. For five or six years any attempt on the part of the officers to arrest Redmond or any of his gang was considered a forlorn hope and a hazardous undertaking.

Redmond in South Carolina Baffles all Efforts to Arrest him by State Authorities.

Redmond, after the killing of Duckworth, extended his territory to a much larger field. Instead of appearing in Transylvania county and a few adjoining counties, he operated in South Carolina and in Georgia. He became known in South Carolina as a desperate character and outlaw, and baffling all ordinary attempts to arrest him, and his illicit whiskey dealing became a nuisance to the good citizens of the State. The authorities being anxious to rid its citizens of this outlaw and his traffic in whiskey, the State authorities offered the sum of six hundred dollars for the apprehension and arrest of Redmond, but this failed to secure his arrest. A portion of the State militia was afterwards called out to secure the arrest of Redmond, which force had a number of encounters with him, but his sagacious mind, keen perception and alluring manners baffled all their skill and generalship, and at last left the Major lord of all he surveyed, king of the woods and cock of the walk. Thus, after the skill of the State militia was exhausted, the State authority was at an end. In 1878, however, a squad of revenue officers from South Carolina pursued and captured Redmond with his wagon and team, loaded with illicit whiskey, and feeling so confident that their long-sought for prey was secure. Redmond, with his characteristic shrewdness, took advantage of an unguarded moment and again made his escape to the mountains, leaving his wagon, team and whiskey to be dealt with as the law might direct. In pursuit of him by the revenue officers they mistook Redmond's brother-in-law for Redmond himself, and endeavoring to arrest him, as he belonged to the outlaw band, he offered that same stern resistance which Redmond was accustomed to do himself. He was shot and killed on the ground in attempting to make his escape. This occurrence, which resulted in the death of one of his gang, and also one that he mainly relied upon when he had a big undertaking to perform, Redmond felt deeply, and was greatly enraged thereat.[9]

Our outlaw had by this time become convinced that he would be executed if ever taken, and the terror which his name caused among the peaceable people of the neighborhood where he might happen to reside, was, perhaps, the one gratification of his life at this time. It was in the highest degree satisfying to his rude vanity when he witnessed the travail of poor abject souls who heard his name pronounced by himself, on some secluded mountain road, on which he might be met at almost any time, going to or returning from some visit to the many illicit distilleries of which he was the *Cerberus*.

Redmond in the State of Georgia.

Raven county, Ga., is one of the most noted counties in that State for illicit distilling and resistance to officers.[10] Major Redmond's fame had ere this time reached this section. He therefore thought this locality would afford a fine field for him to operate in, and to pursue his much cherished occupation of illicit distilling, and changed his base of operations, for the time being, to this new field. All went very well for a while, but, unfortunately for Redmond, Raven county was supplied with field officers, and Redmond, not being a native of the State, these men told him he would have to be content with a Lieutenant's place; but this did not suit the outlaw's ambitious disposition. If he could not be the biggest man in the woods, he was not content with being second in command. Hence, after thoroughly surveying the ground, he decided that his native State, and the hills of Western North Carolina and upper South Carolina, afforded a finer field for him to operate in. Further still, these Georgia moonshiners, being familiar with his fame, had become jealous of him, and thinking, too, that his presence in their midst might operate against their illicit distilling, they failed to give him that encouragement which he expected to receive at their hands. After making two or three unsuccessful attempts to establish what he considered to be his rights, and that honor which he thought his just merit, and after making several narrow escapes from capture by the revenue officials, Redmond made his way back to South Carolina. I have no reliable information which induces me to believe that during his residence in Georgia he was guilty of any greater offence against law or morals than the making of blockade whiskey.[11] The following sensational account of a supposed incident in his Georgia career is wholly without foundation, as I have the best of reasons for knowing. It is taken from one of several sensational lives of Lewis Redmond, to which reference has been made in the first part of this little volume. As a lie out of the whole cloth it deservedly ranks high, and in that connection alone it is offered:

[From Bishop Crittenden's Life of Redmond, pages 76 and 77.]

"Redmond has a Desperate and Bloody Encounter with Deputy United States Marshal Edward Findley, at Shallow Ford, Ga., on the Banks of the Chattahoochie River—He is wounded Several times, but finally kills Findley.

Redmond had sworn to kill Deputy Marshal Edward Findley, for the unprovoked and cowardly murder of one of his lieutenants in the jail at Asheville. Findley belonged in Hall county, Georgia, and had the reputation of being a brave and desperate man. After his discharge by Commissioner McDowell he returned to his home, and thither Redmond followed him, but did not succeed in meeting him. Five years passed away, and Findley had probably forgotten the whole matter. Redmond, however, still harbored revengeful feelings toward the deputy marshal, and swore that if he ever met him, he would have his life, or give up his own.

It so happened that the fourth day of July, 1874, was to be celebrated by the residents of Gainesville, the seat of Hall county, Ga., in an unusually patriotic manner. Redmond was in the neighborhood and determined to join in the festivities. With this object in view he mounted his horse early in the morning, and rode toward the town. He crossed the Chattahoochie river at Shallow Foard, and was ascending the bank on the Gainesville side, when he espied Findley riding toward him. Drawing his pistol, Redmond awaited the approach of his enemy.

When he was in range he fired, and put spurs to his horse to dash forward. Findley returned the fire and also pushed forward his horse. Thus they approached each other, still firing. Redmond was wounded once in the left shoulder, but still kept firing. In this way they emptied the contents of their pistols and neither had been killed. By this time they were as close to each other as it was possible to force their panting and frightened horses.

"I've sworn to have your life!" cried Redmond, springing to the ground and drawing a huge bowie-knife.

"Take it then!" was Findley's defiant reply, also jumping to the ground.

Both were determined, and with flashing eyes and distended nostrils they confronted each other, knife in hand, and watched for an advantage.

"I am Redmond!" cried the outlaw.

"That don't frighten me!" sneeringly replied Findley, who was bleeding from the bullet wound in his cheek. "Come on!"

Redmond sprang forward and the two men closed in a terrible conflict. Their bright knives flashed in the sunlight, and anon dripped with blood. It was a frightful combat. At first neither man seemed to have the advantage. Finally an adroit thrust from Redmond broke Findley's guard, and the keen knife entered to the hilt in the deputy marshal's breast. It was a mortal wound, and with a gasp of despair Findley fell to the ground. Redmond sprang toward him and completed the act by drawing the keen edge of his knife across the wounded man's throat. He was wounded himself in many places, but managed to reach one of the branch distilleries, where he remained until his wounds healed."

Redmond Again in South Carolina—
His Friends Advise him to Seek Other Locality
for his Field of Operations.

In the year 1878 Redmond was again in South Carolina, and upon arriving in that State, he of course assumed command of his old veterans, consisting of desperadoes and moonshiners, and having such resources at his command he felt all confidence in his ability to accomplish anything that he saw proper to undertake. After holding a council of war with his colleagues, it was decided to establish a regular line of communication between the moonshiners of Western North Carolina and the whiskey dealers of upper South Carolina. Redmond set about to find men in whom he could place all confidence—men who lived along the line between where the whiskey was made and where it was to be sold. He soon succeeded in effecting this arrangement and a regular line for the transportation of illicit whiskey was established from East Tennessee down the Tennessee River through Swain, Jackson, Macon, and Transylvania counties, N.C., into South Carolina. This arrangement continued for about two years in successful operation before any suspicion arose that such a traffic was going on, or if any suspicion did prevail, the name of Redmond at the head of it was enough for those people to know, that caused them to keep it a profound secret. But as all unlawful transactions and evasions of the law must come to naught sooner or later, this wholesale traffic in illicit whiskey was finally detected by the revenue officers. The first encounter the officers had with Redmond on this line was in the year 1879. They overtook him about the North and South Carolina line with a wagon heavily loaded with blockade whiskey and seized his wagon and team; but Redmond, with that determination to evade the law and to escape from justice at all hazards, made his escape, barely saving his life, as the officers fired a number of carbines at him while running. His lines now being broken, he was at a loss to know what course to follow, but his strong determination was not to be baffled by small difficulties. He soon recovered from this loss and began operations on the same line on a more extensive scale with probably a few changes in his places of deposit of whiskey. About this time or soon after, some of his kinsfolk, being a little more considerate than himself and foreseeing the difficulty that Redmond was likely to bring upon himself and his friends, persuaded him to change his base and occupy a different field, as his movements were becoming known to all classes in that section. His friends and kinsfolk proposed to him if he would leave the country and emigrate where he was not known, they would give him a wagon, team and outfit for travel. He agreed to do so, and was soon on his way going, as his friends thought, to parts unknown. Three days' travel, however, brought him to Swain County, on the Tennessee River, one of the most mountainous and rugged portions of Western North Carolina. This was near the spot where he was born and where he spent most of his boyhood days. After careful consideration Redmond decided that the place was especially adapted to the business that he wished to pursue—namely, illicit distilling and evading the revenue officers, he set about to secure and make all necessary arrangements. The land then belonged to Mr. T. N. Freeman, to whom he represented his wish to lease the same for the purpose of engaging in stock raising, promising at the same time to put some improvements on the land.[12] He leased the land for three years, built a small cabin and cleared a small patch for a garden. Being thus cut off from the world, he was permitted to enjoy the even tenor of his way for a length of time, but, like a young lion, could not be content in so small a cage as the one he now occupied.

Redmond again in North Carolina, his Native State, where he Continued to live Until his last Arrest.

When leaving South Carolina at the solicitation of friends and kinsfolk, Redmond was careful to make the impression on all that he was going to parts unknown; but when they next heard from him, he was near his old home in Swain county, on the bank of the Tennessee river. As I stated in the previous chapter, Redmond represented to Freeman that his object in coming to this place was for the purpose of farming and raising stock. He went to work, built him a cabin out of logs twenty feet square, a small barn for his stock, which was the extent of his improvements, and with the exception of a small patch he cleared as a blind to leave the impression he was farming for a living. After selecting this secluded sport, which cut him off from the world and the balance of mankind, his name he thought would soon be forgotten, and his deeds would be remembered against him no more; but when we would do well, evil is always before us. Redmond, in his quiet little log cabin, began to reason within himself thus: To raise corn on these rugged hills at 25 cents per bushel is nonsense, to raise stock would necessitate my coming in contact with the outside world to sell these stock, but to make illicit whiskey I can be

"Home of Redmond." Courtesy of the North Carolina Collection, University of North Carolina at Chapel Hill.

cut off from the world, and only have intercourse with men of like disposition with myself. And so the next we hear of Maj. Redmond, he has a large illicit distillery in full operation on the bank of the Tennessee River, within a mile of his house. His fame as a desperado and outlaw soon followed him. His friends and sympathizers flocked to him, and he was at once proclaimed their leader. His gang was again organized, while blockade distilling commenced all over the county at once. When any attempt was made on the part of officers to detect and suppress illicit distilling, these moonshiners all took shelter under Redmond's wing for protection, and Swain county from 1879 up to the time Redmond was arrested, April 7th, 1881, was considered on of the worst blockading counties in Western North Carolina. It was considered more dangerous by the officers to execute the law there than in any section of the State, and this arose principally from the character Maj. Redmond had acquired. We would not, however, have our reader to believe that Redmond was guilty of all that was charged to have been done by him. It is similar to a General in the army, whatever desperate deeds are done by the soldiers under command, whether done within his knowledge or not, the whole is charged to the General, and he is held personally responsible for them all. The same applies to Maj. Redmond. He was the acknowledged chief of the moonshiners, and any violation of the law, such as distilling, selling and resisting officers in that section went to the account of Redmond, the outlaw; and we think justly so, as his fame as a desperate character was heralded all over the country, and an officer was considered in great danger who incurred his displeasure. This gave boldness and energy to all the moonshiners. Consequently in the section of country where Redmond operated it was almost impossible to execute the laws, and while many good citizens would have been glad to have had the illicit traffic in whiskey put down, yet they could not afford to incur the displeasure of Redmond or any of his followers, upon pain of death or great private injury. Those moonshiners had so much faith in Redmond's ability to protect them that they would make threats against any man who dared to report them, and would carry the same out at the risk of their lives. In this way it was impossible for the officers to get any clue leading to the detection and suppression of illicit distilling in the Redmond territory.

Redmond at a Baptist Association in Swain County.

The following incident I have from a reliable party, who was present and witnessed the whole scene:

It is common in the western part of North Carolina for members of Baptist churches to have annually what they call an Association—something similar to a Methodist Conference or a Presbyterian Synod. There the delegates of all the churches meet together and transact the business pertaining to the welfare of their churches. These meetings invariably bring together a large concourse of people, and on one such occasion, in the summer of 1880, in Swain county, North Carolina, Redmond presented himself, and after the hour for service was over, very cordially invited all persons who wished to buy some good blockade whiskey to come out to the woods with him and he would sell them as much as they wanted. A United States Commissioner, who came to hear preaching, was present. Redmond at once discovered him, and with his gang offered every insult imaginable in order to bring on a row; but the Commissioner saw that the odds were all against him, that Redmond was armed and prepared for a fight, and to avoid any difficulty, was forced, with a friend, to make a premature ride from the church to Charleston the same evening, and several hours sooner than they would have done. Thus you see that a man with Redmond's reputation, and following the life that he did, loses all fear of God, respect for religion, and regard for his fellow-man.

Capt. A. C. Bryan and his Squad of Special Force in Pursuit of Redmond in the Winter of 1879.

Letters being frequently sent to the Commissioner of Internal Revenue at Washington, D.C., for relief by the good citizens of Western North Carolina, stating that the illicit traffic in whiskey was assuming large proportions, and that it was becoming a source of great annoyance to the better class of citizens, from the fact that those moonshiners had become so bold in their illicit traffic they had bid defiance to the civil authorities, and rendered the law powerless. These letters were referred to Dr. J. J. Mott, Collector of the Sixth District of North Carolina.[13] Dr. Mott resolved at once to render such aid as he had at his command, to relieve the citizens of this alleged annoyance, and, if possible, to stop illicit distilling in that section. He therefore dispatched Capt. A. C. Bryan, who was in charge of a strong special force, with instruction to make a thorough canvass in all the Western counties, to destroy all the illicit distilleries he could find, to aid the marshals in bringing all the moonshiners to a speedy trial before the proper tribunals, and if possible to capture Redmond, the outlaw, and all of his followers.[14] Bryan reached the vicinity of where Redmond lived and was operating early in the spring of 1879, and went to a distillery said to belong to Maj. Redmond. It was afterwards ascertained that he was a partner in this distillery, but by the aid of his spies and by signals given, when the officers were approaching the outlaw made his escape into the woods about twenty minutes before Bryan reached the distillery, which he found in full operation. Bryan and his squad captured in the distillery at work a man by the name of Walls, who was long obstinate and positively refused to surrender, and had to be taken by force. He swore that he was attending to his own business and that no man had any right to interfere with him.

The feeling which dominates in the breasts of all such men is admirably voiced in the following interview had with Redmond. Speaking for his class he said, or is supposed to have said:

"The custom of distilling liquor from grain and fruit is one immemorial in the western portion of my native State. The people are a hardy, resolute body, and are continually warring with nature for subsistence. A lack of communicative facilities with the outside world necessitates the conversion of our staple products into the smallest possible bulk. As is well known, our principal products are fruit and corn. These are taken to market in the shape of distilled liquor. Before the war there was no tax upon liquors, and when the Federal Congress imposed a duty as a means of affording revenue to pay the interest on the enormous war debt, the burden fell heavily on these hardy mountaineers. For reasons which I shall not here attempt to explain, it is impossible for the small farmers to pay the tax on distilled liquors with profit to themselves. But they must live, and they can only live as their father lived before them, by growing corn and fruit, distilling it into liquor, and selling it to the outside world, free of tax. I believe the law taxing liquor an unjust and tyrannical imposition. We have a right to protest against laws which injure us. If our protest is not heeded, the document which declared us a free and independent nation instructs us to exercise our right and duty, and 'throw off such government,' and the men who are associated with me believe that the law which forbids us to manufacture the products of our own land without first paying the government a tax thereon unjust. We believe that we are right in resisting this law, and to resist it we have mutually pledged to each other 'our lives, our fortunes and our sacred honor.'"[15]

R. A. Cobb and Squad of Special Force in Pursuit of Redmond in February, 1881.

Redmond remained at ease at his favorite occupation from 1879 to 1881, when Capt. Cobb, in charge of the special force, in February, 1881, made a raid into Swain county, where it was reported Redmond was entrenched and operating an illicit distillery.

On the night of the 28th of February, 1881, Cobb and his force left Charleston, Swain county, at 11 o'clock, for Redmond's house, which they reached about 3 o'clock in the morning. Near the house they dismounted and left their horses in the woods—the mountains where Redmond lived being so rugged it was impossible to ride. The men had to crawl on their knees most of the way, and the ground being frozen very hard, it was impossible to avoid making some noise. When within fifty yards of the house Redmond's dogs, being trained to the business, discovered the men and gave the alarm. In an instant the moonshiner sprang from his bed and made his escape through a small door or hole in the rear of his house. He did not have time to even get his pants, boots or coat, but left all behind. The men called to his wife to make a light, which she did very reluctantly. As soon as the light was made the men rushed into the house, but Redmond had made good his retreat in a laurel thicket, from which he called to the men saying: "I will let you off this time without hurting you, but the next time you come back I will be better prepared for you." The men started in the direction of where they thought Redmond was, when he fired two shots at them, which they returned, but no damage was done, and the night being very dark, and Redmond having all advantage of the location, further attempt to pursue him that night was deemed unwise.

The force then came back to Charleston, where Cobb organized for a second attack, having by this time become more familiar with the country, and having secured the services of some additional help. Pending this arrangement Capt. Cobb received a dispatch that the special force was discontinued, and all the job was then turned over to the deputy marshal in Swain county, who carried out the plans as agreed upon by Capt. Cobb, which resulted in the arrest of Major Lewis R. Redmond, the outlaw.

The Arrest of Maj. Lewis R. Redmond, April 7th, 1881, by United States Deputy Marshal K. S. Ray and his Guard.

From the information obtained through the raid just made by Captain Cobb and his squad of special force, Mr. Ray, a Deputy Marshal, who was also in the company with Cobb when the first attempt was made to arrest Redmond, took up the same arrangement, and employing the same guides that were engaged to assist Cobb, left Charleston on the 6th day of April, 1881, on foot, with three days' rations.[16] The party reached the vicinity of where Redmond lived about sunset, and concealed themselves in the woods in sight of his house, and remained there until daylight next morning, when Redmond's dogs discovered them and began to bark, whereupon Redmond took his gun and went to inquire into the cause. Redmond came within thirty yards of where the men were concealed, when one of the men commanded him to halt. At this Redmond threw his gun in a position to fire, when a shot was fired on the opposite side of him. At this time Redmond realized the situation and started to run, when two shots struck his gun and caused one barrel to explode. He did not run far before he fell, but he sufficiently recovered to make a distance of half a mile, having six balls shot into him. He became so exhausted by the loss of blood that he was compelled to surrender. When the party came up with him he was standing supported by a tree, but soon became very sick from the effect of the wounds, and had to be carried to his house in a sheet. His wife seemed to have as much nerve as her husband and bore the shock with great calmness and composure. Redmond was taken to his house and received every attention from the men who arrested him that the surrounding circumstances would admit of. A physician was at once called in—Dr. Lyle, of Macon county, who rendered all the assistance possible, but with all the doctor thought he could not recover.[17] Yet his strong constitution and a determined will survived the shock, and after he remained six days at his house he sufficiently recovered to be removed to Charleston and from Charleston he was taken to Asheville in a ambulance, where he was committed to jail in due form of law. He received every attention from the kind jailor, Col. W. R. Young, that could possibly have been expected.

"The Capture of Redmond." Courtesy of the North Carolina Collection, University of North Carolina at Chapel Hill.

Some apprehensions prevailed that he would be released by his numerous sympathizers and friends, from which a guard of four men was placed at the jail, to prevent any successful attempt to release him.[18] He seemed to bear his confinement with as much composure as it is possible for a man to do that has passed the wild and roving life of Redmond. He seemed to appreciate any little act of kindness that was done or tendered to him. During the Federal Court many conjectures were rife among the masses as to what disposition would be made of Redmond's case. His trial was continued from day to day by the Court, thinking that he would sufficiently recover from his wounds to be able to be brought into Court and arraigned before the bar of justice, to be tried by the laws of his country, for the many deeds alleged to have been done by him. At the Spring term of Count, 1881, bail was fixed in the sum of twenty-five hundred dollars for his appearance at the Fall term of said Court, where it is to be expected an impartial trial will be had before an intelligent court and jury, and if twelve of his countrymen shall decide, after hearing the evidence, that Redmond, the outlaw, is guilty of violating the laws of his country, judgment will be prayed, if not a verdict of not guilty will be pronounced.

Redmond While in Jail Manifests Great Care and Affection for his Wife and Little Children.

I visited Maj. Redmond while in jail frequently and he never failed to speak in the kindest terms of his wife and children at home, and his greatest punishment while in jail was his absence from his home, and his greatest care seemed to be for his little babe. He regretted so much he could not get to see it, but from the character he has established it would seem contrary to his nature to manifest any affection for even his wife and children; but it is said of the great warrior Napoleon after he had conquered nations and caused gallons of blood to be spilt on hundreds of battle fields and had the homage of kings, and potentates, but when he came home and found his little babe lying cold in death, and with his own impress on its tender cheeks, the great warrior and general clasped his hands to his face and bathed his eyes in tears and exclaimed: Oh, my son, my son! So parental care and affection is the same in every condition in life, whether among civilized nations, heathens, savages or outlaws, it is a natural instinct and wisely so for the parents to care for their offspring, either in human or animal kingdom.

Redmond's Financial Condition.

Judging from the reputation that Maj. Redmond has as an incessant blockader, and that he has continued in the business for the last ten or fifteen years, one would think that he had accumulated a nice little fortune during his time. But the experience of all violators of the law in the traffic of illicit whiskey is, the longer a man continues to engage in it the poorer be becomes. Redmond now lives on a small rugged tract of land, a part of it so steep that no human foot has ever trod its surface, and even this tract is owned by another man. His dwelling house is a small log cabin fifteen by twenty feet. The cracks are stopped by mud and straw and yet are open enough for the winter winds to pass through. Two scanty beds for himself and three children supply the furniture. Many an African so surrounded would think he was poorly fixed. A small crib with a rail pen for his stock to shelter under represents his barn. One mule and two oxen make up the stock in trade owned by Maj. Redmond after being engaged incessantly in the traffic of illicit whiskey without suspension since the war. The poor accommodation about his premises may be taken as a criterion of what fortune has in store for all men who pursue a like occupation with Redmond.

A Word of Advice to all Moonshiners, Outlaws, and Persons who Engage in any way in the Illicit Traffic of Whiskey.

In conclusion, permit me to add a word of advice to all persons who are inclined to violate the law in order to evade paying the tax which is levied upon whiskey by the government. The Jews, when our Savior was on earth, endeavored to entrap him, thinking they would prove his disloyalty to their government by asking him if it was lawful to pay tribute unto Caesar or not. He called for a piece of money; he asked them whose superscription it had on it; they told him, "Caesar's." He said unto them, "Render, therefore, unto Caesar the things that are Caesar's, and unto to God the things that are God's." Therefore all good citizens should do likewise, living in the glorious land of freedom that we do, and enjoying the religious and political liberty, having the enjoyment of life, liberty, and the pursuit of happiness, and after enjoying all the inestimable privileges and blessings heaped upon us as American people, we certainly should not hesitate to render unto the government, and unto God the things that are his. From early history of the world to the present time, all governments have taxed their subjects to defray the expenses incident to run its machinery. So the Internal Revenue law is no new thing, but has existed from time immemorial.

Our Saviour also teaches that we must be obedient to the law, both human and divine. He says, "He that disobeys the human law shall be beaten with many stripes, and he that disobeys the divine law shall be punished with the wrath of God." So it has been with Redmond; so it will be with all those who violate the laws of their country. Compare the life of Redmond with that of the most humble citizen who honors and obeys the laws of his country and of his God; see the man who abides by and supports the laws of his county, whether rich or poor, old or young, he moves on in the even tenor of his way. If he has but little, he makes the best of his lot, and is thankful and happy, and when he lies down on his humble cot at night he feels a consciousness within that he is at peace with his fellow-man, his country, and, the best of all, with his God. This makes his slumbers sweet and his dreams delightful. But see the man that is at enmity with his fellow-man, his country and his God. He "fleeth when no man pursueth," and his slumbers are as the raging waters casting up mud and clay. So it has been with Maj. Redmond. He is only 26 years old, and his trials and troubles have already been sufficient to make the account for a many of 80 years. Outside of the remorse of conscience, resulting from the conviction that he had taken his fellow-man's life, he has, for the past ten years, been hunted by both officers and citizens, as the hunter would scour the forests for the roaring lion or the fleet deer. His life has been one continual strain from one difficulty to another—first avoiding arrest, next resisting officers, next breaking the peace, then violating the laws of his county, and finally, through a combination of the special force, Deputy Marshals, and good citizens of the section in which he lived, he was arrested on the 7th day of April, 1881, on the Tennessee River, in Swain county, N.C., was transported from there to the Asheville jail, to await his final trial. Thus you see the result of the life of Maj. Lewis R. Redmond, the famous moonshiner and outlaw, and a similar result will happen to all men who lead the life of that Maj. Redmond led. Take warning in time!

Thus closes my account of the outlaw who is said, in the book to which I have referred, to have gotten that name in this way; but the whole story is false:

"Early in the following spring a large force of marshals established themselves at Asheville, and assisted by a company of United States troops, began to raid through this section of the country quite extensively. They watched the roads closely for blockaders, and it required considerable skill and ingenuity to get through their lines. I made the trip several times, however, and at last excited their suspicions. I now drove four mules, and concealed the liquor under a pile of miscellaneous truck, shucks, chickens, eggs, butter, etc. I always went well armed, and was prepared to make desperate resistance. I would drive slowly, and four members of the band always accompanied me, they making the journey on good, and keeping concealed on each side of the road, in close proximity to my wagon. I made several trips in this manner without adventure; but one evening when but a few miles from Asheville, a squad of soldiers and two deputy marshals, one of whom was the man Crowder, before alluded to, sprang up from their place of concealment among the bushes, and made a rush for my wagon. I knew that prompt action was necessary, and drawing from my pockets a brace of revolvers I dropped the reins and taking cool and deliberate aim at the two marshals discharged shot after shot until the chambers of bother pistols were empty. The smoke cleared away, and revealed both men prostrate in the road. My allies had not been idle, but had attacked the soldiers from both sides of the road. Not knowing our strength, and demoralized by the downfall of their leaders, and this raking cross-fire, they broke and fled. Without waiting to count the number of the slain, I turned my wagon toward the mountain and drove rapidly back, arriving there in safety. That was the last of my blockading. It appeared afterwards that both of the marshals had been killed, five of the soldiers, and several badly wounded. Asheville and all the adjoining country was placarded with printed bills offering a reward of $1,000 for the murders, 'one Redmond' and his accomplices, and the startling adventures which followed this catastrophe gave me the name, 'REDMOND, THE OUTLAW,' which I have borne ever since."[19]

* * *

Since the forgoing was sent to press Redmond has been taken by Deputy Marshal Kennedy, of South Carolina, under warrant of Judge George S. Bryan, of that State, from the Asheville jail to Greenville, South Carolina. There he was put upon his trial and sentenced to ten years' at hard labor in the Albany penitentiary.

He was convicted under eight distinct indictments, not including his murder of Duckworth, which, as yet, goes unpunished.

It seems strange that this man, with six bullets in his body, with no other medical attendance than that of a country physician, and enduring the fatigue of a wagon journey of one hundred miles over high mountains and rough roads from Swain county to Asheville, followed by close confinement in a crowded jail, should yet live to undergo a long trial at the bar, and receive unnerved a sentence of ten years to Albany.

James A. Garfield, President of the United States, dies of a little pistol shot, though he had Bliss for a doctor and koumiss for nourishment, and rode to Long Branch on a rubber bed, and had the White House instead of the penitentiary to cheer him to recovery.[20] Inscrutable Providence that spares the outlaw and dooms the chief magistrate!

Notes

1. John A. Murrell was a famous outlaw from western Tennessee. In the 1820s and 1830s, he was the leader of a small band of thieves who operated along the Mississippi River. Murrell was arrested in 1834. In April 1844, he was released from prison and died seven months later of pulmonary consumption. See James L. Penick, *The Great Western Land Pirate: John A. Murrell in Legend and History* (Columbia: University of Missouri Press, 1981).

2. Lewis was probably born in Rabun County, Georgia.

3. Census enumerators reported that his mother's name was Malinda.

4. Lewis actually resided in Rabun County as a child. Sometime before 1860, Richard moved his family to Transylvania County. Lewis did not live in Swain County until 1879.

5. The information that Cobb provides about Adeline Ladd and her marriage to Lewis Redmond is incorrect. Adeline was born and reared in Pickens County, South Carolina. She and Lewis married in October 1878. They did not move to Swain County until 1879.

6. Lewis mortally wounded Duckworth on March 1, 1876.

7. The *Police News* mistakenly printed, among other things, E. H. Barton's last name as Bastin.

8. Lewis and Adeline married in October 1878.

9. Cobb here is describing the killing of Amos Ladd in June 1878.

10. Cobb mistakenly printed Rabun County as Raven.

11. Evidence that Lewis Redmond moved to Georgia during the late 1870s does not exist. More likely than not, he remained in Pickens County before fleeing to Swain County, North Carolina in 1879.

12. T. N. Freeman was a farmer who lived in Nantahala Township in Swain County with his wife and five children. See *1880 United States Federal Census,* Nantahala Township, Swain County, North Carolina, Roll T9-983, p. 189.

13. Born in Iredell County, North Carolina, and the son of a leading Episcopal divine, John J. Mott was the head of North Carolina's Sixth Collection District from the early 1870s until 1882. Mott used his patronage powers as collector to organize and sustain the Republican Party in western North Carolina. See Gordon B. McKinney, *Southern Mountain Republicans, 1865-1900: Politics and the Appalachian Community* (Chapel Hill: Univ. of North Carolina Press, 1978), 49, 63-64, 72, 96-100, 109, 114, 159, 161-62, 164, 190.

14. In 1877, A. C. Bryan was a gauger ("testing and recording the amount and proof of each barrel of liquor distilled to make sure every gallon was taxed") in North Carolina's Sixth Collection District. By 1878, he had become a deputy marshal. That next year, moonshiners, in response to Bryan's seizure of several illicit stills, burned a barn and several other outbuildings on his property in Burke County, North Carolina. As late as February 1882, Bryan continued to work for the Bureau of Internal Revenue. See Miller, *Revenuers and Moonshiners,* 62; "Enforcement of Internal Revenue Laws," 105, 108; and "Testimony Before the Senate Special Committee to Investigate the Administration

of the Collection of Internal Revenue in the Sixth District of North Carolina," *Senate Miscellaneous Document* 116, 47th Cong., 1st sess. (1882), 389, 575.

15. Cobb quoted this passage from Edward Crittenden's *Entwined Lives*. See Crittenden, *Entwined Lives*, 67.

16. K. S. Ray had been a deputy marshal since at least 1874, when he captured a moonshiner near Brevard in Transylvania County. See *Asheville Pioneer*, March 28, 1874.

17. Dr. J. M. Lyle lived in Franklin in Macon County with his wife and four children. See *1880 United States Federal Census*, Franklin, Macon County, North Carolina, Roll T9-971, p. 482.

18. According to Jeter C. Pritchard in 1912, Adeline gave Lewis a pistol while he was in jail. John Preston Arthur writes, "A girl living in the house found it out, and told Judge Jeter C. Pritchard, who was one of the men guarding him at that time. He told his companion, and it was agreed that he should disarm him. This was done, warning having first been given Redmond that if he moved he would be killed." See Arthur, *Western North Carolina*, 305.

19. Cobb quoted this passage from Edward Crittenden's *Entwined Lives*. See Crittenden, *Entwined Lives*, 72.

20. On July 2, 1881, Charles Julius Guiteau, angry that he had not received a federal post, shot President James A. Garfield on the streets of Washington D.C. On September 19, 1881, Garfield died from his wounds. See Allan Peskin, *Garfield: A Biography* (Kent, OH: Kent State Univ. Press, 1978).

INDEX

Allison, Dick, xxxvi, 52–54, 77, 90
Andrews, Peter, 41–42, 47–49
Asheville (Buncombe County), xix, xxxvi, xxxviii, 7, 39, 51–53, 59–61, 75–77, 81, 86–90, 92–93, 96–97, 101, 104, 110, 118, 121–122
Asheville Citizen, xxxv
Atlanta Daily Constitution, xxxviii
Austin, Gabrielle, xxxv–xxxvii, 101; falsely accused of larceny, 40–45; moves to Asheville, 50–53; Redmond falls in love with, 68–71; saved by Lewis Redmond; 48–50, 64–68; spared by Lewis Redmond, 71–74

Baines, Donald, xlvii–xlvii; "Among the Moonshiners," xlvii–xlvii
Barton, E. H., xx–xxiii, xxx, xxxix, xliv, 12–18, 26
Blacker, Marshal, 81–83, 88
Bradley, D. F., xx, xxviii, xxxix, 27
Bray, Henry, 66–68, 90
Bryan, A. C., xxxv, xxxix, 115–116
Bryan, George S., xxxix
Buncombe County, N.C., 59, 71, 89

Carpenter, L. Cass, xviii, xx–xxiii
Chapman, W. H., xxxii
Charleston News and Courier, ix–x, xiv, xxiii, xxviii, xxix, xxx–xxxiv, xli, xliii–xlix, 2, 11

Civil War, xvi–xvii
Cobb, Robert A., x, xv, xxxv, xxxvii–xxxviii, xlviii–xlix, 98, 116, 117
Columbia, S.C., xlii–xliii
Crittenden, Edward B., ix–x, xv, xxxv–xxxvii, xlvii, 31–32, 78, 101, 110

declining support for the moonshiners, xxxix–xlii
Douglas, Robert M., xxxv
Duckworth, Alfred, ix, xiii, xx, xxx, xxxv, xxxvii, xxxix, xlv, 1, 8–11, 26, 105–8, 122

Earle, William E., xxviii, xxxii, xxiv
Eastatoe Township (Pickens County), xx, xxix, xxxiv, 24
Elmore, Grace, xlii–xliii
Entwined Lives of Miss Gabrielle Austin and Redmond, the North Carolina Outlaw, The, ix–x, xv, xxxv–xxxvii, xlvii, 31–32, 78, 101, 110

Field, W. T., xxix, 2–4, 23, 27
Findley, Edward, 89, 93–94, 110–11

Gannaway, Gideon, 39–43, 46, 48–49, 60, 77
Garlington, A. C., xxxix
Gary, William F., xx–xxi, xxiv, xxx, xxxv, xxxix, 12–13, 15, 20–21, 26

INDEX

Greenville, S.C., xxi–xxii, xxviii, xxxiii, xxxviii, xl, 16–17, 122
Greenville County, S.C., xxi, xxiv, xxvii, xxxii, xl
Greenville Daily News, xxxix, xli
Greenville Enterprise and Mountaineer, xxvii

Hampton, Wade, xix, xxiii, xxix, xxxii, xli–xliv, 23, 26–27, 96, 101
Hashagen, Charlie, 35–40, 53, 60–62, 71–77
Hashagen, John, 35, 37–43, 45–46, 48–51, 60
Henderson County, N.C., xvi
Hendricks, Van B., xx–xxi, 11–12, 15, 20–21, 26
Hendrix, H. B., xxiv, xxx, xxxv
Hoffman, E. G., xxiv–xxvi, xxxiv, 105

industrialization, xl–xli

Keowee Courier, xxvi, xxxiii, xxix–xli

Ladd, Amos, xii, xxvii–xxix, xxxii, xxxiv, 12, 14, 18
"Law and Moonshine," xlvii
liquor taxation, xiii, xv–xviii, xix, xxxi–xxxiii, xxxv, xl, xlii
local color writing, xlvi–xlvii
Lost Cause ideology, xlii, xlv

Mackey, T. J., xxvi, 15, 21–22
McCravy, Edwin Parker, xliv
McDowell County, N.C., 71
McDowell, Irwin C., 88, 92–93, 101, 110
McKinley, C., ix–x, xiv, xxix, xxx–xxxi, xxxiv, xliii, 1
Miller, W. A., xxii
Miller, Wilbur, xvii, xli
Mott, John J., xxxv, 115

National Police Gazette, xxx, xxxviii
New York Times, xxii, xxx, xxxiv, xxxix, xliii
New York World, xxxi
Northrop, L. C., xxvii–xxviii, xxxi, xxxiii–xxxv

Oconee County, S.C., xxiv, xxvi–xxvii, xxxii–xxxiii, xl–xli, xliii–xlv, 90

Pickens County, S.C., xiii, xv, xx–xxv, xxviii–xxix, xxxiv, xl–xli, xliii, 21
Pickens Sentinel, xx, xxiii, xxvi, xxviii, xxxiii–xl

Rabun County, Ga., xv–xvi, 109
Raum, Green B., xx–xxv, xxxi–xxxv, xxxix, xl, xlii
Ray, K. S., 117
Reconstruction, xviii–xix
Redmond, Adeline Ladd, xx, xxv, xxvii, xxxvii, xliii, 103, 105
Redmond, Lewis R., xiii; arrested, xxxvii–xxxix, 115–19; birth, xv–xvi, 103; childhood, xvi, 6, 103; C. McKinley visits, xxix–xxx; death, xliv–xlv; death of Amos Owens, xviii–xxvii; death of parents, xix–xx, 7; denied amnesty, xxxiii–xxxiv; flees to Pickens County, xx, 10, 108; flees to Swain County, xxxv, 112–15; legacy, xlv–xlix; murder of Alfred Duckworth, xiii, xx, 8–10, 104–8; pardoned, xlii–xliii; Pickens County jailbreak, xxiv–xxvi, 21–22; retirement, xliii–xliv; raid on E. H. Barton's home, xxi–xxii, 11–18
Redmond, Richard, xv

Seneca (Oconee County), xliv, 88, 90, 92
Seneca News, xliv

INDEX

Small, Toby, 88, 90–92
Spartanburg County, S.C., xxiv, xxvii, xxxii, xxxviii, xl
Spates, Arthur, 89, 94–96, 101
Springfield Republican, xxxi
Steele, R. E., xxvi
Swain County, N.C., xxxv, xxxvii, 103–5, 111–17, 121–22

Taylor, Sally, xlii–xliii
True Life of Maj. Lewis Richard Redmond, The, x, xv, xxxviii, xlviii, xlix, 98–122

Transylvania County, N.C., xiii, xv, xvi, xix, 27, 103, 105–6, 108, 111

Vance, Zebulon B., xix, 96, 101

Walhalla (Oconee County), xl, xliii–xliv, 90–91
Wallace, R. M., xxiii, xxvii, xxxiii
Washington Post, xxxiv, xxxix
Woolson, Contance Fenimore, xlvi–xlvii; "Up in the Blue Ridge," xlvi–xlvii

Yancey County, N.C., 71

06/09

WITHDRAWN

**Albert Carlton - Cashiers
Community Library**